THE

EMPLOYEE BENEFITS
ANSWER BOOK

THE
EMPLOYEE BENEFITS
ANSWER BOOK

An Indispensable Guide for Managers and Business Owners

REBECCA MAZIN

Pfeiffer
A Wiley Imprint
www.pfeiffer.com

For additional copies/bulk purchases of this book in the U.S. please contact 800-274-4434.

Pfeiffer books and products are available through most bookstores. To contact Pfeiffer directly call our Customer Care Department within the U.S. at 800-274-4434, outside the U.S. at 317-572-3985, fax 317-572-4002, or visit www.pfeiffer.com.

Pfeiffer also publishes its books in a variety of electronic formats. Some content that appears in print may not be available in electronic books.

Library of Congress Cataloging-in-Publication Data

Mazin, Rebecca A.

The employee benefits answer book : an indispensable guide for managers and business owners / Rebecca Mazin.

    p. cm.

Includes index.

  ISBN 978-0-470-52515-9 (pbk.); 978-0-470-91243-0 (ebk.); 978-0-470-91244-7 (ebk.); 978-0-470-91242-3 (ebk.)

  1. Employee fringe benefits.   I. Title.

  HD4928.N6M39 2010

  658.3'25—dc22

2010032313

Acquiring Editor: Matthew Davis

Marketing Manager: Brian Grimm

Editorial Assistant: Lindsay Morton

Production Editor: Michael Kay

Editor: Donna Cohn

Manufacturing Supervisor: Becky Morgan

Printed in the United States of America

Printing 10 9 8 7 6 5 4 3 2 1

About Pfeiffer

Pfeiffer serves the professional development and hands-on resource needs of training and human resource practitioners and gives them products to do their jobs better. We deliver proven ideas and solutions from experts in HR development and HR management, and we offer effective and customizable tools to improve workplace performance. From novice to seasoned professional, Pfeiffer is the source you can trust to make yourself and your organization more successful.

Essential Knowledge Pfeiffer produces insightful, practical, and comprehensive materials on topics that matter the most to training and HR professionals. Our Essential Knowledge resources translate the expertise of seasoned professionals into practical, how-to guidance on critical workplace issues and problems. These resources are supported by case studies, worksheets, and job aids and are frequently supplemented with CD-ROMs, websites, and other means of making the content easier to read, understand, and use.

Essential Tools Pfeiffer's Essential Tools resources save time and expense by offering proven, ready-to-use materials—including exercises, activities, games, instruments, and assessments—for use during a training or team-learning event. These resources are frequently offered in looseleaf or CD-ROM format to facilitate copying and customization of the material.

Pfeiffer also recognizes the remarkable power of new technologies in expanding the reach and effectiveness of training. While e-hype has often created whizbang solutions in search of a problem, we are dedicated to bringing convenience and enhancements to proven training solutions. All our e-tools comply with rigorous functionality standards. The most appropriate technology wrapped around essential content yields the perfect solution for today's on-the-go trainers and human resource professionals.

www.pfeiffer.com   *Essential resources for training and HR professionals*

Contents

Introduction   ix
Health Care Reform   xiii

1 The Benefits Package: Why Should I Have a Plan? What Should It Include?   1

2 Paid Time Off: How Many Vacation Days Do I Have to Give?   17

3 Enrollment and Changes: How Do I Obtain Information and Communicate Value?   39

4 Medical Plan Basics: What's the Difference Between a POS and an HSA?   55

5 Dental and Vision Plans: Are Checkups and Eye Exams Enough?   73

6 Choosing and Working With Brokers: How Do I Get the Most Out of the Broker Relationship?   83

7 Benefits That Save Payroll Taxes: What's Involved in Flexible Spending Accounts, Transportation, and Tuition Assistance Plans?   95

8 Retirement Plans: What Do I Need to Know About Pensions, 401(k) Plans, and Nonqualified Plans? 111

9 Benefits That Provide Economic Security: Do Employees Expect Life Insurance and Disability? 137

10 Benefits Buffet: From EAP to Concierge Services What Else Do Employees Want and What Should You Provide? 147

11 When Employees Leave: How Does COBRA Work and What Else Do I Need to Do? 165

12 Cost Control: What Can Employers Do to Rein in Benefits Costs? 181

Resources 195
Resource Guide for Health Reform 203
Tools and Templates 205
The Author 229
Index 231

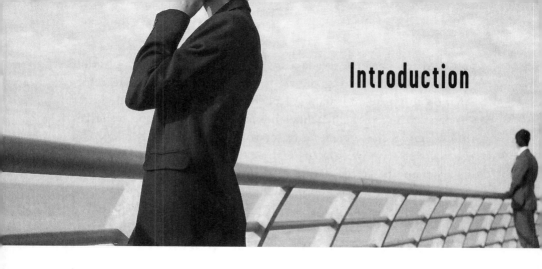

Introduction

PROVIDING EMPLOYEE BENEFITS IS A LOT LIKE OWNING a car. The product is really expensive, costs keep rising, and there are numerous options that are so complicated that you need an expert to keep them running. The 2010 passage of health reform has added new models and increased complexity, both today and for the future, as the regulatory time line is implemented and federal agencies issue clarifications, regulations, and guidance. For most people a Summary Plan Description (SPD) and the added layers of the Patient Protection and Affordable Care Act (PPACA) are about as comprehensible as the worn brake rotors a mechanic takes out of an SUV. Companies spend hundreds of thousands or millions of dollars each year for employee benefits and yet feel so little control. Any other purchase with a similarly sized price tag is made only after lengthy processes that weigh the pros and cons of multiple bids. Benefits decisions and accompanying administration are also very personal with the potential to directly affect everyone in the room with a voice in consideration of the information. Convene a meeting of owners or senior executives to present a new health benefit option or 401(k) provider and be prepared when attendees look at details and announce, "I'm not sure my wife likes this hospital" or "Where is the index fund we have in the current 401(k)?" When CEOs have a question about Short Term Disability they do not want to call an 800 number; internal resources should be available for a quick clarification. This book was written to give employers tools to respond to everyday inquiries and gain a better position and outcome by asking the right questions and obtaining information to create and manage coherent policies based on a clearer understanding of the benefits landscape. Knowledge and resources allow employers to create a framework for employee benefits as a business strategy with goals and a budget that can be juggled to meet changing needs and a platform for questions, review, and decision making. This approach changes the paradigm from reacting to steep price increases with dismay and complaints to planning and allocating resources to meet organizational needs.

The Employee Benefits Answer Book has been written to:

- Help business owners and executives make better-informed decisions and enable more effective plan administration.
- Provide managers with guidance about their own benefits and in explaining company policies.
- Create a trusted resource for human resources professionals in establishing and maintaining employee benefits plans.

The concept of *The Employee Benefits Answer Book* sprang from my experiences as a human resources executive, consultant, and consumer. As the senior HR executive for a start-up company I was responsible for implementing plans from scratch and maintaining them within budgets through multiple changes of ownership. This experience strengthened my perspective as a consultant where I once worked with an employer to decentralize and update benefits administration for multiple locations throughout the United States during the same season that my husband changed jobs. It did not take long to spot the key reasons why my client's employees had not opted for a new lower-cost health plan during the previous open enrollment; the difference in employee contribution was minimal, the selection was at the bottom of a list and no one had "sold" the plan. Identifying the best coverage choice for my own family was much more difficult. I found myself sitting on the floor surrounded by plan descriptions in an effort to compare the choices. When I contacted both the company and insurer with questions I consistently stumped call centers because I was not a plan member.

The explosion of new benefit options and designs has made the task of sorting through information even more daunting. This book is organized by topical area in an easy-to-use question-and-answer format enabling readers to zero in on the subject of interest. From vacation days to retirement you will find clear explanations and definitions in plain language that does not require benefits expertise. Checklists, charts, and specific illustrations clarify the contents of each chapter with real-life examples of employer actions that are "worth repeating" or "better forgotten." Sample forms, formats, and letters can be found in Tools and Templates. While you may locate the answer you need about life insurance in Chapter Nine: Benefits That Provide Economic Security, I encourage you to spend some time reading Chapter One: The Benefits Package: Why Should I Have a Plan? What Should It Include? Here you will find direction for identifying a benefits strategy referenced throughout the book as the guiding principle for decision making.

Just as this book is all about clarification for business owners and managers, they are reminded that the time, effort, and money spent on employee benefits can be wasted unless it is backed up by consistent, effective communication to employees. I often work with employers who provide an array of rich benefits only to face criticism and frustration from employees who do not understand points of access or who take action based on misguided direction from a coworker. You will find examples and recommendations throughout the text and are encouraged to make benefits communications an ongoing, year-round, activity. Headline news about health reform adds urgency to the need for clear, understandable information delivered through a variety of formats. The dry, complex nature of the topic should not preclude the use of creativity; employers have taken advantage of social media, cartoons, and readily available online video to get the benefits message across. The program does not have to be an all-inclusive benefits university; bite-size items targeted to the audience will build results. The newest, youngest employees may be most receptive to a reminder that their dental plan covers cleanings twice a year, whereas the parents of preteens search for information about the plan maximum for braces.

In creating an accessible volume, decisions were made to devote more space to common items, those that tend to confuse, or viable choices that can be overlooked due to complexity. Through this design and in response to the escalating pace of change, *The Employee Benefits Answer Book* will be a valuable navigation tool to set direction and avoid getting sidetracked along the way.

Rebecca Mazin

Health Care Reform

How and When Does the Patient Protection and Affordable Care Act Affect Employer Sponsored Plans?

THE PATIENT PROTECTION AND AFFORDABLE CARE Act (PPACA) signed into law in March of 2010 contains many potentially sweeping changes for employer-sponsored health benefits and at the same time leaves numerous definitions and regulations yet to be determined. The Department of Health and Human Services (HHS) has the primary responsibility for promulgation of rules and clarifications with additional involvement by the Departments of Labor and Treasury. Even as guidance is issued there will be components that are challenged and reinterpreted for many years to come—in a process similar to action taken on other legislation that affects employers. Definitive answers may not be available on all aspects but it is important that employers familiarize themselves with mandates and take action on deadlines and requirements that are not fluid. An overview of the law is easier to understand in the form of a time line, as the PPACA will be enacted in phases beginning in 2010 through 2018. This approach should also help avoid an entirely reactive response by planning for changes in advance of implementation. It's important to remember that the Act does not require employers to provide health insurance; it does contain financial incentives for the smallest employers and, effective 2014, creates penalties for employers with more than 50 employees who do not provide access to a company sponsored plan. Employers who are not currently offering health insurance should not wait until June 2013 to obtain quotes for coverage. Researching the marketplace and identifying options and choices for purchasing will facilitate decision making, even if a determination is made not to offer a plan. Proactive steps will produce data that plays an important role in forecasting to meet business and organizational strategy.

One of the potentially confusing aspects of the Affordable Care Act is the applicability of some sections to "grandfathered health plans." A grandfathered health plan is any group health plan that was in effect on the date PPACA was enacted, March 23, 2010.

Plans lose grandfathered status if they:

- Significantly cut or reduce benefits such as deciding to no longer cover people with diabetes.

- Raise coinsurance charges; if the rate is 20% at the time PPACA was enacted the plan will no longer be grandfathered if it is increased by 30%.

- Significantly raise copayments; grandfathered plans will be allowed to increase these by no more than the greater of $5 or a percentage equal to medical inflation plus 15 percentage points. If a plan raises copayments from $30 to $50 over the next two years it will lose grandfathered status.

- Significantly raise deductibles; grandfathered plans can only increase these deductibles by a percentage equal to medical inflation plus 15%, which would be 19–20% based on recent calculations. Using this formula, a $1,000 annual deductible could be increased to $1,190 in 2011.

- Significantly lower employer contributions; grandfathered plans cannot decrease the percentage of premium paid by the employer by more than 5 percentage points. The employee share of the premium cannot jump from 15 to 25%.

- Add or tighten an annual limit on what the insurer pays.

- Change insurance providers.

Don't be intimidated by all of this complicated language about maintaining grandfathered status. For many employers the potential loss of grandfathered status will not have a significant impact. They may already provide the benefits that will be required of nongrand-fathered plans, or the cost savings resulting from change could out-weigh any financial burden of compliance.

2010

Provisions Applicable to All Group Health Plans Effective January 2010

Small Business Tax Credits

Small employers who already offer coverage, or are planning to start, may be able to take advantage of a tax credit if they:

- Employ the equivalent of fewer than 25 full-time workers. A busi-ness with 10 full-time and 20 part-timers, who each work 25 hours per week, could still qualify; and
- Pay average wages to all employees below $50,000 a year; and
- Cover at least 50% of the cost of health insurance for employees.

The credit is effective January 2010 and employers can claim it retroactively. The tax credit is worth up to 35% of the premiums busi-nesses and nonprofit organizations pay for health insurance based on a sliding scale that includes wages and number of employees in the calculation. The full credit is available for firms that employ fewer than 10 equivalent workers who earn average annual wages below $25,000. The maximum value of the credit increases in 2014 to 50% but it is not intended to be available forever. It includes a gradual phase out.

Provisions Effective for Plan Years Beginning on or After September 23, 2010

Extension of Coverage to Dependents

The law requires that coverage be extended to dependents up to age 26. Half of all states already mandate an extension of coverage, most commonly to age 25, although it can be higher, as in New Jersey where it is up to age 30. The federal requirement includes children who may be working or married, as long as they are not eligible for another employer-sponsored health plan. Employers are not required to extend benefits to the children of these covered dependents. Any additional cost for this coverage will not be considered taxable income for the employee or dependent and employers can collect any increased contribution as they would for adding any other eligible dependent.

Eliminate Lifetime Coverage Limits/Regulate Annual Limits

Plans can no longer include a lifetime maximum for benefits to be paid on behalf of employees or dependents. The law also restricts annual limits on specific coverage that provide essential health services to be defined by HHS. Essential health services will include basic care, hospitalization, and prescription drugs, among other things. Employers are likely to be allowed to maintain annual maximums for ancillary services such as chiropractic care until 2014 when most annual maximums will also be prohibited.

Prohibition on Rescission of Coverage

Insurers can no longer deny coverage for any reason except in cases of fraud. This includes a prohibition on dropping benefits for eligible participants and beneficiaries.

Ban on Pre-Existing Condition Exclusions for Children

All employer-sponsored plans must cover any pre-existing condition, without a waiting period, for all dependents up to age 19.

Break Time for Nursing Mothers

Tucked into PPACA is a section that amends the Fair Labor Standards Act (FLSA) to require employers to allow "reasonable break time" for nursing mothers to express milk for children who are up to 12 months old. The law also requires that employers provide a location that is "shielded from view and free from intrusion by coworkers and the public." Organizations with fewer than 50 employees can claim an exemption from the requirement if it would result in undue hardship that causes significant difficulty or expense. Breaks that are longer than 20 minutes can be unpaid, but employers may already be subject to more stringent statues in one of the 24 states and the District of Columbia that have passed laws requiring break time for breastfeeding mothers.

Provisions Effective for Plan Years Beginning on or After September 23, 2010

Covering Preventive Services

Preventive care coverage as defined by Health and Human Services must be provided under employer-sponsored plans without cost sharing. Where beneficiaries have a choice between in-network and out-of-network care, both must be provided with no out-of-pocket expenses. Preventive services already include annual checkups, healthy child visits, breast cancer screenings for women, and immunizations; this list could be expanded.

Emergency Room Copayments

Any copayment for an emergency room visit must be the same wherever care is accessed when a plan allows coverage in both in-network and out-of-network hospitals Plans are also prohibited from requiring any type of preauthorization for emergency room visits.

Primary Care Designation

Plans that require participants to designate a primary care physician must allow women to identify an ob-gyn for this purpose and pediatricians for dependent children. Plans cannot require authorization or referral before ob-gyn visits.

Nondiscrimination Testing

Fully insured plans must meet the same nondiscrimination requirements applied to self-insured plans that include rules that the plan does not favor highly compensated employees in eligibility rules. Highly compensated employees are defined for this purpose as the five highest-paid officers, those with 10% ownership in the company, and the highest paid 25% of all employees. Plans meet nondiscrimination requirements if they satisfy tests that determine eligibility for the majority of employees. The tests should be performed by a qualified professional. This provision is likely to make it difficult to have separate plans for highly paid individuals that cover additional costs not covered in the company's health plan. These executive plans have been in place to reimburse expenses not paid for by the regular plan.

Independent Appeals Process

Plans must allow participants access to effective independent internal and external appeals processes to appeal decisions made by their health insurance plans.

2011

Long-Term Care Insurance

The Community Living Assistance Services and Support (CLASS) Act makes available a voluntary long-term care insurance program to be financed by voluntary payroll deductions. Participating employers automatically enroll employees who pay premiums in order to receive a basic daily cash benefit for home-based or residential services in the event of a disability. Eligibility for payment requires a lengthy participation period and employees can opt out of the plan. Long-term care insurance is a relatively complicated product, and this program will require extensive communication that hopefully includes materials developed by the appropriate federal agency.

Grants for Wellness Programs

Beginning in 2011 health reform makes $200 million available for up to five years for grants for employer-sponsored wellness programs.

Employers can apply for grants if they:

- Employ fewer than 100 employees who work 25 or more hours each week and

- Did not have a workplace wellness program in place on May 23, 2010.

The Department of Health and Human Services is responsible for developing the criteria required for this program.

Elimination of Savings Plan Reimbursements for Over-the-Counter Drugs

As of January 1, 2011, participants in Flexible Spending Accounts, Health Reimbursement Accounts, and Health Savings Accounts can no longer use these funds to cover the cost of over-the-counter medications not prescribed by a doctor. This includes all previously covered items such as pain relief and allergy medication obtained without a prescription. For many employees this will represent a big change in habits so communication of the restriction should begin well before January 1, 2011.

Increase in Health Savings Account Withdrawal Penalty

Employees who make withdrawals from Health Savings Accounts for non-qualified expenses will be subject to a 20% tax penalty. This is a doubling of the penalty of 10% in effect up to December 31, 2010.

Auto Enrollment into Health Plans for Large Employers

Employers with more than 200 employees will be required to automatically enroll newly eligible individuals covered under their sponsored plans. Employees will have the opportunity to opt out of coverage. The law is silent on the specific effective date of this requirement. Some interpretations have set inception at 2014, while others project an earlier implementation. Rules are expected to be issued by the Department of Health and Human Services. Automatic enrollment should help boost participation as it does for 401(k) plans.

Simple Cafeteria Plans for Small Employers

The IRS Code Section 125 that allows employers to provide tax-free benefits has been amended to provide simple cafeteria plans that include a safe harbor from discrimination for employers who employ an average of 100 or fewer employees during either of the preceding two years. Once an employer qualifies they can retain this status until they employ 200 or more employees in the previous year.

2012

W-2 Reporting of Value of Health Benefits

Employers are required to include the value of employer paid health benefits on annual W-2s beginning with the form issued in 2012. This form will reflect 2011 costs.

Uniform Summary of Coverage

The Secretary of Health and Human Services will develop standards for employers to create a Uniform Summary of Coverage to be distributed to employees. The goal is to utilize language that is "culturally and linguistically appropriate" in a document that is no longer than four pages using 12-point type. All communications are important and this is a step toward further clarity but should not be relied upon as the only form for disseminating information.

Provision Effective for Plan Years Beginning on or After September 23, 2012

Comparative Effectiveness Fee

Employers pay an annual fee to support comparative effectiveness research of $1 per group health plan participant, per year, in plans beginning with the plan year after September 23, 2012. The fee rises to $2 in 2013 in the subsequent plan year and may be indexed to increases in national health care expenditures until it is phased out.

2013

Cap Flexible Spending Account Contributions

Beginning this calendar year employers must limit contributions to health Flexible Spending Accounts (FSAs) to $2,500 per year.

This maximum may be adjusted annually based on the cost-of-living adjustment.

Notices of Exchanges and Subsidies

Beginning on March 13, 2013, employers must give written notice to current employees, and new employees when they are hired, that describes Health Benefits Exchanges, premium subsidies, and whether the employer's plan meets minimum coverage requirements. Guidance for contacting the Exchange to request assistance will be included along with the availability of premium tax credits in the event that the employer pays less than 60% of the total costs of benefits.

Taxes on High Earners

The Medicare payroll tax on earnings over $200,000 for individuals and $250,000 for married couples who file jointly increases to 2.35% from 1.45%. These same wage earners will also pay additional taxes on unearned income.

2014

Individual Responsibility for Coverage and Establishment of Health Exchanges

U.S. citizens and legal residents will be required to have qualifying health coverage or pay a tax penalty. In order to extend the availability of plans, state-based Health Benefits Exchanges and Small Business Health Options Program (SHOP) Exchanges will be established to enable individuals and businesses with up to 100 employees to purchase coverage. These exchanges designed for individuals and small businesses will be expanded to cover larger employers in 2017.

What Are Essential Health Benefits?

The Exchanges established in 2014 are required to offer Qualified Health Plans that meet a list of specified plan features for marketing and provider networks and include Essential Health Benefits. The

Secretary of Health and Human Services will determine the details of Essential Health Benefits that are referred to in a number of sections of PPACA.

Essential Health Benefits will include at least the following:

- Ambulatory patient services
- Emergency services
- Hospitalization
- Maternity and newborn care
- Mental health and substance abuse disorder services, including behavioral health treatment
- Rehabilitative and habilitative services and devices
- Laboratory services
- Preventive and wellness services and chronic disease management
- Pediatric services, including oral and vision care

Employer Responsibility to Provide Plans or Pay Penalty

Employers who *do not* offer health coverage will be required to pay a penalty if:

- They employed an average of at least 50 or more full-time employees, defined as individuals who work at least 30 hours a week, during the previous calendar year and
- Have at least one employee who enrolls in a qualified health plan through an Exchange and receives a premium tax credit during any month in the current calendar year.

The penalty amount will be:

- $2,000 per full-time employee per year, calculated on a monthly basis. The first 30 employees will be excluded from the calculation.

Premium credits will be made available to individuals with incomes above the Medicaid eligibility and below 400% of the poverty level to help purchase benefits through the exchange. The subsidies will be made available to help employees who meet specified income levels purchase benefits through the Health Insurance Exchange. These employees are also described as purchasing subsidized insurance through the Exchange.

Employers who *do* offer health coverage will be required to pay a penalty if:

- They employed an average of at least 50 or more full-time employees, defined as individuals who work at least 30 hours a week, during the previous calendar year; and

- Have at least one employee who enrolls in a qualified health plan through an Exchange and receives a premium tax credit during any month in the current calendar year.

And either of the following occurs:

- The employer's coverage is considered "unaffordable" because it costs the employee more than 9.5% of household income; or

- The employer pays less than 60% of the cost of a plan that includes minimal essential benefits.

The penalty amount will be the lesser of:

- $3,000 for each employee receiving subsidized coverage through an exchange; or

- $2,000 for each full-time employee.

These fees have been referred to as shared responsibility or free rider penalties.

Employers will not be required to pay a penalty for any part-time staff, those who work less than 30 hours a week, even if the individual receives a premium credit and coverage through the Exchange.

Free Choice Vouchers

Employers who offer coverage will be required to provide a voucher to employees who earn less than 400% of the poverty level if employee contributions toward premiums are between 8 and 9.8% of income. These Free Choice Vouchers will equal the amount of monthly employer contributions and allow employees to enroll in an Exchange plan. Employers who offer Free Choice Vouchers will not be subject to the penalty levied for plans that are considered unaffordable as described above.

Limits on Deductibles and Cost Sharing

Maximum out-of-pocket health plan expenses cannot exceed the amount identified by the IRS for High Deductible Health Plans paired with Health Savings Accounts. The limit, indexed each year, was set at $5,950 for single coverage and $11,900 for family plans for 2010. Small group health plans that provide essential health benefits as defined by HHS cannot have deductibles that exceed $2,000 for single coverage and $4,000 for family coverage. Up until 2016, states have the option of defining small group plans as either employers with the equivalent of fewer than 50 or 100 employees. As of 2016 small employers are defined as those with 100 or fewer employees.

Eliminate Annual Limits

Plans can no longer maintain annual limits on the amount of coverage for individuals for essential benefits as defined by the Secretary of Health and Human Services. Plans may continue to place maximums for certain medical procedures or treatments identified as nonessential health benefits.

Eliminate Preexisting Condition Exclusions

All employer-sponsored plans must cover any preexisting condition, without a waiting period, for all employees and all of their dependents.

Limit Waiting Periods for Coverage to 90 Days or Less

Employer-sponsored benefits commonly have waiting periods that establish eligibility for enrollment. As of January 1, 2014, these waiting periods cannot be longer than 90 days.

Coverage of Routine Costs for Clinical Trials

Plans with effective dates on or after the first of this year must cover the routine costs for care of employees and eligible dependents who participate in clinical trials.

Rewards for Wellness Plan Participation

Employers can offer employees rewards that equal up to 30% of the cost of coverage for participating in a wellness program and meeting specific health-related standards.

Reporting Requirements

Employers will be required to submit a new set of data to the IRS about employees and health plan features, including minimal essential benefits and employee contributions. Statements that include this information will also be sent to employees no later than January 25, 2015.

2018

Excise Tax on High-Cost Plans

High-cost plans will be subject to a new 40% excise tax effective January 1, 2018. High-cost plans are identified as those that exceed $10,200 a year for individual coverage and $27,500 for family coverage.

MEDICARE, RETIREES, AND ADDITIONAL COMPONENTS

Health reform legislation filled more than 2,000 pages with an array of sections that cover insurance providers, Medicare recipients, and others. Information related to employer-sponsored retiree health benefits, both as part of health reform and existing plans, has not been included and these offerings are not described in this book, as they are more likely to be provided by the largest employers and are being cut more often than instituted. There will be changes as PPACA requirements are defined by federal agencies during this timetable and in years to come, due to experience, new regulations, the function of the Exchanges, and advances in health care itself.

WRAP UP

What's an Employer to Do?

With the many questions and inevitable interpretations of health reform it can be tempting to adopt a wait-and-see attitude and take action only when absolutely required. This approach could be costly when you don't have the time to identify the best options or pay unanticipated penalties.

This checklist should assist in a transition:

☐ Apply for tax credit and wellness program grants if you meet requirements for business size and employee income threshold.

☐ Review the time line to identify potential plan changes.

☐ Discuss plan change requirements with broker or plan provider.

☐ Communicate plan changes to employees.

☐ Compare plan to Essential Health Benefits as published by the Secretary of Health and Human Services.

☐ Review cost structure to ensure that employer contribution is at least 60%; calculate potential free rider penalty to decide if cost-sharing structure will change.

☐ Obtain information about Small Business Health Options Program (SHOP) Exchanges (for employers with fewer than 100 employees up to 2017 when they are slated to cover larger employers). to review available plans and costs for comparison purposes.

☐ If no plan is currently offered, obtain quotes for coverage by the beginning of 2013, well before the 2014 requirement. These may not be valid for the following year but will provide an idea of costs and parameters with the options to institute some benefits.

☐ Calculate potential costs of penalties for not providing coverage, and make decisions about future benefits.

☐ Track and comply with record-keeping requirements.

Always consider your benefits strategy and ask questions until you understand and are able to make well-informed decisions. The new regulations may add layers of complexity—but this does not mean that employers should pay for benefits they do not understand, whether through an existing provider or the Exchanges. Crunching the numbers and ensuring that billing, enrollment, and changes are accurate as described in Chapter Twelve, Cost Control, are essential steps toward meeting new requirements and identifying opportunities for savings. Incorporating health reform mandates into your overall approach to benefits may mean some changes in non–health plan areas but these will not be made without a foundation of knowledge and planning. Implementation of PPACA over a number of years will also likely coincide with changes in your workforce as an aging population retires, or remains on the job longer, and younger workers are hired. As the employee benefits landscape continues to change, increasing your knowledge through understanding of the concepts included on these pages will be a resource to facilitate transitions.

CHAPTER 1

The Benefits Package

Why Should I Have a Plan? What Should It Include?

WHETHER YOU ARE CREATING A BRAND-NEW BENEFITS plan or maintaining an existing program, it's essential to use a guiding framework for decision making and implementation. Don't feel bad if you can't outline a benefits strategy; most employers are likely to draw a blank if asked to describe one. This important first step is often skipped in favor of the too common organizing principles of keeping up with the company down the block and responding to specific needs of the most senior decision makers. These approaches can result in unnecessary offerings or a nasty surprise when the cost spikes for an item provided to satisfy a very small group. Other employers concentrate their energies on keeping up with spiraling costs, accepting annual increases without question as inevitable. Organizations that look at the big picture change the focus of employee benefits from staring into a black hole to a business strategy.

WHAT IS A BENEFITS STRATEGY?

A benefits strategy provides a blueprint for decision making at the point where financial considerations intersect with the employment

> WORTH REPEATING
>
> ### Never Doubt the Benefits of Ice Cream
>
> Dixon Schwabl earned the honor of number one on the 2008 Best Small Company to Work for in America list. This 70+ employee marketing and advertising firm in Victor, New York, gives all employees a paid "Make It Happen Day" to volunteer with the nonprofit of their choice—and treats staff to ice cream once a week during the summer.

relationship. This is the foundation for your answer to the question, "Why should I have a plan?" Organizations may describe themselves as seeking to be "an employer of choice." Though adopting this mantle will mean different things in different industries and workplace cultures, employee benefits will always be an important part of the equation. If you aspire to be named as one of AARP's Best Employers for Workers Over 50, your focus will include health and pension offerings and retiree health coverage. The Great Place to Work Institute, the research organization that interviews more than 100,000 people to identify the Fortune 100 Best Companies to Work For and the Best Small & Medium Companies to Work for in America, notes on-site fitness centers, number of holidays, health and wellness programs, and retirement among valuable factors in reaching rankings but makes special reference to unique initiatives as important components of employee satisfaction.

Three Questions About Your Benefits Strategy

As you work to frame your company's health benefits strategy, you need to answer three basic questions.

1. What Role Do Benefits Play in Recruitment and Retention?

If you are competing for the same hires against employers who provide premium benefits, this will become a factor in your decisions.

It does not mean you automatically risk losing employees if you don't offer identical plans. Your work environment may include perks or a culture that has a greater impact on job satisfaction. The inclusion of cost-effective voluntary benefits can also be a powerful way to add value to an employment package. These are extremely attractive to a diverse and changing workforce and typically are paid for primarily by employees through easy-to-handle payroll deductions.

Benefits offerings will play a different role during the various points in career and life paths. Work environment perks and more creative lifestyle initiatives inspire the newest and youngest members of the workforce. Middle and upper managers who have been building a résumé for seven to ten years are more likely to focus on health and economic security as they settle into family life.

If you value longevity, benefits that reward length of service must be a key component. Employers who tolerate higher turnover to encourage a constant flow of new perspectives will focus on elements with short-term results. Organizations that employ a greater percentage of temporary or part-time staff in response to seasonal fluctuations will provide only minimal benefits to this segment of the staff and more robust offerings to the full-time contingent. Include the potential of changing demographics, such as the upcoming retirement of baby boomers when identifying these considerations, but take care to ensure that single employees won't feel slighted by spending that is heavily tilted toward family needs.

Employee engagement for all employees increases with benefits understanding and satisfaction. An employee who spends 20 minutes at his or her desk on hold waiting to talk to an insurance company representative, and is then told to call another number, will be unhappy and share this discontent with coworkers.

2. What Benefits Are Offered by Employers in the Same Industry or Geographic Area?

A survey of other companies' benefits should be conducted once each year before benefits plans are renewed or updated and whenever a new offering is contemplated. Useful information is available from benefits and human resource professional organizations, foundation research, local and regional business groups, and

---

WORTH REPEATING

Don't Play the Matching Game

A brand-new hospitality company surveyed competitors to find that benefits provided by well-established companies in the market were virtually identical. The offerings did not seem to match newer concepts and employee populations so they focused on budget and worker needs in creating plans. Before long other companies were copying the start-up.

---

industry or trade associations. Data can be obtained without charge or at a range of price points for specific information or targeted surveys from consulting firms. Published information can be augmented by a project undertaken by an internal staff member who has an understanding of benefits terminology.

There is no need to panic when your most valuable employee brings you a glossy multipage brochure describing every imaginable benefit—from personal concierge to long-term care—offered by the "hot" company across town. This information can be integrated into existing results or trigger a new benefits survey. An effective approach identifies the offerings of employers who draw from the same pool of candidates, evaluates the competition, and has the potential to yield information about new or creative options. The local geographic area will be the source for information about positions that can be filled from the immediate population, but a broader survey is needed for roles that require recruitment from a wider talent pool.

Review the complete information to identify your best options in response to the competition. A new, large employer with very generous benefits can pose a threat with the potential to poach your talent. Although it may not be realistic to match all the expensive items, you can select those that are most important to your staff. Convene focus groups or conduct an employee survey to differentiate the real wants and needs from components that are nice but not essential.

Combine any efforts to seek employee input with education about the contents and costs for employer-sponsored plans. Remember that the life stages of your workforce will change. In a new location with a very young population, internal survey results may place a very low priority on long-term savings. Enrollment, vesting schedules, and company contributions should be tweaked before a retirement savings plan is eliminated in favor of providing an on-site holistic healing clinic. Disseminate the results of employee input, along with clear explanations and information, as the basis for decision making. In response to employee feedback, demonstrate sound responsiveness by offering a plan that includes a dental benefits provider affiliated with a large local practice, and fiscal responsibility in explaining that housing a day-care center is just too expensive.

3. How Much Can You Spend Now and in the Future?

Providing employee benefits is a significant financial commitment but it does not have to be a blank check. Dollar amounts included in forecasts and budgets, whether they are for one, three, five years, or longer, should be backed up by information from benefits decision makers. Yes, it is difficult to project expenditures, particularly for health care, but budgeting can be used to drive plan design and employee cost-sharing equations. When a renewal quote includes an unanticipated double-digit increase and immediate cost savings cannot be found, steps can be taken to stem the trend for subsequent years; this is the time to lay the groundwork for the potential of significant changes including an entirely new plan design or patterns for employee cost sharing. Scaling back employee plans is never popular and will be more likely if multiyear forecasts are not created.

Calculations are commonly represented as a percentage of wages. The United States Bureau of Labor Statistics (BLS) reported that the national average cost of benefits for all civilian workers was 30.2% of wages at the end of 2008. This represents a rise in 2 percentage points from 2003 when the same statistic was 28.2%. Average costs range from 27% to more than 33% of payroll dollars based upon industry, location, and occupation. BLS publishes statistics broken down by broad regions (the 14 largest metropolitan areas in the country), as well as by worker characteristics. Don't be shocked if the benefits percentage in your organization is significantly higher. BLS statistics bundle information from all employers, whether or not they offer benefits plans, including those who only provide mandated coverage or hire large numbers of part-time employees. Statutory benefits cost employers a relatively stable average of 8% of compensation. Unemployment and worker's compensation payments will vary based on employer experience and industry trends. Begin building the cost structure by using statutory benefits as a base and identifying the additional spending you are prepared to make to create a total budget.

When staffing levels fluctuate, identifying costs as a percentage of payroll will be the most useful measurement. A zealous accountant may seek specific projections when demographics change. This makes sense when 100 new employees are added primarily from a population of recent college graduates who will be working for many months before they are eligible for medical coverage—but should not extend to initiating a questionnaire that asks employees about plans for starting a family.

WHO IS GOING TO BE ELIGIBLE FOR BENEFITS?

Eligibility decisions have two parts: who will be able to participate in plans and when does coverage start? Coverage can be based upon employee classification or status but must be administered consistently within each group. The definition of who can participate will be included in any agreements written by plan providers. Employers should have published definitions of the difference between full- and part-time status and any other classification used in their workplace, such as temporary or casual. Employers should consider aligning a description of full-time status eligibility for health benefits with the PPACA that defines full-time employees as individuals who worked at least 30 hours a week during the previous calendar year. These should be in writing, provided to employees, and specifically included in each plan eligibility description.

What Benefits Should I Give to Part-Time Employees?

Employers commonly limit part-time employee benefits to prorated vacation and holiday pay. After completing competitive research

BETTER FORGOTTEN

But I Thought They Were Part-Time

A real estate management company provided benefits for all full-time employees and gave everyone an employee handbook, but there was no definition of full- or part-time. The office manager made decisions when people were hired. One employee who had been working a full week reduced her hours to one shift on the weekend in order to finish college. Eight months later the office manager noticed the drop in hours, terminated the employee from the plan and sent out a COBRA letter. The employee protested, citing the lack of definition of employee classifications. It took many more months, premium dollars, and extension of the COBRA start date before the discrepancy was settled.

and creating your benefits philosophy, you may decide that these workers should also be able to participate in health benefit plans and other options. If your organization relies on a stable, part-time workforce, this decision will make more sense. A fluctuating staff with limited hours can incur additional indirect costs due to complicated and time-consuming administration.

The design of 401(k) and defined benefit retirement plans create an exception to an employer's ability to broadly define eligibility. Federal law governing employer-sponsored retirement plans requires employers who offer these plans to include all employees who are at least 21 years old and work 1,000 or more hours during an eligibility year.

When Does Coverage Start?

Policies about waiting periods for eligibility will be driven by competitive data and administrative considerations. It will be easier to enroll and track employees if there is some consistency in these dates. Imagine the headaches created at a company that enrolls employees for medical coverage after 60 days, dental at the end of six months, allows sick days with 120 days on payroll, and awards vacation time off upon completion of nine months of service. Though it may not be possible, or desirable, to identify a single eligibility date for all benefits, using the same time frame as much as practicable will simplify record keeping and communications. One date can be used for health coverage and paid time off, while entry into the retirement plan requires a longer waiting period. Record keeping is also made easier when enrollment and eligibility begin on the first day of a calendar month. Check payroll and HRIS capabilities to identify capacity for tracking and deductions to match plan parameters.

The most common waiting periods for health coverage are 30, 60, and 90 days. Effective January 1, 2014, the federal PPACA will preclude waiting periods that are more than 90 days. These have lengthened with the availability of COBRA continuation. Longer waiting periods are suitable when there is high turnover during the early days of employment, unless the lack of benefits is one of the reasons for the churn. If health benefits enrollment dates become an issue during a hiring negotiation it is not necessary, or advisable, to seek or create a plan exception. The better approach is to offer to reimburse COBRA expenses or the cost of individual insurance, thus saving money and preserving consistency. A time-off policy exception will make sense for the department manager who has a ten-day summer vacation planned six months before he would be eligible for any paid days off. You can determine whether you will pay all or part of the time off and include the exception, in writing, in an offer letter. Don't feel obligated to continue wages during a vacation taken during the first few months of employment; the individual who is changing jobs is probably being paid for unused days by his or her previous employer.

What About Benefits for Employees' Domestic Partners?

Benefit coverage for employees' domestic partners have been increasing in popularity since they were first offered during the 1980s. In 2008 35% of U.S. private employers, including 52% of Fortune 500 companies, extended eligibility for health care benefits to domestic partners. Your benefits provider will be able to tell you if adding this benefit will have an impact on premiums. Once you make the decision to offer domestic partner coverage, you will need to identify the documentation required for eligibility. Employers in locations where any type of government registration of domestic partner status is available can require proof of registration to provide the benefit. Where local registration is not available, the requirements from a nearby municipality can be incorporated into your policy. Any standard you create must be applied consistently; don't offer domestic partner benefits to all employees and then require proof of registration for same-sex couples while covering a heterosexual couple simply because "everyone knows they've been living together for ten years."

The cost of providing health insurance for domestic partners must be considered taxable income and included on annual W-2 forms. Employer payments for qualified health benefit plans available for employees, their spouses, and dependents are not treated as taxable income; a domestic partner, whether same-sex or not, cannot be considered a spouse under federal law. Avoid year-end surprises by communicating this information at the time of enrollment.

Can I Put My Brother on the Plan?

Check eligibility rules carefully before you set up company-sponsored group benefits with the intent to cover your extended family. The employer who decides to cover his elderly parent should be prepared to identify the nature of the employment. Putting a parent on payroll as a consultant, when she lives thousands of miles away and does not have any visible responsibilities, creates a red flag for a fraud investigation.

Should the Benefits Philosophy Be Summarized in a Written Statement?

Business plans and decisions are more effective when they are focused on a goal. A benefits philosophy can create this goal or guiding principal.

Here are two examples:

The ABC Company provides benefits that ensure complete coverage for all employees and their families in the event of major health care expenses and loss of income due to a serious illness, allow for savings and accumulation of funds for a comfortable retirement, and offer time away from work for vacation and personal matters. ABC employees are provided with the knowledge and tools needed to effectively participate in mandatory wellness programs to improve health and be active consumers of care through educated purchasing decisions.

XYZ Inc. provides employee benefits at a variety of levels that respond to individual needs identified through constant communication and input. Each year the annual benefits budget will be identified and communicated to all employees. Annual benefits budget increases will not exceed 8% over the previous year for all options combined.

A well-thought-out benefits philosophy statement should not be kept a secret. It can provide the core of an explanation to staff of the reasoning behind benefits decisions, demonstrate consistency, and be used in recruitment materials.

WHAT BENEFITS ARE EMPLOYERS REQUIRED TO PROVIDE?

The most costly workplace benefits, health and retirement, are not mandated by law. When provided, these are often highly regulated by states and the federal government.

Does Health Reform Change Everything?

The Patient Protection and Affordable Care Act of 2010 (PPACA) does not require employers to offer health coverage, but as of January 1, 2014, it does assess penalties on an employer of more than 50 employees who does not offer health benefits, and it contains a number of specific requirements that affect employer-provided plans. The PPACA also establishes a national voluntary long-term-care plan that is paid for through payroll deduction effective January 1, 2011. A time line of these items is included in a separate chapter.

Both unemployment insurance and workers' compensation are mandated by federal legislation but administered by each state. The many variations in regulations and administrative requirements make it impossible to cover these comprehensively in this volume. This overview will provide generalized information and direction for additional resources.

Workers' Compensation

For almost a century workers' compensation has protected both employers and employees. The availability of medical coverage and compensation protects employees in the event of a work-related illness or injury while employers are shielded by law from suits for damages by the affected employees. Benefit levels are mandated by each state and can vary widely in both the amounts paid and the processes for administration. In all states workers' compensation laws prohibit individuals from seeking additional damages from their employers for workplace accidents and sickness.

Workers' compensation expenses are paid through specialty insurers and state-administered funds. This kind of coverage is experience rated; the higher the level of expenses the higher the costs. For a new or very small employer the experience rating will be based upon a common industry and geographic area. Although workers' compensation often seems like a black hole of uncontrollable expenses, employers can take steps to reduce illness and injuries through effective workplace safety and monitoring programs. Workers' compensation carriers will provide additional resources for these efforts.

Cost savings can be achieved in states where employers are allowed to direct or manage care. Check with your insurer to see if you can designate specific providers or require second opinions. When employees are out of work for extended periods of time, keeping in touch on a regular schedule will continue a connection to the job and can hasten a return to work. Employers also reduce expenses by instituting light-duty programs or reduced work weeks that return people to the workplace gradually and provide impetus to get back to their "real" jobs. It is important to understand reporting requirements and specifics about injuries covered away from an employer's

BETTER FORGOTTEN

Weekend Warriors Increase Costs

One employer found that their most serious workers' compensation claims that increased costs and resulted in significant lost time from work came from members of the new company-sponsored soccer team. The lengthening disabled list ended the team's playing career after one season.

premises. It's easy to see how the painter who falls off a ladder at a worksite will be covered by workers' compensation. The twisted ankle during the sack race at the annual company picnic and the broken hand of the star pitcher on the company softball team will probably be covered under workers' compensation too. Contact the agency that administers workers' compensation in your state for specific definitions.

Unemployment Insurance

Unemployment insurance (UI) benefits are designed to provide a safety net for employees. Employers pay both federal and state unemployment taxes as a percentage of earnings up to a maximum amount of taxable wages. Employers pay into state funds at a rate determined by their level of claims or experience, and eligible individuals are paid benefits using formulas that include wages and weeks worked during a specified period. An employee terminated during the first week of employment may be eligible for unemployment benefits if he or she has worked the required number of weeks at a previous employer.

Although it is certainly in an employer's interest to take steps to reduce the UI rate, contesting every claim is not the best approach. In the event of layoffs these benefits serve their intended purpose of allowing individuals to remain actively searching for work while collecting a base amount. Employees may also be eligible for partial unemployment if their earnings are cut due to a reduced workweek; this payment could dissuade valuable staff from using the time off to find a new job. Disseminating up-to-date information about UI benefits to employees at the time of a layoff or reduction in hours demonstrates concern and clarifies misconceptions. Contact your state department of labor to obtain instructions and directions to facilitate processes and minimize frustrations.

Respond promptly to any information requests concerning UI claims; delays can incur fines and determinations may be based only on information provided by the individual out of work. When an employee is fired you choose whether or not to contest the claim for unemployment benefits. Determination of eligibility is based on the factors supporting the termination decision; UI benefits are delayed or not given to individuals who are fired due to misconduct. The definition of misconduct applied in these cases is much narrower than the standards used by most employers and varies by state. Obtain clarification of these rules from in-house human resources, an external consultant, or specialist in responding to UI claims and the state agency that administers unemployment benefits. In the event of a termination involving a difficult individual, it can be prudent not to contest the unemployment claim in an effort to avoid or minimize additional actions by an angry former employee, or as an offer of good faith to conclude the employment relationship without ill will. Never create a false record by describing different circumstances surrounding a termination; the best response may be none or simply "The employer does not wish to contest this claim at the present time."

WORTH REPEATING

Call My Payroll Provider

A multilocation employer contracted with a service through their payroll processor to respond to all unemployment insurance claims. Independent consultants or those linked to a payroll company can keep up to date with all of the details required for administering UI. The dollars saved in adjusted claims and other reviews more than pay for the cost of the service.

Are There State Specific Requirements for Other Benefits?

Six jurisdictions extend the safety net to include compulsory Short-Term Disability (STD) providing income in the event of non-work-related injury or illness. California, Hawaii, New Jersey, New York, Puerto Rico, and Rhode Island require all employers with at least one employee to participate in an STD plan. The specifics of STD vary by location, but in all cases noncompliance can result in fines and penalties. The benefit is extended to employees regardless of full- or part-time status and is based upon where the individual works. If a company headquartered in Connecticut employs sales-people in Rhode Island and New York, STD must be provided in the two states where the benefit is compulsory, whether they work out of space with the company name on the door or function effectively from a home office.

The benefit amount varies by state and individual earnings but should certainly be communicated as part of a benefit package. California also extends disability, for a specified period, to Paid Family Leave to allow employees to care for a seriously ill child, spouse, parent, or registered domestic partner, or to bond with a new minor child.

Don't I Have to Pay for Regular Sick Days?

There are no federal requirements to provide paid time off for sick days, vacation, or even holidays. Identification of these benefits days will be an employer decision based on the considerations outlined here. A detailed description of paid time-off benefits is included in Chapter Two.

What Do I Need to Know About Federal Law That Regulates Employee Benefits?

ERISA, the Employee Retirement Income Security Act, is the federal law enacted in 1974 to govern employer-sponsored benefit plans. ERISA does not require employer-provided plans but it does govern regular plans that are established in two categories: Employee Welfare Benefit Plans and Employee Pension Benefit Plans.

Employee Welfare Benefit Plans defined by ERISA include any employer-offered plan that provides benefits for:

- Health insurance
- Group life insurance
- Long-term disability coverage
- Severance pay
- Vacation pay
- Apprentice or other training programs
- Day-care centers
- Scholarship funds
- Prepaid legal services

Benefits covered by ERISA as Employee Pension Benefit Plans include:

- Profit-sharing retirement plans
- Stock bonus plans
- Money purchase plans
- 401(k) plans
- Employee stock ownership plans
- Defined benefit retirement plans

What Are SPDs and 5500s?

All plans covered under ERISA are governed by a set of reporting and disclosure requirements. Summary Plan Descriptions (SPDs) that describe eligibility, claim procedures, and appeals must be provided to participants within 90 days of employee eligibility and after any significant modification. Other amendment changes require updated SPD distribution every 5 years and every 10 years if there are no plan changes. Your benefits broker or provider can create or furnish these SPDs. They may bundle distribution in regular mailings and the requirement can also be satisfied by providing online access to these documents. The SPD is a summary of a full plan document which, in accordance with ERISA, must be made available upon request to employees and their beneficiaries. Ask for a full plan document for each covered plan as part of the annual renewal process. Ensure notification compliance by distributing the current SPD as part of annual open enrollment communications.

Whereas SPDs comply with an internal requirement, Form 5500 reports must be filed with the IRS. The Form 5500 is due on the last day of the seventh month after the end of each plan year. For plans that follow a calendar year, the 5500 report is due on the following July 31st. Welfare Benefit Plan 5500s include data about participation and can be completed by a benefits professional or broker and are filed electronically. Completing the 5500 report for retirement plans is an extremely complex undertaking typically performed by external accountants with expertise in this function.

ERISA prohibits employers from discriminating or retaliating against participants or their beneficiaries in exercising their rights under covered plans. The wide reach of these provisions results in enforcement powers within a number of agencies, including the Departments of Labor and Treasury and Pension Benefit Guaranty Corporation.

Approaching employee benefits with a guiding strategy, a view of the competitive landscape, and a basic understanding of legislative requirements will facilitate decision making. The result will be the difference between a collection of initiatives with the potential for conflicts and mounting administrative headaches and a responsive program that enhances the employment package.

WORTH REPEATING

Get the Cost Up Front to Avoid Sticker Shock

An employer with a staff of more than 750 researched 401(k) plan providers, asking for details of all plan fees including recommendations for an accountant to complete the filing and the potential cost of the annual 5500 reporting. The employer verified the information with references. Providers who did not respond were taken out of consideration and the employer had a solid basis when budgeting for the benefit.

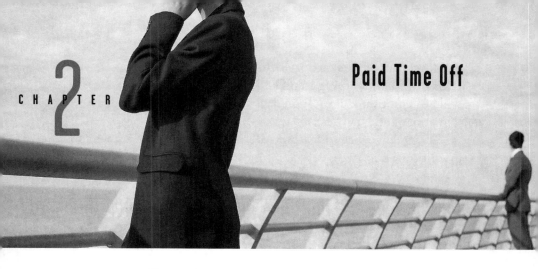

2

Paid Time Off

How Many Vacation Days Do I Have to Give?

V ACATION AND HOLIDAY PAY TOP THE LIST OF BENEFITS provided by private sector employers in the United States. More than 90% of these employers offer full-time staff compensation for vacations and 89% grant paid holidays. The variety of paid time off expands for some organizations to include leave in a range of categories from birthdays to bereavement. Policies may also create a bank of time in the form of Paid Time Off (PTO) to be taken for reasons at the employee's discretion. A handful of states legislate varying forms of pay for jury duty and a few cities have created employer requirements to provide sick days.

VACATIONS

Vacation policies are designed to aid recruitment and retention and allow employees time off from work to rest and recharge.

Do I Have to Give Everyone Two Weeks off?

Vacation plans commonly reward longevity by providing an increasing number of days as length of service progresses. New employees are unlikely to expect to be able to earn their wages while taking the month of August off and veterans with ten years of service will be demotivated if vacation days are limited to one week between Christmas and New Year's Day.

The following chart featuring BLS data indicates the averages for *all* full-time employees.

	AFTER 1 YEAR	AFTER 3 YEARS	AFTER 5 YEARS	AFTER 10 YEARS	AFTER 15 YEARS	AFTER 20 YEARS	AFTER 25 YEARS
DAYS OF PAID VACATION	9.2	11.3	13.7	16.5	18.0	18.9	19.5

Conduct or review research for your industry, types of positions, and location before using this information to adopt or change your own schedule of vacation allotments. The same national data reports that 28% of managers and professionals earn 20 days of vacation after 10 years of employment, whereas 44% of service workers can take five days off with pay at the end of a year on the job. Nonprofits and public employers are recognized as having the most generous vacation allocations. This is often described as a tradeoff for lower government and nonprofit rates of pay. Part-time employees in any sector are the least likely to receive significant, if any, vacation allowances.

If you are creating a policy for the first time or reviewing an existing one, it's a good idea to err on the side of offering a more conservative number of vacation days. A subsequent increase can be promoted with fanfare; any conversation about shrinking the number of available days will be greeted with an adverse reaction.

Can the VP of Sales Get Five Weeks of Vacation?

Vacation eligibility can be tailored to groups of staff; for example, the management team is designated as eligible for more paid time away from work than hourly employees, or there can be greater allocations for positions at director or vice president levels and above.

Individual situations can be acknowledged by granting additional vacation time at the time of hire or after. Make certain that any special arrangements will not be considered discriminatory. When a hiring manager promises an extra week of vacation to every white woman brought in as a department head but minority female and all male counterparts are granted only the regular vacation days—even after they too asked for exceptions—these actions could provoke claims of discrimination under ERISA and federal employment law.

Exceptions are most common for individuals hired away from senior positions where they had accumulated enough time to earn up to four weeks of vacation. Before rushing to match 22 paid days ask the individual if she had used all the time in the past. A better tactic may be to agree on a schedule to earn the days as employment progresses that will satisfy all parties. Document any exception to the vacation policy in writing in an offer letter or memo to the employee to minimize misunderstandings that can pop up when there are management changes or the employee leaves. In many states, absent a written description, disputes about pay are settled in favor of the employee; thus, an amiable handshake could become an expensive gesture.

When Can Employees Take the First Vacation Day?

Identifying the number of days available is essential but it's only the first step in creating a coherent policy. Vacations are calculated, earned, and accrued using an endless variety of methods. Too often there is disagreement about this process between accounting, line managers, and even human resources that causes confusion and the potential for misinformation resulting in employee discontent. An employee thinks he has seven vacation days, accounting tells him eight, but the boss says he can't take any until after the end of the year.

A clearly written vacation policy answers two questions:

1. How are vacation days earned?

    There are employers who calculate vacation earnings based on hours worked beginning on the first day of employment. For example, if new employees earn one vacation day after every 26 hours worked, at the end of a year of 40-hour work weeks they have gained 10 days of vacation. Other organizations use specific calendar dates to determine vacation totals. This format might specify that employees hired before June 30th are eligible for five vacation days following January 1st of the subsequent year. These illustrations represent very different approaches and do not describe entitlement for longer-term employees. Consider recruiting strategies and consult with accounting and payroll services when identifying a policy that best fits your organization. Processes that can be easily tracked in payroll or HRIS systems will ensure accuracy, minimize administrative headaches, and provide more consistent information to employees.

2. When can employees take earned vacation?

Employers commonly require a waiting period once at the beginning of employment, or during each vacation year, whereas some employers allow requests for time off as soon as the benefit is earned. Operational needs can result in the establishment of mandatory weeks when the workplace is shut down, functioning with minimal staff, or the designation of blackout periods when business levels prohibit vacation time off. These can be written into a policy and announced as the need arises. Many employers differentiate between accrued and earned vacation in communicating to employees. Accrued vacation describes the formula used to award the time that turns into earned vacation when the employee becomes eligible to use the days. For example, "Full-time employees of the ABC Company begin accruing one day of vacation for every 160 hours worked on their first day of work; this time can be taken after six months of employment." Accruals are also used under accounting standards to tally the financial cost of the vacation to the employer. Whenever these terms are used it is important that employees understand the difference between the two and that policies do not mix the terms up in a description that ends up altering the intent.

What Does a Vacation Policy Look Like?

Because vacation is considered an Employee Benefit Welfare Plan under ERISA, you must have something in writing that describes specifics.

Here's a brief policy sample describing vacation earnings and eligibility:

> *Beginning on their date of hire until December 31st of the calendar year in which they are employed, full-time employees of XYZ Enterprises accrue .75 of one vacation day for each complete calendar month they work. Beginning on January 1st for each of the next two calendar years of full-time employment, employees of XYZ enterprises accrue .833 vacation days for each complete calendar month they work. Employees can request this time off to be taken at any time during the calendar year after it is accrued.*

The policy can be further clarified using a chart to describe eligibility:

XYZ Enterprises Vacation Eligibility

Length of Service	Number of Days Earned as of January 1st
Less than one year	.75 day for each complete calendar month worked
One to three years	10 days
Three to five years	12 days
Five to ten years	15 days
Ten years or more	20 days

Examples can make communications even clearer, such as, "If Sue was hired by XYZ Enterprises on April 20, 2010, on January 1, 2011, she will be eligible for 6 vacation days and on January 1, 2012, she will have 10 days earned."

Can Employees Take Earned Vacation Whenever They Want?

XYZ Enterprises would not be very productive if Sue and all her colleagues took off each year from January 2nd through January 15th because they had earned the time. Effective vacation policies include specific steps necessary to request and receive approval for time off. Separate the processes for verifying eligibility, the number of available days, and compatibility with work requirements, and always include a statement that eligibility does not guarantee that vacation will be granted as requested. For scheduling purposes, decisions about the length of notice can include different requirements based on the number of days in question. Two consecutive weeks can necessitate a request at least 90 days in advance, whereas two days to extend a weekend or holiday can be sought at the beginning of the previous work week. Minimize mistakes and miscommunication with procedures that identify the approval path, include written documentation, which can be as simple as an e-mail, and provide for follow-up and receipt. Designate due dates for all vacation requests for popular summer or holiday weeks with the understanding that business demands can result in a variation in requirements by department; for example, requests will not be granted by Accounting when calendar year end closing activities are at their peak, but a function that realizes a drop in activity just before Christmas will be very willing to allow employees to take off the last week of the year. Employers may require that vacations be taken in five-day or full-week intervals, whereas others do not allow vacation time off longer than five consecutive days. Don't include restrictions simply for convenience; they should be based on a real business reason that can be explained to employees.

Vacation approvals should not be based solely on seniority; employers typically approve requests on a first-come, first-served basis. Write this into the policy to avoid a ten-year veteran attempting to bump an individual with three years on the job who had requested the time off many months in advance to take a cruise.

BETTER FORGOTTEN

But the Night Manager Told Me I Could Go on Vacation

A restaurant manager decided that a bartender had abandoned his job when he didn't show up for work for two weeks. The employee came in at the end of the period ready to work as if nothing unusual had happened. When the restaurant manager confronted him with the intention of termination, the bartender replied, "The assistant manager who works at night approved my vacation." Make certain the approval process is clear and provides availability of a written acknowledgment.

Can Employees Use Their Time in Partial Days?

There are three main considerations in deciding whether to allow employees to take vacation in partial days.

1. How will the time be tracked?

   Payroll systems can easily account for time in days, hours, and even fractions of hours. Maintaining records that track two hours of vacation on Tuesday and three hours the following Friday may sound like a nightmare or it may be an automated breeze with up-to-date information available on demand for employees and their managers.

2. How does a partial vacation day affect workload?

   Will the employee have to be replaced during her absence and, if so, is someone available for the short shift? Or does the individual catch up later with a coworker picking up the slack?

3. Can exempt employees be paid partial vacation days?

   Employees who are classified as exempt from overtime, as defined by the federal Fair Labor Standards Act (FLSA), receive a salary for each week no matter how many hours are worked. Vacation time is considered a benefit, not hours worked, so exempt employees can receive pay for part of a day's earnings from this compensation category.

   In any partial vacation day policy avoid confusion by clarifying available time increments and the request process. Working until lunch, using a half day of vacation approved in advance on the day before a long holiday weekend, may be perfectly acceptable.

WORTH REPEATING

Follow the Steps, Take Your Vacation

A professional services firm simplified a long list of rules for vacation requests into Steps 1 through 5 for employees to follow. The initial response of "You're treating us like babies" dissipated when employees realized that following the easy steps, in order, resulted in a quicker answer if requests were denied and better tracking for correct payment.

Calling in from a break to request a few hours of paid time to take advantage of bargains at a big sale would not be allowed.

How Do We Handle the Employee with 60 Vacation Days?

Employees want a generous amount of paid days away from work yet many never use up the time they earn. The International Vacation Deprivation Survey, conducted by Internet travel company Expedia.com since 2000, has consistently found that more than 30% of Americans do not take all of their vacation days. In some cases employers allow the days to pile up, accumulating backlogs of 40 or even 60 days while employees continue to earn new paid leave. It is unlikely that the boss is looking forward to approving requests for 14 weeks of vacation.

These jumbo vacation allocations create a potential financial burden by accumulating days to be paid at the higher rate in effect when the time is taken and, in states and municipalities that mandate payouts of earned and unused vacation, when employment ends.

There are a few ways to reduce these obligations:

- Make a one-time payment of all outstanding vacation not taken before the end of the previous accrual period.

- Identify a payment at a reduced rate or pay for a portion of the days, requiring the employee to take the remaining time before a specified end date.

- Create a schedule indicating a date by which the days must be used up or will be lost.

- Allow employees to transfer these days into a bank of hospital or disability days to be used in the event of a hospitalization or longer-term illness.

- Allow employees to donate these days to a leave bank to be used by other employees facing serious illness or to care for a family member.

Check state laws before selecting a course of action. In states where vacation time is automatically considered wages, there will be restrictions on any scheme that potentially limits payouts. A combination of these strategies can also be used. Once the steps are put in place to

BETTER FORGOTTEN

Two-Week Maximum Carryover, Every Year

An energy company thought they were limiting vacation accumulation with the statement, "Employees must take their vacations during the calendar year and the vacation time may not be carried over the year's end unless approved, in writing, by the manager. Such accumulations shall not exceed two weeks." This was interpreted by employees, and supported by wage and hour, to mean two weeks each year. Make certain that any carryover limitations are clear enough to avoid misinterpretation.

reduce huge vacation accounts it is essential that practices are established to avoid this pattern for the future. Too many employers go through financial pain to eliminate outsized vacation earnings without implementing any policy changes and face the same situation five years later.

Include one of these options in policies to prevent vacation buildup:

- Adopt a "use it or lose it" policy, if allowed in your state. Employees are not allowed to carry unused days over into the next vacation period.
- Extend a grace period for using up a specified number of vacation days that includes a requirement for prior approval.
- Allow transfer of some excess vacation time to hospital or disability days or leave sharing banks.

Any extension or bank must contain a cap on the number of days allowed. The problem is not eliminated when 50 vacation days are simply turned into an equivalent number of hospital days.

What's a Leave Sharing Bank?

Leave sharing programs allow employees to help coworkers respond to extraordinarily difficult situations, without requiring

---

WORTH REPEATING

It's All One Policy Now

A midsize service provider was bought by a larger company. The parent organization had a different vacation structure and the smaller employer had allowed time earned for vacation to pile up in supersized numbers. The employer extended the new policy at the same time that it established parameters for handling the vacation backlog. Not everyone was happy about the result but the company was able to move forward with a clear, consistent policy without the cloud of extra unused days.

---

direct cash donations, by donating paid time off to be used by others who have exhausted this benefit. The employer manages the bank and accepts applications from employees to draw time in the event of specifically defined situations. Employees who donate leave cannot designate the recipient of their time and a leave program should not be created in response to one personal tragedy.

The IRS has approved special tax treatment for donors, recipients, and the employer for leave banks designed to respond to a prolonged absence due to defined medical emergencies and major disasters that cause an employee substantial income loss. A tax professional should be consulted to ensure guidelines are clear and that potential liabilities are understood. State laws may limit the types and amount of leave that can be donated, adding complications that should be navigated by benefits professionals or an attorney with applicable expertise.

What Happens to Unused Vacation When Employees Leave?

Decisions about distribution of unused vacation should consider potential costs and state law. Seventeen states require unused vacation to be paid out; 20 allow employers to determine the parameters of this policy. Where state requirements exist they can include: payout of all time accrued and earned, even if the employee is not yet eligible to take the days; payment for earned days only; or employers can restrict post-termination payouts as long as the policy is communicated in writing.

Absent state requirements, include specifics in your written policy to avoid claims and disputes after the employment relationship ends. A fair policy errs towards paying unused vacation to longer-term staff upon resignation but saves money by denying payment to short-term employees in high turnover spots. For multistate employers the legislation in force is based on the location of the employee, not the main office. Adopting site-specific policies will add to confusion, cause potential discontent, and create continued headaches if employees relocate. Review the complete policy at least once each year to ensure continued compliance.

HOLIDAYS

Holiday closures are the norm in many industries but cannot be accommodated in seven-day-per-week operations.

Do I Pay Employees Extra When They Work on a Federal Holiday?

Federal holiday designations do not specify a requirement for premium pay or even any time off. Employers can designate their own holiday schedules, including popular regional, state, or company-specific days, and associated pay practices. The fewest rules will be attached to the organization that regularly closes on a holiday and no one works.

Follow these steps to create a coherent policy:

Step 1: Identify the Holidays to Be Observed

There's no reason to spend time trying to identify the perfect holiday schedule; it's easier to publish the days to be observed in advance of each calendar year. The number of days and specific holidays can be changed based on business demands and other schedule considerations. When January 1st is a Saturday you may choose to celebrate New Year's Day on December 31st, or a Thursday Independence Day can spur a four-day weekend to include July 4th and 5th. The U.S. Office of Personnel Management publishes a schedule each year of the days on which federal holidays will be observed by its agencies. Use this information, your competitive data, and identification of locally observed holidays to write your own list. The updated annual list is clearer than a handbook description that is full of caveats, "If a holiday falls on a Sunday it will usually be observed on the following Monday." Distinct groups or categories of employees can be eligible for different holiday lists as long as the benefit is applied consistently within each designation.

Step 2: Establish Eligibility Rules

Choose one rule for all full-timers or create a distinction between exempt and nonexempt employees. A single standard will grant the holiday benefit as of the date of hire to comply with wage and hour requirements to pay exempt employees for a full work week when they are ready and willing to work. In a workforce with a large hourly contingent and higher turnover, a waiting period makes sense to save money and encourage retention. To facilitate administration, set the eligibility date to coincide with other benefits. Many employers deny hourly nonexempt employees holiday pay if they fail to report to work on the scheduled days before and after the holiday. The employee who extends Thanksgiving to a three-day celebration may be disqualified from earning holiday pay. Applying the same rule to exempt employees exposes a potential land mine of wage and hour violations; check federal and state statutes carefully before adopting this stance. A seven-days-per-week operation that does not close for holidays should also include specifics to describe pay parameters for employees who are scheduled to work but call in sick on these days. Holiday pay need not be paid to any employee out of work on an extended unpaid or disability leave of absence. Make certain to put all eligibility rules and qualifications in writing and check for compliance with state laws.

Step 3: Designate Holiday Pay Rates

Holiday pay, for employees who have the day off, is typically paid at a rate of one full day of pay. If you choose to provide this benefit to part-time employees, compensation can be set at a specific amount, such as four hours' pay, or on a prorated amount based on average hours worked. Employees who work on a designated holiday can be paid a premium for the time they work or simply receive holiday plus regular pay for the day. The formula must be clear and in writing, and the categories identified correctly on the pay stub. In a difficult staffing situation consider announcing a one-time premium to provide a much-needed incentive.

Any pay schedule for working on a holiday needs to clearly designate, "for hours worked." Don't write, "Employees who work on a holiday will earn time and one-half plus holiday pay." This can be interpreted to mean that they receive 20 hours of pay even if they only work four hours and your intent was to pay them 14 hours.

WORTH REPEATING

This Year Memorial Day Work Earns Double Time

A nonprofit operator of group homes knew that the combination of a popular concert in the area, the forecast of good weather, and regularly scheduled staff needed at a special event would make it very difficult to find enough employees willing to work on Memorial Day. The employer extended a one-time-only offer announcing that all employees would be paid double time for the hours worked on this day, plus holiday pay. Just enough employees responded to the offer to ensure that no one had to work overtime and there were no service interruptions.

SICK DAYS

The factors involved in offering sick days have some similarities to those described for other items in this chapter with the addition of potential specific unique considerations.

Are Six Sick Days Enough?

More than 70% of employers offer full-time employees sick leave through policies as different as honor systems that place no limit on days, disability coverage for lengthier periods, and allocations of three, five, six, or ten days a year. Your own policy should fit within your benefits strategy and may make this time available through a Paid Time Off bank or, as a deterrent to absenteeism, you may decide not to offer paid sick time. Employers in Milwaukee (*law currently blocked by court injunction*), San Francisco, and Washington, D.C. are required to cover between three and nine paid sick days each year with varying eligibility based on size of employer, length of employment, and number of hours worked. Beyond legislative requirements, sick days provide employees with continuation of pay when they cannot work and the potential to minimize illness in the workplace. Presenteeism, the tendency of an increasing number of employees to show up at work sick, reduces productivity, prolongs illness, and increases the likelihood of spreading disease to coworkers.

There are four specific issues to review regarding your sick leave policy:

1. How many sick days should you provide and how are they earned?

    Sick-day allowances are routine and generous in public employment and nonprofit sectors, but the wide variation in private employer offerings makes it tough to use comparison data for this decision. Think about the impact on your company before you commit to twelve sick days as offered to government employees in your state, even if you hire people with similar skills. Can you cover for the absences or afford a fat check to a departing employee that includes a month or more of accumulated sick pay? Consider eligibility for short-term disability, flexible schedules to accommodate medical treatment appointments, or other benefit days that can be used to manage this time off. When an annual number is agreed on, create the schedule for earning sick time. Unlike vacation, sick time does not typically increase with longevity, with the exception of adding to the nominal number of days during the first few months or year of employment.

2. What are the eligibility criteria?

    Administration will be easier if waiting periods and full- and part-time eligibility are matched to vacation-day rules. Eligibility criteria should also define if and when sick leave can be used for situations other than an employee illness. Some state laws require employers to allow available sick leave use when an employee needs to care for a seriously ill family member. It is common, and required by some state laws, for sick leave to be allowable to care for an ill child and cover time away from work for doctor appointments and medical procedures for employees and to accompany immediate family members. The policy can specify that sick time cannot be used for personal or vacation time.

3. Will you allow partial sick days?

   If you are covered by the Family Medical Leave Act (FMLA), an employee can be eligible to take intermittent leave in partial days. FMLA does not require payment for intermittent leave but it makes sense to allow the employee to receive the pay and use up available time. This provision would not make it necessary to allow sick time in the same increments for time off in a way that does not qualify under the FMLA. An employee arriving at work an hour late, twice a week, in order to accommodate chemotherapy can use sick time, but your policy may not allow use of the same benefit for routine dental work. Make certain that any distinction is incorporated clearly into your policy. Exempt employees can be paid partial sick days if they have the time available. Here again, check with your state department of labor; if paid sick time is not available you will most likely be required to pay exempts for a full work week.

4. How do employees request a sick day? Do sick days have to be used by the end of the year?

   Establish the procedure that requires employees, or an immediate family member if they are unable, to contact work when they will not be in for any eligible reason. This can be by phone or e-mail and needs to include the option of contacting more than one person; the designated immediate supervisor may not be available. The policy should state whether the employee must request sick-day pay or it will be included automatically for eligible occurrences. Be clear about any requirement for daily call-in during an extended absence. The team members on the receiving end of sick calls should be trained to obtain and record basic information for any call in case the conversation can be identified as a request for an FMLA leave.

Employers have long sought notes from a doctor for multiple-day absences, often making this a requirement for receipt of sick pay. Doctors' notes are easy to get and may contain protected personal medical information that should not be viewed by supervisors. Limit any request to a note clearing a person to return to work, which is perfectly acceptable and desirable after an employee has lost time due to a highly contagious disease.

Some employees consistently use all available sick time each year, while others never miss a day. "Use it or lose it" policies for sick days are more common, but they can backfire when the employee who feels that sick days are an entitlement, not a benefit, develops a sudden unexplained illness during the last week of the eligibility year. Allowing a carryover of some sick days can cover periods of an extended illness or be used to create a bank of days to be applied specifically for hospitalization, disability, or outpatient surgery. The number of hospital or disability days that can be accumulated should be capped. Employers may also choose to reward perfect attendance with a payout of some of the days.

Are Unused Sick Days Paid When an Employee Leaves?

State law requirements for sick-day payouts are less common than for vacation; check with your department of labor to ensure compliance. Don't assume that time must be specifically labeled "sick days," if carryover days have been converted into other types of leave; check to see if these are considered sick time under state legislation. Written policies should always specify the distribution, if any, of any unused time.

JURY DUTY

Both federal and state laws protect an employee's right to take time off from work for jury service. Federal law does not require any payment for this time and, though state statutes vary, they may require a small stipend of $40 or $50 a day, or full payment for a number of days; more than 60% of employers reported paying a jury duty benefit beyond any requirements.

The components of a policy on jury duty include:

1. Notification Requirements

    Ask employees to submit any jury duty summons to a specific individual, their supervisor, department manager, payroll, or human resources as soon as it is received. Employers may routinely write a letter to seek a postponement of every jury duty notification. In order to expand jury duty pools the permissible excuses for delay or exclusion have shrunk. If a postponement must be requested, be prepared to commit to a specific time frame for service. Employers should review and retain a copy of the juror summons. In many locations potential jurors do not automatically show up for the first day of jury duty; they may call in or log on in advance to find out if they need to report. This requirement will trigger scheduling considerations: must the employee be replaced in case he cannot come to work? Daily contact may be necessary to identify the specific date when jury duty will begin.

2. Number of Days; Paid or Unpaid

    Employers can limit the total number of days that employees can take for jury duty, whether or not they will be paid. Start by identifying payments required by your state and the amount of time you are willing to cover. One option can be five days of jury duty paid with an employee option to take unpaid time, or use other available paid leave, for an additional five days. In states where a small stipend is offered you may write, "Employees will be paid for up to ten days of approved jury duty at their regular rate of pay, less any stipend received; any additional service will be unpaid." Employers are not required to pay an employee who is serving on the jury for a five-week malpractice trial.

3. Returning to Work

    The policy may require proof of service and any payment in order to authorize the benefit or confirm unpaid leave. Workplaces with weekend, evening, or overnight shifts will need to identify any exceptions or modifications. If an employee who regularly works on Saturday and Sunday serves on a jury for five weekdays, is he entitled to five days of jury duty leave even if he works the weekend; or does he get the weekend off; or is he paid three benefit days and two work days? Will jurors who are released early be expected to return to work? There is no reason to pay an employee a premium during jury service, and it is reasonable to require a return to work if the time remaining in the workday is at least four hours.

BEREAVEMENT LEAVE

Employers demonstrate care and concern by commonly offering time off for employees affected by a death in the immediate family. Time off helps employees deal with grief and the attendant responsibilities, and can be supplemented with other forms of leave.

Draft a policy that includes these components:

- A definition of immediate family including an employee's spouse, parent, children, siblings, grandparents, and grandchild. In deference to blended families employers increasingly add stepparent, stepchildren, father-in-law, mother-in-law, brother-in-law, sister-in-law, son-in-law, daughter-in-law, or domestic partners.
- The number of days that will be paid; three days is a standard minimum. Some employers choose to add a greater benefit for a long-distance funeral.
- Any documentation that must be submitted to obtain payment for the leave, such as an obituary, death certificate, or funeral home information.
- Consider offering a one-day funeral leave to allow an employee to attend the funeral of a close friend who is not a family member.

The additional leave for nonfamily members may seem generous but it is a better step than considering other requests on a case-by-case basis. This ensures that the policy is applied uniformly and enforced consistently.

TIME OFF TO VOTE

No employee should ever be discouraged from voting, and the majority of states prohibit employers from disciplining employees for exercising this right. More than 30 states legislate time off to vote, mostly paid, and specify the number of hours to be offered, usually before or after a shift when polls are open. Check polling hours for individuals living in one state and working in another to ensure that the proper time off is given. A call to the state department of labor will answer specific questions and direct you to useful written information.

OTHER DAYS

Employers need not confine paid days off to the same formula offered for the past twenty years. When identifying options take the time to ensure that changes are understood by employees and do not cause an unanticipated administrative burden.

Can I Take Off for My Birthday?

Ask around and you will hear a list of other paid days offered by employers: birthdays, anniversary days, floating holidays, personal days, even leave for children's school activities. The employer that provides four days in additional categories has added administration and record keeping. If my birthday doesn't fall on a workday, can I be paid for it and earn six days of pay in one week? If I can't take my employment anniversary day off can I wait six months and add the day to my vacation? It makes more sense to view paid time off as a total number of days and add these extras to another category. The easiest record keeping combines different types of days into one leave category with a Paid Time Off (PTO) policy.

WORTH REPEATING

I Used the Week to Help the Community

California-based data storage provider NetApp offers employees Volunteer Time Off (VTO) to support employees who choose to serve their communities, with a benefit of up to five days per year with full pay to spend time performing volunteer work.

PAID TIME OFF (PTO)

Combining vacation, sick, and personal days into one policy of Paid Time Off (PTO) simplifies tracking and reduces record keeping and paperwork. The very act of creating one account or bank of leave results in a more flexible benefit and encourages good attendance. PTO days can also be used by employees for holidays not recognized in a standard formula, thus making them less likely to feel slighted by having to use a vacation day.

How Many PTO Days Do I Provide and When Do Employees Earn Them?

Decisions about the number of PTO days, eligibility, and earning schedule should be made using the same factors in consideration for vacation and sick days. This does not mean you need to total all potential days and the result will be the perfect number of PTO days. Employers should weigh the usage of benefit days, particularly sick days, and think about when they are earned to determine PTO allocations. For a new plan, or one considering a change, the annual potential is likely to be lower than the total of more traditional benefit day offerings. It is important that PTO plans include all the guidelines in a regular vacation policy such as the method for requests, partial days, a cap on carryover, and specifics about payouts after an employee leaves.

How Do I Turn Vacation and Sick Days into a PTO Plan?

It is essential that employees feel that they are not losing benefits in the transition to a PTO plan. The best communications will include individualized information for all employees that details the balance of their days. Make certain these are correct and use examples of how the time can be earned and used. If implementation of a PTO plan will make what is perceived as a significant change in the total number of days available, consider introducing the plan gradually based on seniority. The potential for extra record keeping due to a temporary extra day or two will be balanced by acceptance and long-term clarity.

Adding benefits such as a leave sharing plan or ability to roll over unused days into disability or hospital days will also ease the transition to a new plan.

Should All Benefit Days Be Paid Out of a PTO Bank?

No, keep jury duty, bereavement leave, and most likely holidays separate. In states where some type of jury duty pay is mandatory, employers are unlikely to be able to require the use of PTO for these days. For bereavement days you may want to limit the definition of immediate family; employees can use PTO in the event of the death of an extended family member or friend, or to extend allocated leave. Most employers will continue to offer a regular holiday schedule when scheduling and payroll are pretty consistent with the workforce. For a 24/7 operation it would be atypical but potentially helpful to include the number of holidays in PTO. This can resolve issues about religious observances and, if you provide a premium for working on generally recognized holidays, it can encourage employees to work knowing that they still have an extra day of PTO.

How Do State Laws Treat PTO?

Because most states treat PTO as vacation time, it may become part of any required payouts after employees leave. Employers in these states should calculate the potential cost before making the decision to implement PTO. The benefits could outweigh the cost, controlling vacation allotments could make the price tag minimal, or traditional vacation and sick leave benefits may make more sense.

PART-TIME EMPLOYEES

Your approach to paid time off for part-time employees will be dependent on your benefits philosophy. For employers who rely on a core staff that works only 10 hours a week, the money spent on prorated holiday and vacation pay can ensure consistency. When this segment of the workforce is characterized by high turnover, any costs beyond those required are probably not justified.

Do I Have to Give the Same Paid Days to Part-Timers?

You might be required to give part-time employees jury duty, short-term disability, sick days, or voting leave if they are mandated by your state or municipality. If this requirement exists, or you decide to offer other types of paid days off, establish separate eligibility and accrual rules for part-time employees. All communication should specifically state what full-time employees are eligible for using the term "full-time" in each description, with separate statements describing part-time coverage.

Communicate Consistently

The best paid-leave plans can be sabotaged by poor communications. If an owner, payroll supervisor, and office manager cannot agree about the application of a vacation policy, then employees are certain to be just as confused. Additional problems surface if promises are made or practice is inconsistent with written policies. Wage and hour investigations will err on the side of an employee when policies are unclear or unavailable. Create clear documents to be revisited, revised, and reissued once each year to ensure understanding and correct application.

CHAPTER 3

Enrollment and Changes

How Do I Obtain Information and Communicate Value?

BENEFITS ENROLLMENT AND CHANGES CREATE THE triple challenge of fully informing plan participants, maintaining confidential employee personal data, and ensuring accurate and timely notifications to providers. These processes, when performed correctly and effectively, can make the difference between employee satisfaction or frustration and anger. These tasks don't create the necessity for in-house staff experts, typically available only to large organizations; there are readily available resources for employers of all sizes.

NEW EMPLOYEE ENROLLMENT

The new employee enrollment process sets the tone and expectations for the entire benefits experience.

When Do Employees Sign Up?

The first day of any new job can be an exercise in information overload. In addition to manuals, files, computer codes, and telephone instructions, many recent hires receive thick booklets describing benefits with a list of plans and providers. Individuals who live in one state and work in another can be handed a bigger stack that includes geography-specific plans. On-boarding is not complete without the task of providing personal identifying data for a W-4, I-9, direct deposit, and company property among an endless list of forms. The next day the new staff member is reminded, "Please get those benefit forms back to me by the end of the week so we can enroll you in the plans." If benefits do not kick in for 60 days the employee might receive a terse e-mail 59 days later announcing, "We have not yet received your completed benefit enrollment forms. If they are not returned by 5:00 PM today you cannot enroll in the XYZ Company benefits plan until the next open enrollment, eight months from today."

PPACA changes the communication for employers with more than 200 employees by requiring automatic enrollment into their sponsored plans upon eligibility. Employees will have the opportunity to opt out of coverage. The effective date of this requirement is unclear.

The following components change this paradigm to a truly effective introduction that responds to employee needs:

- Create a **Benefits Overview** listing available options along with enrollment dates that can be used as a tool during the recruitment process and when employment begins.

- Hand out **detailed information and contacts** in response to early requests that includes telephone numbers and e-mail contacts of knowledgeable resources to respond to questions about the plans.

- Schedule **introductory meetings** to answer questions including clarifications, to learn from the inquiries of others, and to offer assistance to complete paperwork. Accommodate multiple locations or shifts by supplementing in-person sessions with Web-based or conference call communications. Use different formats or times to allow for the inclusion of a spouse or another family member who is frequently the benefits decision maker or individual responsible for paperwork completion and retention. Add additional resources by scheduling a representative from a provider or broker.

- Use a **variety of communications methods** to announce meetings and provide information. In a sea of e-mail the announcement about benefits orientation may not stand out or become a top priority. Supplement e-mail with letters home and telephone reminders.

- Understand applicable **requirements of the PPACA** in order to provide correct information to employees. Employers are in a great position to clear up misconceptions before employees call an external agency.

BETTER FORGOTTEN

Makes Sense?

The employees at a small start-up Web publisher were very happy that a benefits plan was being introduced. The information meeting was conducted by a representative who used a string of jargon when very quickly describing all of the specifics. Every so often he paused and looked at the audience to ask, "Makes sense?" They all nodded their heads but it was clear that the torrent of information was a blur, and they did not know the difference between a precertification and approved lab facilities. These explanations need to be in the simplest terms possible with time allowed for the presenter to ask, "What questions do you have?"

Doesn't All This Information Belong in the Employee Handbook?

Employee handbooks are not the best communications format for benefit plan details and could actually be problematic. Benefit specifics, particularly those related to health plans, change more frequently than other company policies. Different provisions for groups or classes of employees can add a great deal of length and could create discontent when comparisons are made. If benefit-day policies are consistent among all staff members, particularly when they are state mandated such as jury duty and time off to vote, describe them in a handbook paragraph or two.

A list of other offerings that includes disclaimer language to allow for changes, as in the following example, will suffice.

Your Benefits

Town Industries offers a number of benefit plans to eligible employees including:

- Medical and Dental Coverage
- Short- and Long-Term Disability
- 401(k) Plan
- Life Insurance
- Paid Time Off (PTO)

The provisions of the plans, including eligibility and benefits provisions, are found in the Summary Plan Descriptions (SPD) which may be revised from time to time. Those documents, along with any updates the company gives you, should be your primary resource for information about your benefit plans. If you see any conflicts between the SPDs and other information, you should rely on the official plan documents. Town Industries may add to, modify, or rescind any benefits provided after notice to you.

What Is a Benefits Handbook?

A benefits handbook is a step-by-step guide that combines provider information into a coherent document. The concept expands on a basic benefits overview and is presented in a loose-leaf binder, file folder, accordion file, or via company intranet, containing sections for each benefit describing processes and procedures, with places for SPDs, other descriptions, forms, and personal document retention. Life and disability carriers often provide a binder or folder in this format as a guide for employer processing of enrollment, billing, and claims.

A complete benefits handbook will include a section of Frequently Asked Questions (FAQs) that can be written from experience with actual inquiries and a glossary of terms. A good first step is a company-specific glossary of terms and valuable communications tools to increase understanding.

If the knowledge, skills, or external expertise are not available to create a benefits booklet, stick to SPDs and information created by providers and brokers. Providers frequently have information, including enrollment forms, translated into different languages to accommodate a multilingual workforce. Carefully review any communication pieces before they are distributed to make certain

BETTER FORGOTTEN

Right Benefits, Wrong Company Name

At the beginning of a plan year an employer received a box with 100 new descriptions of the dental plan for distribution to participants. The content was correct with one exception, another employer's name was at the top of each sheet.

that the audience will understand them and that they reflect your specific plan.

Don't forget that ERISA mandates that all employees must receive SPDs for each plan. Newly eligible employees must also be apprised of their rights and responsibilities under COBRA if coverage, ends or they experience a qualifying event. See Chapter Eleven for a description of the Initial COBRA Notice.

What's the Best Way to Process All of These Forms?

Processing benefits enrollments requires accuracy and timeliness. If an employer offers options for medical, dental, and vision coverage, many employees begin by completing three separate forms, often with similar information, to be double-checked and then faxed to the appropriate provider. Small employers tend to rely on a broker for processing, in which case all three forms are faxed to the adviser's office. Multiple steps increase the potential for errors; Social Security numbers, addresses, and even selections can be incorrectly coded somewhere along the way. Faxing forms may require follow-up phone calls to ensure that the correct person received and will process the documentation. Online enrollment can increase accuracy and creates a record of the transaction, facilitating responses to employee queries about eligibility. Providers offer tutorials and secure access codes that should be limited within your organization. If this task cannot be completed within the organization and enrollment forms continue to be faxed to a broker, make certain the broker is completing enrollments online whenever possible. Faxing a form twice only increases the likelihood of mistakes and delays.

A universal enrollment form can be used to minimize paperwork and further reduce the potential for missteps. Employees fill in personal information at the top of the form and indicate selections and details in designated spaces. The same form can be used for health plans, life insurance, voluntary offerings, and changes to any selections. A broker or benefits consultant can design a universal enrollment form that will be most useful for processing online enrollments but, as long as providers agree, can be transmitted via fax. Regardless of the form or format used, cutting out steps also helps protect individual data. Benefits enrollment forms contain a wealth of personal information that should never be left in a pile on the top of a desk available for photocopying by a night cleaning crew.

Where Do I Keep All This Information?

The Americans with Disabilities Act (ADA) and the Family Medical Leave Act (FMLA) require that all medical information regarding employees be kept in separate files in a secure location distinct from personnel files. Set up a separate benefits file for each employee to hold plan enrollment and change forms and paperwork regarding reasons for sick days, medical leaves, or ADA accommodations. Audit benefits files once each year to remove and destroy unnecessary and inappropriate items. There is no reason to retain the 1995 medical plan enrollment form, particularly when it is for an insurer that no longer provides your coverage. Older documents may also contain information about family medical history that pose a potential conflict with the Genetic Information Nondiscrimination Act (GINA) provisions that went into effect in November 2009. Never toss discarded items in the trash; they should be shredded or pulverized.

Enrollments, changes, and other documentation for life insurance, dependent care accounts, and flexible spending accounts should also be retained in the benefits file. One exception is life insurance beneficiary forms; it's helpful to retain these in one location for easier access. 401(k) information should be held in individual distinct files. These can be in the same secure location as benefits files. Tracking for non-health-related plans such as jury duty, transportation reimbursements, education assistance, and employee discount programs can be retained in personnel files.

Employee Changes

The life cycle events of marriage, birth, divorce, and death all have the potential to affect individual benefits. Less dramatic changes, such as moving or a switch between full- and part-time status, also have a ripple effect on coverage.

It's a Girl! Do I Send Flowers?

It is the employee's responsibility to report changes in personal status that affects coverage, including adding a dependent through birth, adoption, or marriage. Flowers can be a nice gesture but make certain to send enrollment forms, or instructions, for medical and dental plans along with life insurance beneficiary forms in case the employee wishes to make a change. New dependents must be added within a period of time specified by the plan, generally thirty-one days. Check the dental plan for specifications; don't wait until a two-year-old develops a painful toothache to find out that he cannot be covered until the next open enrollment. When an employee marries, he or she may choose to add the new spouse or drop coverage in favor of the plan offered by the new spouse's employer. Remind employees that after the enrollment period ends they will have to wait until the next open enrollment to make any changes in these benefits elections. In the event of divorce or death, employees are also responsible for notifying their employer that coverage should end.

BETTER FORGOTTEN

The Insurance Company Knew I Had a Baby!

A call center employee had a baby fully covered under the company health plan; she used in-network benefits and obtained all of the necessary pre-approvals before the birth. Six weeks after the baby was born, the employee called the provider to ask when her son's member card would be sent out. She was told that the baby was not enrolled in the plan. The employee was supposed to contact the HMO within 31 days of the date of the birth; dependents are not automatically enrolled.

Two Plans—Which One Is Used First?

Employee coverage under a spouse's plan or Medicare creates the potential for coordination of benefits with health plans. One plan becomes primary, paying initial claims, and the other is secondary, to be accessed to cover remaining costs. Avoid confusion by obtaining, understanding, and disseminating a clear definition of how your plans treat coordination of benefits.

While employees are responsible for notification of life events, proactive guides as simple as a one-page sheet will remind employees and add to satisfaction. These can be included in the benefits handbook or created separately. Think about ages and stages to identify the targets for these: marriage; birth or adoption of a child; divorce; children aging out of medical coverage; and employees turning 65.

OPEN ENROLLMENT

Each year the time period before a plan renewal is called open enrollment, the window of opportunity for employees to make changes in plan options, if available, and allow staff who had previously opted out of coverage to select a plan. Changes are not allowed in between open enrollment unless they are the result of a life event such as marriage, birth or adoption of a child, divorce, or death of a spouse.

Exceptions are granted for special enrollments available to any benefit-eligible employees who had been covered for health benefits under another plan but lose coverage for these narrow reasons:

- They are no longer eligible for Medicaid.
- Their children lose coverage under a state child health plus plan (CHIPS).
- They are no longer covered as a beneficiary under a spouse's plan.

Open enrollment presents the perfect opportunity for employers to convey value, in both personal and financial terms, and details about benefits. Approach the process with the view that employees are consumers in these transactions with a need to understand the options available and what's in it for them. Planning for the process from the first notice through enrollment and changes will improve results and satisfaction.

Use this checklist for a more effective open enrollment:

☐ Establish a time line for all communications and due dates.

☐ Create strategy for communicating changes including costs and employee impact.

☐ Coordinate information in materials created by providers with that in materials developed internally or by consultants.

☐ Schedule meetings for all locations, in person, online, or via conference call.

☐ Check all materials, including Web-based and telephone-based processes.

☐ Audit enrollments and changes after effective date.

Use as many communications channels as possible, e-mail, face-to-face meetings, teleconferences, Web-based information, and mailings home. Representation from various parts of the organization can improve the open enrollment process. A team, or at least a meeting, that includes representatives from human resources or administration, payroll and accounting, and operations can spot potential snags, create buy-in, and raise questions that will head off griping and save time. Tailor messages to demographics and individuals as much as possible. This can include targeted examples and total compensation statements that state the value of all benefits delivered as a simple but effective customized tool to each employee.

WORTH REPEATING

Benefits Are Fashionable

A multistore women's retailer created an internal brand for benefits communications that matched its image. One mailing to employees looked like an ad and read, "Looking for the perfect accessory to complete that perfect look? Try a healthy bod, teeth and eyes. Don't miss out on this season's most exclusive event—Open Enrollment—your one chance each year to take advantage of the amazing benefits Bebe offers to keep you looking and feeling sexy and sophisticated." Tailor your message to reflect your culture.

How Do I Deliver Bad News?

No one wants to hear that out-of-pocket costs are increasing or plan design is changing, but they won't be surprised. One key to delivering this news is to do so directly without sugar coating or hiding information. If premiums have increased by 11% and employee contributions will go up by 7%, present all of the data. Even with all the press about the high costs for employer-sponsored health care, many people are shocked to learn just how much the premium is the first time they see it in a COBRA notice. If your employees are contributing $220 each month toward medical coverage for a family, they should know that you are paying at least $800. The number has a greater impact using annual totals, "Our company pays more than $10,000 each year for your family medical coverage." When the percentage, or dollars, that you contribute compares favorably to geographic, industry, or data for similar-sized employers, include this information in your explanation.

The following chart drawn from BLS data provides an example of comparative information.

Medical Plans—Percentage Share of Premiums Paid by Private Industry Employers and Employees

	SINGLE COVERAGE		FAMILY COVERAGE	
	EMPLOYER SHARE	EMPLOYEE SHARE	EMPLOYER SHARE	EMPLOYEE SHARE
All workers	81	19	71	29
Retail trade	76	24	65	35
Utilities	85	15	79	21

Presentations to participants and letters home should draw on this information and explain, "Employee contributions for family medical coverage will increase $20 per month to $269.25; this represents only 25% of the monthly premium of $1,077.00. XYZ Industries' employees will continue to pay far less than the average of 29% paid by employees in U.S. private industry." Cost information will make more sense if it includes relevant amounts broken down by pay period so employees know exactly what will be deducted from their pay.

New plans or terminology necessitate additional careful explanations. If a prescription plan is adding a fourth tier, make certain to have copes of the lists for each segment along with information on generic alternatives and mail order programs where these are available. Use examples of potential situations as often as possible. A description that reads, "Using an out-of-network allergist could mean that you may have to pay $225 for the first four visits to satisfy your deductible" means a lot more than, "Accessing providers out of network can incur additional costs" or "The plan pays 80% after deductible." The greater level of communication and information will correlate with increased satisfaction with benefits plans.

Avoid these common open enrollment mistakes:

- Representatives answering the provider's toll-free number cannot respond to questions, particularly from individuals not yet enrolled in the plan. Check the number and give hints and instructions for calling.

- The sign-up period is rushed into a few days. Be clear with brokers or providers about deadlines and expectations in order to allow adequate time for information and instructions.

- The newest options are listed at the bottom and there are no explanations of changes. Always include a description of changes and new choices in all forms of communications.

- Online enrollment systems are cumbersome and frustrating. Take a test run to make certain they are user-friendly and the path and screens can be navigated by your participants.

Does the Plan Year Have to Start on January 1st?

January 1st is the most common plan year start, making the fall open enrollment season a race for both employers and providers. Smaller companies can feel slighted when the HMO they just selected puts more energy into signing up 1,750 participants from a large group. The plan year does not have to coincide with the calendar year; your broker and provider will probably be happy to service a plan that begins on May 1st. Moving away from the crush could initiate more attentive service and present additional data for pricing and forecasting. The January 1st date is often used to coincide with

> BETTER FORGOTTEN
>
> ## *Medical in January, Dental in April*
>
> A brand-new employer established benefits plans when the first group of employees was hired during April of the inaugural year of operation. When the team grew to more than 500 employees, the company changed health plan types and moved the medical plan contract renewal to January 1st in order to coincide with budgeting. For the next three years the company scrambled to communicate benefits changes twice within a few months, first for medical and then for dental three months later. During the fourth year the plan renewal dates were negotiated and changed to coincide.

financial planning, but actual costs are frequently unavailable until November, long after budgets have been approved. You may be able to extend a plan year, and hold a rate for a few months, to create a new open enrollment date.

So I Can Tell Employees Everything They Need to Know Once a Year, Right?

Open enrollment should not be the only time to educate employees about their benefits. Only one-third of employees and employers agree that benefits communication educates employees effectively, yet there is a very high correlation between benefits satisfaction and job satisfaction. Simple surveys along with involvement from a variety of disciplines can identify the biggest gaps in knowledge.

Enlist brokers, providers, and independent sources for content throughout the year:

- Hold a health fair that can include a blood drive, blood pressure screening, home safety tips, and a chance to ask questions of representatives from providers.
- Choose a monthly topic for communications by e-mail and posters. Don't confine the topics to medical and dental plans; include vacations, life insurance, and any other benefits.

- Send a quarterly letter home that highlights a benefit with illustrations of how it works.

- Customize an online benefits portal that employees and their beneficiaries can access for general health information and plan specifics.

What About the 401(k)?

Open enrollment and communications for 401(k) are essential but should be distinct from health plan initiatives as the information is very different and can affect a larger group of employees. Use the same variety of tools and formats available for other plans, and consider adding to them with additional financial education. Employees increasingly turn to their employer as the primary source for personal financial information. This can be accommodated through plan representatives and independent advisors and financial planners. If employees receive preferential accounts at a local bank or have access to a credit union, these can also be good sources for financial information tools and educators. Independent representatives should be given information about all benefits that affect financial security in addition to the 401(k), including life insurance, disability coverage, and long-term care. Seek out advisers and educators who are not focusing on selling additional products, but if they do, make certain that the connection and optional nature of any purchases are made clear to employees. Review any presentation to ensure that the audience will understand all of the verbiage and concepts. When presenters ask people about risk tolerance, don't be surprised if they are greeted by blank looks.

Employers can enroll participants into 401(k) plans automatically through a concept called elective deferral. The automatic

---

WORTH REPEATING

The Midnight Meeting

During a 401(k) plan provider change, a hotel company scheduled meetings for employees who worked the overnight shift. The plan provider and broker sent representatives to these meetings and the employees never felt they were left in the dark.

enrollment boosts participation but still requires clear communication of the benefits of the 401(k), as employees may opt out of the plan at any time. See Chapter Eight for more details about elective deferrals.

Changes in Status That Trigger Changes in Eligibility

Benefits eligibility can be affected by changes in employment status from full- to part-time, a temporary furlough, or a leave of absence. Employers should be aware of and track changes to ensure consistency.

Do Employees Stay on the Dental Plan If They Are Laid Off?

Plan definitions will indicate whether they cover full-time, part-time, or other employee categories and likely include the word "active" in the description. Before employees are temporarily furloughed or idled due to a facility shutdown, review coverage definitions to clarify the status. You can certainly still consider them full-time if they are scheduled to return to work. Conflicts can arise if definitions include the requirement for a minimum number of hours worked. If employees lose eligibility, even temporarily, you are required to offer continuation of coverage under COBRA, or make a decision to modify the definition allowing benefits to remain in force without a break.

Employees out of work on an approved FMLA leave of absence must be allowed to retain coverage and can be required to make contributions at the same level as any active employee. FMLA notifications must include the costs and due dates for any employee payments. Employers can end coverage and offer COBRA to employees who are out of work on an unpaid leave of absence or due to a work-related injury lasting beyond the time allowed for FMLA eligibility. If you decide to limit coverage in these situations, make certain that the policy is in writing, given to all employees, and reinforced when an employee takes an unpaid leave or is out of work and receiving workers' compensation benefits for an extended period and applied consistently.

What If I Tell Employees Too Much?

Employers are in a critical position to provide information and answers, yet most do little more than hand out benefits booklets created by providers and dutifully include Summary Plan Descriptions (SPDs). Distributing SPDs is important and required by law but rarely transmits the easy-to-understand information that employees and their families need. SPDs, even short ones, are great cures for insomnia. Use the wealth of information in this chapter that employers don't usually think about to make a huge difference in your employees' benefits experience.

What's the Difference Between a POS and an HSA?

EMPLOYER-PROVIDED MEDICAL PLANS HAVE UNDERGONE dramatic transformations within the past thirty years and the pace of change continues to increase. Driven by ballooning costs, legislative initiatives, and shifting demographics, employers and providers are constantly searching for ways to better manage these offerings.

IS ANYONE STILL COVERED BY AN INDEMNITY PLAN?

In 1980 employees could reliably expect to be covered by employer-sponsored indemnity or fee-for-service plans that provided reimbursement for covered health services within designated limits. The plans typically featured first-dollar coverage or an annual deductible as low as $50 per employee after which 80% of expenses were reimbursed. Employees paid a bit more to satisfy a family deductible when covered dependents became ill but never had to dig too deep, because the reimbursement rate rose to 100% when they reached a low annual out-of-pocket expense maximum of no more than a few thousand dollars. Employees took very little responsibility in the process; after visiting the doctor they submitted completed claim forms to the designated individual at their company. The "benefits lady" checked the forms, kept copies, and sent them off to the insurer. Employers managed fat files full of individual health information and monitored processing every step of the way.

Generous coverage, minimal oversight, and increasing medical costs fueled staggering premium increases. Today indemnity plans are offered by only 4% of U.S. employers who provide health benefits. Twenty-first-century fee-for-service options feature much higher deductibles and out-of-pocket maximums without the personalized in-house employer claims service, which is now prohibited by legal protection of personal medical information.

MEDICAL PLAN OPTIONS

Employer-sponsored health coverage has been transformed from the one-size-fits-all concept to an array of choices with selection driven by company size, industry, and geographic location.

Providers and employers have created a list of plans that are referred to most commonly by acronyms but which can also be combined and tweaked to constitute entirely new products.

Health Maintenance Organizations (HMO)

The first HMO plans were started in the 1930s as cooperative efforts for employers to provide medical care to specific portions of local populations in a few cities. Touted as an alternative to curb health care expenditures, HMOs grew in popularity during the 1970s and 1980s. The model seeks to reduce costs by requiring that all participants receive care at designated locations. In the strictest sense services are provided by practitioners who are paid flat fees or salaries, thus creating the opposite of a fee-for-service plan. Some HMOs operate their own full-service clinics where members go to take care of all medical needs from flu shots to CAT scans and all doctor visits in between. HMOs may also be referred to as an Exclusive Provider Organizations (EPOs).

HMOs have evolved to include doctors who may not work out of one site but care exclusively for plan members, and other doctors who treat patients from a variety of sources. These plans are likely to feature lower, fixed fees, called copayments or copays, for doctor visits and tests, with an occasional deductible. Participants can receive a grid that clearly lists the cost to them for all services. This creates a popular option for families who live near an HMO center that has a good reputation in the community or anyone who prefers recommendations for health care services without needing to navigate a long list of options. It is essential that employees understand that there are no benefits available outside of the HMO network, with very limited exceptions for out-of-area travel.

The popularity of HMOs has declined as costs have risen and other forms of managed care have evolved. The appropriateness of this choice will depend on cost, availability, and local reputation.

Preferred Provider Organization (PPO)

PPO options provide the flexibility of using any provider with the cost savings benefits of managed care. PPO members usually pay only a copay for any service covered by a provider in the recognized network and have the option of receiving care out of the designated list that is covered at significantly reduced rates and commonly requires a deductible and coinsurance. Out-of-network coinsurance under a PPO plan is likely to pay for 70 or 80% of what are identified as reasonable and customary expenses after the deductible has been satisfied.

PPO providers achieve savings by negotiating fee reductions and setting reimbursements based on these schedules. Individuals covered by a PPO usually have the freedom to mix and match care by selecting the provider of their choice from within the network or seeking others outside the network. They will most likely be asked to designate primary care physicians at the time of enrollment but will not be required to use them. Out-of-network care is, however, discouraged by the requirement to navigate rates and reimbursements that may not repay a full 80%, even after a deductible when schedules of reasonable and customary charges are applied.

Slow Down—What Are Usual, Customary, and Reasonable Charges?

Health insurers set reimbursement rates for care, procedures, lab work, and hospital stays. These usual, customary, and reasonable (UCR) rates or charges are based on information from the community and can vary by geography. The highest rates are most likely to be found in large cities and locations with elevated cost of living; the payment for gall bladder surgery in Miami might exceed payment for the same operation in Memphis. Plan designs typically include a payment schedule set at a percentage of what the insurers consider usual, customary, and reasonable charges. Employers choose between, for example, rates of 70, 80, or 90% of UCR charges. If a plan reimburses employees for out-of-network care at a rate of 70% of 80% of the UCR rate, and a specialist visit costs $275, the benefit amount (70%) will be based on $220 (80%) for the care as long as the $275 is within reasonable and customary limits. In this scenario, the plan pays $154 and the employee is responsible for $121. If, in this case, the insurer identifies the usual, customary, and reasonable rate as lower than $275, the claim will be paid based on the reduced fee schedule. Few out-of-network providers will accept reimbursement at lower levels. It is important to understand the mechanics of these calculations before employees are upset by unexpected expenses.

Point of Service Plans (POS)

Point of Service Plans operate very similarly to PPO plans, with the addition of the primary care physician as a gatekeeper to authorize treatment. In a POS the selected primary care physician is required for referral to specialists and additional care with the goal of managing care that results in reducing costs. A POS plan will also add the option of out-of-network coverage with a deductible and coinsurance.

WHAT DO EMPLOYERS HAVE TO DO WITH CONSUMER-DIRECTED HEALTH CARE?

Consumer-directed health care is a catch-all term for employer-sponsored plans that are designed to encourage participants to monitor costs and take a more active role in decision making about health services.

High-Deductible Health Plans

High-deductible health plans (HDHP), the newest responses to ever-rising costs, have significantly expanded the alphabet soup of insurance approaches. Also termed consumer-directed or consumer-driven health plans (CDHP), these choices combine higher than typical annual deductibles with tax-advantaged savings that employees can use to pay for covered expenses and save for future medical expenditures. HDHPs create an incentive for better-informed decisions and cost consciousness when participants pay expenses from a fund they control, especially given the potential for rolling over unspent money into accounts that can accumulate for future use.

The earliest forms of these savings plans were made possible on a limited basis by 1996 federal legislation which was expanded in 2003 and again in 2006 to allow the current formats. The regulatory evolution has made adoption of HDHPs easier and, after a slow start, they have grown steadily and are now offered by more than 20% of employers who provide benefits. A broad range of health plan designs can be created incorporating Health Savings Accounts or Health Reimbursement Arrangements.

Health Savings Accounts and High-Deductible Health Plans

There are three key features of HDHPs paired with HSAs:

1. The health benefit plan must have a minimum annual deductible at or above the annual rate set by the IRS; in 2010 this amount is $1,200 for an individual and $2,400 for a family.

2. Each eligible participating employee has an HSA account set up with a trustee—such as a bank, insurance company, or anyone already approved by the IRS to be a trustee of Individual Retirement Accounts (IRAs)—into which an annual maximum amount can be contributed as designated annually by the IRS. For 2010 HSA account maximums are $3,050 for an individual and $6,150 for family coverage.

3. The IRS sets an annual limit, indexed each year, on out-of-pocket expenses that employees are responsible for after which plans generally pay 100% of expenses. For 2010 the maximum annual combination of deductible and other out-of-pocket expenses for HDHPs is $5,950 for self-only coverage and $11,900 for family coverage.

Who Puts Money into the Account?

Contributions into an HSA can be made by the employee, employers, or both, in a variety of ways:

- Employees can be allowed to contribute earnings on a pre-tax basis through a salary reduction plan, also referred to as a cafeteria or Section 125 plan.
- Employees and their friends and relatives may make contributions directly into the account at intervals of their choosing, within plan guidelines.
- Employers can choose to make contributions into employee accounts, and designate the timetable for these deposits.
- Employee and employer deposits are combined to calculate the total allowable annual contribution; in 2010, $3,050 for an individual and $6,150 for a family.
- Employees who are 55 years old or older can contribute an additional $1,000 per year.

Employees cannot make contributions into an HSA if they are enrolled in any other health coverage, including Medicare, that is not an HDHP. When spouses are enrolled in separate HDHPs with an HSA, the deposits in both accounts combined cannot exceed the annual family limit.

Can the Money in an HSA Earn Interest?

HSAs can be set up in interest-bearing accounts and investment vehicles similarly to IRAs. Plans can impose rules requiring minimum deposits.

What's the Tax Advantage of an HSA?

HSAs are described as having a triple tax advantage; that is, employer and employee contributions, any interest earned, and qualified distributions are all exempt from federal income tax and deductions. Employee after-tax contributions, and those made on their behalf by friends or relatives, can be considered an "above-the-line" deduction, which allows participants, including those who do not itemize deductions, to reduce taxable income by the amount contributed.

So How Does All This Pay Doctor Bills?

Employees have the option to receive reimbursement for covered medical expenses by requesting funds from their HSA or using after-tax dollars. As plans are likely to have minimums on distributions, some participants choose to cover small expenses themselves, thus allowing the HSA balance to grow. The HSA works like a checking account; employees can only be reimbursed from actual deposited funds accessed through a variety of channels including a debit card, checks, or withdrawals that participants can use to pay covered expenses. Because employees own these accounts they do not have to receive approval for payments made by an employer or third-party administrator. Employees simply use the account to draw money for covered expenses and keep receipts for tax filing purposes, similar to the way in which charitable contributions are handled. If an employee depletes the account balance before meeting the plan deductible, he will have to pay out of pocket to cover expenses. Participants can request reimbursement at a later date as the account balance grows.

WORTH REPEATING

Yes, a Flu Shot Is Preventive Care

After a credit union in Arizona switched to an HDHP, they were surprised to learn that employees were being billed for flu shots as office visits and not as preventive care, which was to be covered at 100% under the plan. An HDHP will only be successful when employees learn to review all of the lines on provider bills.

Health savings accounts can be used for a wide variety of qualified medical expenses from acupuncture to alleviate pain to wigs for a patient who has lost her hair due to a medical condition. Many employees will be interested in reimbursement for glasses, contact lenses, and solution. Expenses can be paid from an HSA for dependent family members who are not covered by the HDHP and also be used to pay premiums for COBRA, Medicare, and long-term-care insurance.

Can I Still Access In-Network Care and Get Free Physicals?

These plans can include access to preferred provider networks, a PPO or POS component that provides eligibility for lower negotiated fees. When in-network options are made available, expenses for out-of-network services can be excluded in calculating the annual maximum combination of deductible and out-of-pocket expenses that must be reached before the plan pays 100% of covered medical expenses. This formula encourages the use of in-network care. The IRS allows HDHPs to be structured to provide preventive care with no deductible, a separate deductible set below IRS minimums, or a small copay. HDHPs will be required to comply with PPACA coverage requirements for preventive care as described elsewhere in this book. For these purposes the IRS defines preventive care to include physicals, tests, a range of screenings, and weight-loss and tobacco-cessation programs.

Where Does the HSA Money Go at the End of the Year?

If an employee has a balance in an HSA at the end of the year, the amount rolls over into the new year, whether or not the individual remains covered by the plan. When coverage continues, the employee then has a potentially larger account to draw from. If the employee enrolls in a different plan he can still access his HSA for reimbursement of covered expenses not paid for under a new plan.

What Happens When an Employee Leaves, Retires, or Turns 65?

Individual HSAs are portable; employees take them when employment ends and can continue to access the balance for covered expenses. Participants can only make contributions into the account if they are covered by another HDHP. Employees are also prohibited from making contributions into an HSA when they enroll in Medicare, usually at age 65.

HSA account holders can make withdrawals that do not cover qualified medical expenses but must understand that the amount will be considered income for tax purposes and, if they are under 65, could be subject to a 10% tax penalty on the amount withdrawn. The penalty doubles to 20% after December 31, 2010, under new requirements in federal health care reform.

Health Reimbursement Arrangements and High-Deductible Health Plans

Health Reimbursement Arrangements (HRAs) are tax sheltered accounts funded only by the employer that can be used for reimbursement of allowable medical expenses. Employers own these accounts and employees may not make contributions into them. There are no legislated minimum and maximum deposits for HRAs. Employers can elect contribution amounts and designs and retain the ability to make changes each year.

Does an HRA Pay for Expenses Just Like an HSA?

Employers identify plan design parameters that drive how the funds are used. The HRA may pay for first-dollar expenses or require that employees pay all or part of initial expenses out of pocket. HRAs can be used to pay out for all of the items recognized as qualified medical expenses by an HSA, or the employer may decide to limit distributions to cover, for example, only deductibles and copays. Contributions made to an HRA are tax deductible for employers and not taxed as income for employees. HRAs can be established as a stand-alone account or used in combination with any kind of employer-sponsored health plan; they don't require an HDHP. An HRA can also be offered alongside an HSA or Flexible Spending Account (FSA). Unlike HSAs, employees who are covered elsewhere may be included as HRA participants; employer contributions into an HRA do not affect employee or spouse maximums allowed into HSAs or FSAs.

Do HRA Funds Roll Over at the End of the Year?

Plan designs can allow for rollover of HRA funds at the end of the year, or for use during retirement, and also impose a maximum on accumulations in an account. Because employers own these accounts, they are not portable after an employee leaves; the participant cannot cash out or take withdrawals at any time for nonmedical expenses. Employers can use the dollars left in forfeited accounts to fund future contributions for active plan participants.

Which Is Better, an HRA or HSA?

The portability and long-term potential of HSAs can make them very attractive to employees, particularly when employer contributions are part of the plan. This flexibility is paired with limits in employer control over deductibles, contribution amounts, and participation in other plans. Employers can design attractive plans without making any contributions. The employer-only feature of HRAs may be viewed as a negative but comes with fewer rules on contributions, greater control over disbursement of the funds, and limits on cost exposure through maximum allowances in accounts and retention of balances when an employee leaves.

Both accounts are designed to encourage employees to be more knowledgeable about health care expenses. As participants become savvier health care consumers, they increase the potential for accumulation of funds that can be used when expenses mount. Employers save money through reduced premiums of HDHPs and may realize lower expenses from cost-conscious, healthier participants. Studies have showed cost savings, but with only 4% of U.S. employees eligible for HPHPs they are not widespread enough to earn a ringing endorsement. One of the first steps in decision making about this or any plan design is to obtain a model that includes cost comparisons of available options.

These Are Really Complicated; Do Employees Understand Them?

HDHPs require extra layers of education and communications that must be tailored to the employee population. Start communication about HDHPs as soon as you make the decision to adopt one, long before the first day of open enrollment. When an HSA is introduced, employees must be guided in how to enroll in both the health plan and the savings account. Multiple channels of communications, including models—especially online calculators that provide specific examples—will be required to reach participants and beneficiaries. Follow-up is critical for effective decision making and satisfaction; if the plan year begins two months after open enrollment meetings, spread the message again at the New Year with a wave of instruction including examples of how HSAs or HRAs work in terms of routine and unexpected medical costs. Reeducation and ongoing instruction will use a variety of formats including Web-based information with simple explanations in videos, call centers, and in-person meetings. Many employees may not access any medical care until six or eight months into the year. The first time the employee looks at frequently asked questions about the new plan should not be after her emergency appendectomy in July. The additional time spent will translate into better benefits plan usage.

When HDHPs are one option among employer offerings, better understanding will spur sign-up and retention. If employees don't comprehend the new coverage or are frustrated, fallout will negatively affect morale and future enrollments. You may decide to offer an HDHP as the only available plan. If so, be prepared when a less-sophisticated workforce finds it difficult to navigate potentially complex HSA or HRA rules. Make certain that the process and

---

WORTH REPEATING

It Was Worth Taking the Time

A regional bank converted the health plan covering all employees from a PPO to a HDHP with an HSA. They scheduled three weeks of informational meetings, allotting 45 minutes for each session. After the first few gatherings it became evident that there was not enough time to provide clear explanations and respond to all of the questions. The meeting schedule was changed to accommodate 90-minute time slots.

communications are targeted to the specific audience to increase the potential for turning employees into confident medical consumers.

PLAN COMPONENTS

Once a decision has been made to provide employer-sponsored health benefits, there are components that will be required by certain states and federal law.

What Does an Employer-Provided Health Plan Have to Cover?

Prior to federal health care reform, there were only a limited number of federal laws that affect employer health plan components. These include minimum inpatient stays after the birth of a child, parity between annual and maximum benefits for mental health, including substance abuse, and for medical and surgical care and coverage for certain breast reconstruction after cancer treatment. PPACA includes a range of requirements from coverage for adult children up to age 26 to limitation on benefit maximums. These are phased in, with many definitions yet to be determined, from 2010 through 2014. An explanation and time line for implementation is provided in the Health Care Reform section at the beginning of this book. In addition federal employment laws require that all employee benefits are provided in a nondiscriminatory fashion. In addition to these disparate items, many state and local mandates may affect health plans. Multistate employers can face the additional challenge of different requirements. Even if you have only one remote salesperson, working from a home office in another state, check local laws to ensure compliance.

Are Employees Going to Thailand for Gallbladder Surgery?

A small but growing number of employer health plans cover medical tourism, sending employees around the world to Thailand, India, Singapore, and a host of other locations for elective surgery. The costs, including travel and even resort stays for recuperation, can be up to 70% lower than costs in the United States. Before sending employees to pick up a visa, make certain that the option is voluntary, and check out the American Medical Association guidelines on medical tourism to review all the contingencies for travel, care, and follow-up treatment.

Prescription Drug Benefits

Prescription drug benefits are an integral part of any health plan package in partnership with medical coverage.

What's a Pharmacy Benefits Manager and Do I Need One?

Pharmacy Benefits Managers (PBMs) provide managed pharmacy benefits for more than 75% of individuals covered under employer-sponsored health plans in the United States. The industry is dominated by a handful of large national companies with smaller PBMs meeting a little less than half the need. The influence and reach of PBMs have increased as prescription costs have grown at a significantly faster rate than expenses for other medical care. PBMs have the ability to negotiate prices with pharmaceutical companies and use buying power to create options with generics and preferred drugs being offered for reduced copayments.

What Do Tiers Have to Do with Prescription Drugs?

Prescription drug benefits are commonly organized into three- and four-tier structures that arrange items according to member cost or copayment. The lowest tier, say $5 or $10 for a 30-day supply, is for generic drugs; the second and third, with copays of $20 to $35, include preferred or formulary drugs. Plans with a fourth tier set the top as high as $50 to $75 to encourage use of less-expensive generics or alternatives from other tiers that can be prescribed to treat the same symptoms. Plans may also limit participant benefits to in-network pharmacies and refuse to cover nonformulary drugs altogether. PBMs encourage mail order delivery of maintenance drugs at significant savings by eliminating the cost of the retail pharmacy; using this route, a 90-day supply is likely to cost the employee the same as a 30-day prescription purchased in person.

WORTH REPEATING

My Manager Understands the Plan

A Midwest-based company that operates photo studios in depart-ment stores trained the managers from each location in the details of the health benefits plan, including tools for communicating information to all local employees. The result for this employer was better employee satisfaction and effective plan utilization through clear, correct guidance. Use your management team to spread the word.

The prevalence of drug marketing combined with new medi-cations and generics makes the ever-changing topic an important educational opportunity for employers. Communications should certainly not recommend specific therapies but can point employees in the direction of reputable information sources, including provider resources and suggested questions to ask physicians and pharma-cists. Employees may not be used to routinely asking, "Is there a less expensive drug or generic?"

Health Advocates

Third-party guidance provides valuable assistance to employees navigating the health plan maze and creates the potential for increas-ing satisfaction and aiding cost control.

Is There Any Way to Replace the Helping Hand of the Benefits Lady?

When complexity becomes overwhelming, plan members are facing mounds of paper and can't get answers from the standard 800 numbers, a health advocate can step in to resolve the situa-tion. Health advocates, or personal health advocates, provide access to independent experts—professionals with backgrounds in health care and insurance who navigate claims, identify providers, and assist with scheduling appointments among a myriad of supports.

WORTH REPEATING

There Is a Cost-Effective Option in Anchorage

A nationwide employer with almost twenty locations from Charlotte to Anchorage had a self-insured PPO in place for all locations. In Minneapolis and Anchorage there were local plans that took advantage of area negotiations to offer rates that could not be matched by the national plan, as it did not have network providers in these locations. After reviewing all of the potential costs it made sense to separate these two locations into individual plans.

The independent nature of the product helps protect against distribution of employee health information that should not be divulged to employers.

The service can be paid for by the hour or made available for all beneficiaries and billed at a monthly rate based on the size of the employee population. Health advocates can increase employee satisfaction and save plan dollars by reviewing billing and processing. They will be most welcomed by employees faced with the choices inherent in an HDHP, but they must be introduced clearly as a neutral third party so as not to be seen as an arm of the insurance provider.

Self-Funded or Fully Insured—What's the Difference?

Employer-provided health insurance is paid for in one of two ways: fully insured or self-insured (or self-funded). The decision on funding will be based on employer size, type of plan, available information, and risk tolerance.

Fully insured plans require employers to pay monthly premiums; the insurance company assumes the financial risk for providing coverage to those under the plan. Premiums will be affected by the number of employees, population characteristics, and health care use, but they will be set for each coverage category during the plan year, facilitating expense forecasts. Small employers, with fewer than 200 employees, are more likely to choose to pay premiums for fully insured products.

Employers assume the risk in a self-insured arrangement by paying for claims, plus administration fees, through an insurance company or third-party administrator (TPA) or administrative services only (ASO) arrangement. In order to protect assets, employers purchase catastrophic or stop-loss coverage that will pay for very large claims. Self-insured plans are exempt from state insurance laws, making them attractive to multistate employers who can use this flexibility in plan design to offer one or fewer plans across locations. More than 85% of the largest employers, with 5,000 employees or more, offer self-insured health plans, primarily in the form of a PPO.

Plan administrators and brokers have the ability to create a comparison between fully insured and self-insured choices by modeling potential costs for different plan designs. The task can be made difficult by the lack of availability of history of claims for a group but, once established, it can become a baseline for periodic review. Price may not be the deciding criteria in identifying the third-party administrator that best fits your needs. The local network affiliated with a regional TPA can be a strong selling point, and availability of access to wellness and disease management programs can be another consideration.

Is a Mini-Med Plan a Type of Band Aid?

Offering a plan option with limited benefits, targeted to cover only short-term expenses, can be an attractive choice for employers in high turnover industries, particularly those with a young workforce. These have been referred to as mini-medical, limited-medical, limited-benefit, or fixed-benefit plans. The relatively inexpensive offerings help employees cover noncatastrophic medical expenses. With an annual cap of only a few thousand dollars and low or no deductibles, these plans cannot be described as comprehensive but are undoubtedly better than the alternative of no plan at all.

With monthly premiums that can be at least 50% less than major medical coverage, limited benefit plans can be an effective vehicle for offering coverage to part-time employees, low wage earners, and as a short-term solution during waiting periods for regular plans. Make certain that you and your employees understand the specifics of the policy before a catastrophic claim occurs that will not be paid. Mini-med plans must be reviewed carefully for compliance with PPACA as requirements phase in through 2014. It may be impossible to offer a compliant plan in this category based on restrictions on annual and lifetime maximums and the definition of Essential Health Benefits.

CHOOSING A PLAN

Finding the right health plan can seem like a daunting decision. The information in this book will undoubtedly help, and when offerings do not meet expectations, or situations change, it's important to remember that options are available to meet the range of employer needs.

How Do I Make the Right Choices?

There is no one right or wrong plan for every employer. Your selections will represent a compromise between budget, available options, and employee wants and needs. Use the information here to ask as many questions as possible during any presentation by a broker or plan provider. Benefits professionals use a dizzying amount of jargon and abbreviations from costs represented as PEPM (per employee per month) to census data (information about group members) that contains PHI (protected health information)—and new terms are created all the time. Ask for comparisons, even if they are between one more affordable plan and another that is way beyond any budget. The discussion can spur thinking about changes in design and tweaking. Find out if there are specific, potentially optional, covered items that affect premiums. Alternative medicine, surgery to promote weight loss, and in vitro fertilization are examples of treatment that might be limited or not included in plan coverage.

Preferences can be accommodated by offering a choice between two or more plan options. This decision is most effective when there is a clear difference between offerings and a cost differential between employee contributions, for example an HMO or a High Deducible Health Plan with a PPO and an HSA. If a plan requires a minimum number of participants or costs skyrocket as a result of diminishing group size, it may become impossible to present alternatives.

Can My Employees Be Eligible for State Health Insurance?

Low-income or part-time wage earners may be eligible for state-administered Medicaid programs or other plans provided to those whose wages rise above Medicaid thresholds. All states administer benefits for children under the federal Child Health Insurance Program (CHIP) that insures children in families qualifying based on income level determined by the state, ranging from 160 to 400% of the federal poverty level. Contact your state department of health or labor to learn more about these programs and obtain information to pass on to appropriate employee populations.

Whew, This Is Still Pretty Confusing—Now What?

In summary, the complex nature of employee health coverage frequently drives company owners to accept plans, even in the face of huge rate increases, without question. The very act of requesting clarification, explanations, and possible alternatives will often unearth changes that can meet employee needs within an agreed-on budget.

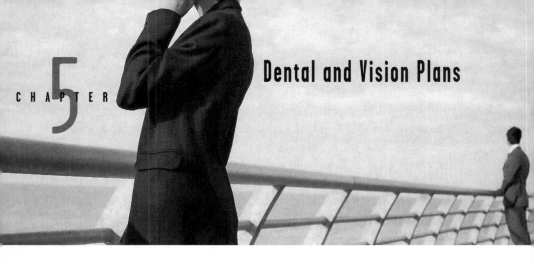

Are Checkups and Eye Exams Enough?

DENTAL AND VISION ARE THE HEALTH CARE BENEFITS that don't receive half the attention afforded to costlier and more complicated medical coverage. Employer-provided dental coverage is widespread; more than 94% of employers with over 100 employees offer plans, as do almost 90% of smaller workplaces. Vision coverage is less prevalent; it is included as a component in more than 75% of employers' packages.

TYPES OF DENTAL PLANS

Employer-provided dental benefits became common in the 1970s and, like medical, they were delivered in a traditional indemnity model, typically by the same carrier administering policies for both; thus, eligible employees were essentially covered under one plan. This formula shifted dramatically as managed care spread first to medical and then to dental plans, and mergers and acquisitions left many insurers discontinuing dental offerings while others began to specialize in these products. Today more than 95% of employer-sponsored dental plans are purchased as a freestanding product, distinct from medical coverage.

Are the Options Just Like Medical?

Although dental plans are offered as indemnity, networked or preferred provider plans, and Dental Health Maintenance Organizations (DHMO or DMOs), there are key differences that affect both design and usage. Dental plans focus on and promote preventive care with very low or no copayments; dollars spent on cleaning and x-rays have been proven to save money by diminishing the need for fillings and replacing teeth. Annual maximums that range from $500 to $2,500 reinforce the focus on predictable costs, unlike medical insurance plans' capacity to pay for catastrophic claims. Newer plan designs have instituted graduated maximums for participants enrolled in the second and third year, and the ability to roll over unused benefit plan dollars to be used in subsequent years. If, for example, a participating employee only uses $750 of a $2,000 annual maximum, the plan could allow an amount equal to the unused portion to be added to the annual benefit cap in the subsequent year, creating an individual limit of $1,250. Plan design would indicate details about rollovers including a ceiling on accumulations. These variations can create incentive for taking responsibility to obtain necessary preventive care and to watch costs.

Is the PPO the Best Option for Dental?

Preferred Provider Organizations (PPOs) are the most common but not overwhelmingly dominant dental plan design. Indemnity, direct reimbursement, or fee-for-service plans are actually offered by more than 35% of employers who include dental plans in the benefits mix. The ability to control costs through caps combines with availability of utilization to make these viable.

Indemnity coverage includes the freedom to obtain service from any dentist, whereas a PPO allows participants to choose an in-network or out-of-network provider. Selecting a participating dentist reduces employees' out-of-pocket expenses. In a DMO covered members must access the benefit through a member dentist. These providers are likely to be paid a fixed per-participant monthly fee, called capitation, to provide care, regardless of utilization. Participants are restricted in their ability to change providers and can only do so at specified intervals. Hybrid dental plans that combine DMO and PPO features allow employees to switch between the two, within limitations, and the capability to include a common plan across different locations. Dental health benefits designs can be fully insured or self-funded.

Plan Components

Dental plans have not been regulated under PPACA but there are still common definitions used in this type of coverage.

What's the Difference Between Restorative and Major Restorative Treatment?

Dental insurance plans break down types of services and rates of reimbursement or coverage.

Preventive Care will be included with minimal fees or none at all. Plans do place limitations on the frequency of cleaning and check-ups, most likely twice a year, and allow screening x-rays on a recommended schedule.

Restorative Care, or basic restorative care, designates fillings, extractions, periodontics, and endodontics. Indemnity plans typically pay 80% of usual, customary, and reasonable (UCR) charges associated with these procedures. PPOs publish two reimbursement schedules for restorative care with a higher benefit level for in-network providers at predetermined rates. DHMOs are likely to provide a rate sheet for restorative care that states, for example, that a filling will cost the member $15.

Major Restorative Care, or major care, involves crowns, bridges, and dentures that will generally be covered by an indemnity plan at

50% of reasonable and customary rates. PPOs apply a dual schedule that includes a higher in-network reimbursement; DHMOs apply fixed rates. All three formats will commonly request an authorization or predetermination of benefits before any major restorative care is approved for coverage. Dentists are familiar with this requirement and understand that it must be completed in advance of any procedure in order for the patient to receive coverage for the care.

Orthodontia is treated as an entirely distinct benefit category within dental plans with a separate deductible, payment schedules, and lifetime per-participant maximum. Plans that provide orthodontia may also limit the age for coverage and specifically exclude adults.

Both indemnity and PPO options are likely to have a deductible that can be designed in a myriad of ways. It can include preventive, basic, and major care, with a separate deductible for each, and an additional requirement for orthodontia.

Multipage charts of dental coverage details are lengthy and complicated. They can be demystified with examples that will be particularly helpful if you are trying to steer employees to lower cost in-network choices. Dental plan components have not necessarily kept pace with changes in dental care. Ask when the plan was last updated and find out whether the coverage schedule reflects current best practices in oral health.

Consider these items in this review:

- Are white fillings for back teeth eligible expenses? Many plans pay only for amalgam (silver) fillings for those teeth we don't see, whereas dentists are consistently using white for all fillings.

- Is screening for oral cancer covered? This involves a simple procedure.

- How often can crowns and bridges be replaced? Plans are often priced to provide replacement more frequently than is statistically necessary, say every five years, but crowns and bridges have been shown to last longer. Ask for an explanation and statistics to back up coverage.

- Are more frequent cleanings available for individuals with periodontal disease? These people are likely to realize multiple health benefits from cleanings four times a year, with the potential to minimize longer-term dental and medical problems and costs.

BETTER FORGOTTEN

That's Covered Under the Medical Plan

An employee who lived in one state and worked in another underwent oral surgery at his regular dental practice. The work was considered medical care in the state where the worker lived but he did not find this out until after the fact; he paid a premium because he used an out-of-network provider and failed to get preapproval. Remind employees to contact the dental plan carrier before any procedure beyond checkups and routine fillings.

Plan Selection Tips

It's unfortunate that dental plan decisions are often a rushed afterthought following the review of the more costly medical benefits. It's worth planning more time for this evaluation, as employees who have dental benefits actually use them more frequently than medical.

Consider your benefits strategy and these points when identifying the best plan to meet company needs:

- Identify the type of plan suited for your employee population: indemnity, network, DHMO, or a choice.
- Cost of plan and expectation of employee contribution.
- Understand how reimbursement relates to usual, customary, and reasonable rates; the employer typically chooses the percentage, 100%, 80%, and so on.
- When selecting a network find out how many dentists practice near work or where employees live. A great network is useless if it is too far away for convenience.
- Annual and lifetime maximums should be competitive but will influence cost.
- Establish any exclusions from coverage, such as cosmetic procedures or age limitations on orthodontia.
- Where does orthodontia fit in, if at all?

Are There Dental HSAs and FSAs?

Employee dental expenses are considered health care costs that can be paid with HSA, HRA, and FSA funds. Employers do not need to set up separate accounts. These tax-favored accounts provide participants with the ability to budget and plan costly dental care that can be scheduled, such as orthodontia, crowns, and dentures.

Can the Employee Skip Medical and Just Take Dental Coverage?

It is to an employer's advantage to allow participation in all or parts of health benefit offerings. An employee may choose to obtain medical as a beneficiary under a spouse's plan, and individual or family dental coverage in your package. The availability of this mix-and-match approach can save money by avoiding duplication and increase satisfaction by allowing employees to choose the options that meet their needs.

Dental Discounts

Employers who are not yet willing to commit to dental insurance can take a first step by participating in dental discount programs. These are available through benefits providers, national and regional programs, and even local group practices. Dental discount programs can require a modest annual membership fee that allows access to care by participating providers at discounted rates. As with PPO choices, make certain that the provider network is a match with the demographics of your workforce. Discounts will lose most of their advantage if an employee has to pass every dentist in town and drive 75 miles for care.

VISION PLANS

Dental and vision plans provide benefits that are much more than simply nice to have. Plans that are well researched and communicated effectively enhance the health of a workforce and fit into a benefits strategy that promotes satisfaction, recruitment, and retention.

Should You Sign Up for a Chain Store Discount?

Vision care discounts can be as simple as distribution of cards from a local eye care provider that announces eligibility for 10 or 20% off exams, lenses, and frames. A more detailed discount plan will include a chart of prices for specific services accessed through a list of eye care professionals and optical retailers. This can involve an annual membership fee or specific enrollment procedures.

Isn't Vision Care Covered Under the Medical Plan?

Comprehensive vision care, including eye exams, glasses, and contact lenses, is not a typical component of a medical benefits plans. Beyond discount programs, employer-sponsored vision care insurance covers routine eye examinations and prescribed eyewear available on a schedule, usually every 12 or 24 months. Vision plans feature low premiums, minimize participants' costs, and offer purchases through providers in a designated network. Plans may include deductibles and reimbursements for a relatively small part of costs for exams, glasses, and contact lenses obtained out-of-network.

There are nationwide providers that feature networks across the country. As with any network, it is essential to identify compatibility with employee needs. With vision care this may also require some comparison shopping. Employees won't appreciate a benefit that involves a selection of five frames from two retailers when nearby big box stores offer an array of fashionable eyewear at steep discounts. Prices for contact lenses are extremely competitive, so these too must

---

WORTH REPEATING

I See Clearly

An employee was concerned about the cost of an eye exam that included regular screening for glaucoma due to family history. She was scheduled to visit a provider out of the vision plan network. The visit to the eye doctor for a medical condition was covered under this part of the health benefits plan, not under the vision plan. Here's another opportunity to provide communication that creates clarification and increased satisfaction.

---

be part of any value assessment. An effective survey starts with a call to the carrier's toll-free member number in order to obtain information and identify customer service quality.

Look for ease of administration when choosing a vision plan. Enrollment and changes should be quickly accomplished through a simple Web portal, without complicated forms. Employers and members should have quick and easy access to up-to-date benefit and provider details. Check these and the materials that vision plan providers create for participant education to make certain that they match your employee population. Do you need printed explanations in Spanish, or Chinese? Ask your broker or plan representative if these are available.

Will the Plan Cover Laser Vision Correction?

Vision plans can include the ability to obtain laser eye corrective surgery at discounted rates. Again this will be through approved laser vision care facilities. The availability of laser vision correction is likely to be an option when selecting a plan and will affect the premium.

How Much Do Vision Plans Cost?

Group vision coverage carries the smallest price tag of all health benefits, with monthly rates averaging less than $30 for family coverage and hovering around $5 for an individual. Though many employers offer vision plans as a voluntary benefit requiring employees to pay the entire premium, subsidizing the cost can provide added value for a minimal investment. Regular eye exams have the potential to identify vision problems before the employees, or their children, realize the necessity for glasses, and also help spot other medical conditions. When employees don't sign up for the plan they can face sticker shock midyear if the need for bifocals is diagnosed. Whoever pays the premium, vision plans should be offered as a stand-alone benefit to minimize duplication of coverage. Employees may choose only vision care that is not available through a spouse's employer that covers their medical and dental.

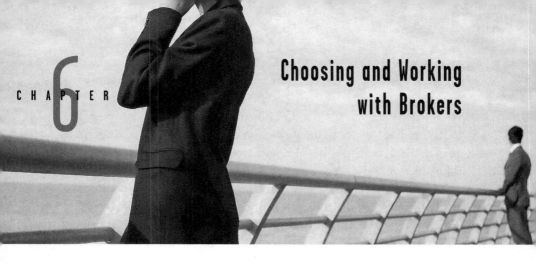

CHAPTER 6

Choosing and Working with Brokers

How Do I Get the Most Out of the Broker Relationship?

BENEFITS BROKERS ARE POTENTIALLY FABULOUS resources for employers in identifying, selecting, and administering the full range of plans. The best brokers will be trusted advisers; the least effective can cost an employer through administrative errors, premiums for unnecessary benefits, expensive fines, and even litigation for noncompliance. Broker relationships are often passed down, inherited from family or generations of leadership without alteration, even in the face of dramatic changes in the benefits landscape. These long-standing arrangements can produce excellence but should be reviewed periodically to make certain they continue to serve the best interests of the company.

CAN I OBTAIN COVERAGE WITHOUT A BROKER?

Benefits coverage can be contracted directly with a provider in certain situations. There is no need to contact a broker in order to sign on to a plan through a business or professional association. The individual who services the plan for your local chamber of commerce will probably be a broker. In this situation, a different broker can access a comparison quote for an alternative option that may contain variables not included in the choices offered by the association.

Other benefits, such as Qualified Transportation, can be easily structured using companies that specialize in administering these plans; these benefits are also available through payroll providers who offer access to a variety of voluntary programs. A broker can review all of the components in the package to ensure a fit with your overall strategy or simply act to connect you with necessary resources. Employers also choose to use a broker, even if not compulsory, to facilitate research, service, and representation.

Plan providers may not deal directly with the smallest groups or businesses in the earliest stages of development for health, life, disability, and retirement products; in this case, a broker will be required to establish this contact. Carriers don't give any discounts for dealing directly, even though brokers receive their compensation through commissions from the insurance company. If you have not found the right broker, or have not been using one, the representation can be established at any time.

FINDING A BROKER

It is not difficult to find a broker interested in representing employers in the benefits market. In this very competitive environment spending some time to find one, or a team, that meets company-specific needs is well worth the effort.

Are All Brokers the Same?

The role of the broker has evolved with the dramatic changes in employer-provided insurance. It is unlikely that one agent is the best choice to manage all business insurance needs; health, life, workers' compensation, disability, property and casualty, business interruption, and liability require many different areas of expertise. Today's brokers are specialists either in smaller firms, or staff members in large regional or national companies. The agent that sells your homeowners and auto insurance may also be well equipped to review individual disability, or have a partner with competence in this area, but

---

BETTER FORGOTTEN

Sorry, I Was Busy with a Client in Europe

A service company thought that partnering with a senior VP at one of the largest global benefits consultants would add clout in negotiating a January 1st renewal on behalf of the company's more than 2,000 primarily low-wage workers in eighteen locations across the United States. The VP was frequently out of the country during the summer and early fall but provided updates on premium estimates and sought additional data to hold an anticipated health plan increase to 8%. At a November meeting to discuss final numbers, the insurance company presented a 16% rate jump. When the employer asked about other options, everyone looked blank, making it clear that this group was not a high priority.

---

he or she is unlikely to have the depth of knowledge and expertise to manage an increasingly complex employee benefits market.

The relationship yields the greatest value when the broker is matched with the business and employee needs, enabling the broker to become a partner in executing the benefits strategy. The largest global consulting firms have the ability to provide complete service through sheer size and competence but are less likely to be as attentive to the needs of small to mid-sized employers. If your point of contact is more focused on a client with a workforce of thousands, a depth of knowledge won't add value; however, the global reach will be a necessity for employers, no matter how small, who hire individuals scattered across continents. The location and size of the agency is less important than their reach; a team of twelve in Boston can have sufficient national contacts to service a client in Boulder.

Do I Start by Searching the Web for "Employee Benefits Broker"?

Millions of results pop up when you type "employee benefits broker" into your favorite search engine. A more targeted approach begins by networking in the community you already know. There are bound to be brokers in local business groups, and you can obtain referrals from professional associations, vendors, and your circle of friends and neighbors. This is one time when industry competitors with similar workforces can be a great resource.

It does not take a juggling act to engage different agencies. It's conceivable to appoint four, divided by general business insurance, health benefits, workers' compensation, and retirement. Agents will seek to add to their business by working on the less-complicated life insurance and disability in tandem with other policies, but brokers who are confident in their specialty will also refer you to a network for the best service for another product.

What Questions Do I Ask a Potential Broker?

Use this reference list of interrogatories:

1. What sets you apart from your competitors? Differences include philosophy, size, and the background and experience of principals. Key players can be effective if they are working in a brokerage with roots as a family business but will have an entirely different perspective with a resume that includes employment for a health insurer.

2. How many clients do you have? How many have been clients for at least five years? The length of relationships is more important than volume, which will vary by types of coverage and group size.

3. What size and types of industries do you service and for what kinds of coverage? This is where comparables will be helpful, particularly for workers' compensation and disability.

4. How do you remain up-to-date on legislation and changes in the marketplace? Concrete examples are a more reliable predictor than a response of, "I read a lot."

5. What other services do you offer? These can range from enrollment, providing required notices, claims assistance, and on-site meetings to COBRA administration, customized benefits brochures, benefits statements, online enrollment and materials. Ask

about any costs associated with each of the options; some will be routine and free of charge while others will only be available on a fee basis.

6. How do you handle renewals? Savvy brokers will respond with a general timetable that involves the employer and communication with carriers.

7. How do you get paid? The broker should clearly explain commissions and any other fees that are paid by carriers or billed to you. Transparency will enhance trust in the relationship.

8. Will there be a dedicated account manager and, if so, who will that be? A designated individual can answer employee questions, particularly for a company that lacks a benefits professional. You want to understand the roles of anyone servicing your account and have confidence in his or her ability.

9. How do you help employees who have claim and service issues with carriers? Seek specific examples, and listen for a resolution. There is no reason to be content with, "We make some phone calls."

10. How long does it take you to respond to client phone calls and e-mail?

11. Have you ever been disciplined by a regulator?

12. Could you describe a recent success story? Look for details of improved service and satisfaction or lowered costs. This is much more specific than, "The new client was very happy."

If the answers fail to meet your expectations, or don't even address the inquiry, move on. Courting new business should bring out the best in anyone; they are either not interested or do not have the level of competence and service orientation you need. Conversations with other clients will round out the information and help with the selection decision.

What Do I Ask When I Check References?

Request the names of three to five references from any agency under final consideration. More than one reference provides a greater chance to identify comparable needs and results.

Drill down to obtain specifics from friendly sources by asking:

- How has this broker responded when you have had claims and billing issues?
- Does the office work with employees to resolve claims issues or are they directed to the insurer?
- How long have you been a client and why have you continued this relationship?
- Who is most helpful at the agency and why?
- What can this broker do to improve the level of service they provide?

With so many agents to choose from, one key factor in a successful relationship is the comfort level and personal trust with everyone involved in the account. Agents and staff need to be sharp and knowledgeable but also able to explain concepts and costs in an understandable way without overusing jargon and industry abbreviations. Sit down with a potential adviser and ask for a description of the advantages and disadvantages of High Deductible Health Plans with Health Savings Accounts. This is not a conversation to have during a networking reception when you are introduced to a broker, but for a dedicated in-person meeting. If you don't understand the answer or the broker can't answer your questions, continue interviewing other agents. Plan to meet members of an agency's team that services similar accounts. There is no reason to settle for a broker who is a great negotiator but cannot back up a plan with an acceptable level of ongoing service. The time and frustration involved in difficult dealings will overshadow plan design elements and even better rates. Changing brokers does not necessarily mean changing plans or carriers.

THE BROKER RELATIONSHIP

Because brokers are most likely to earn their income through commissions from insurers, the arrangement does not involve a complex agreement for a fixed period. The specifics of any consulting work that includes additional fees can be spelled out in individual agreements.

What Is a Broker of Record Letter?

A broker of record letter formally designates an agency as acting on your behalf and representing you in negotiations with a specific carrier. The broker of record letter is written on company letterhead by the insured and terminates any relationship between a current broker and the carrier; they are no longer authorized to negotiate on behalf of this client with the designated provider. This is also the document that enables a broker to earn commissions on the policy. If you work with one broker who obtains contracts for medical, dental, and life insurance through three different companies, each will receive a separate letter that defines this arrangement.

Agents don't need the broker of record documentation in order to go into the marketplace and obtain quotes for coverage. Your existing broker can act without this designation if they are seeking rates from competing carriers for comparison during planning and the renewal process. If you are considering new brokers, they can research alternative insurers in an effort to gain your business; however, they cannot discuss coverage details with a provider when an agent is already designated as your broker of record.

How Often Should I Talk to My Benefits Broker?

Early in the relationship the effective broker will learn about your benefits strategy, identify your needs, and evaluate the plan. This conversation should be repeated at least once each year when planning for renewals, or whenever there is a major business change.

In a perfect world without questions about benefits, bills, or claims, there is no need to talk to a broker frequently; once a quarter for health and retirement plans is adequate. Brokers should keep you up-to-date about trends in claims and legislative initiatives that affect the plan, and ask about employee feedback even when there are no ongoing issues. The dialogue is important in situations when frequent contact is not essential, because health plan renewals are never too far off; these contracts are overwhelmingly written to cover just twelve months. If one broker manages life insurance, long-term disability, and some voluntary benefits, then interaction once a year is fine, as claims under these policies are rare. As activity increases so do service needs. If you are ever disappointed by the service received from anyone in a broker's office, don't be shy about bringing this to the attention of the key contact on the account. They want to keep your business and should take steps to meet your expectations. If they cannot meet service levels, it may be time to change brokers; you can always return after the glitches have been corrected.

How Often Should I Change My Benefits Broker?

None of these steps is meant to suggest that benefits brokers should be rotated every few months or even every year. The best relationships are long-standing, span many years, and work well for the company. Change should only be sought if service is consistently unsatisfactory or in the event that an agent cannot respond effectively to requests for new products. If the owner of the agency in place has been playing golf with the company founder for 25 years, it is very possible that the brokerage has kept up with industry changes and client growth. If not, it's time to issue a request for proposals to a few different brokers, but include the current one in the process, as they may make changes in order to keep the business. They may also be retained as the broker for a smaller piece of the business with another agent or agents representing the organization for insurance that matches their expertise in the market.

BROKER SERVICES

Brokers can provide a range of additional services beyond contract review and negotiation (or none at all). Such services may involve partners that the agent pays for or a fee arrangement that should include some preferential pricing, based on the relationship.

What Can I Hand Over to the Benefits Broker?

At minimum, a benefits broker should be able to handle enrollments and changes for small employers who do not have the staff to process these tasks. For speed and accuracy these should be Web-based transactions, but employers must never transmit employees' personal data by e-mail. Enrollment forms may be faxed or sent. It might be just as fast for a company employee to be trained in Web-based enrollments and

WORTH REPEATING

The Broker Audits Bills Every Quarter

Chatham Consulting Group Inc., based in New York, leverages relationships with national carriers to service clients in multiple states. They use their record-keeping strength to automatically compare all client bills and enrollments once each quarter. The exercise saves premium dollars by identifying incorrect rates and finding mistakes in enrollments, changes, and terminations that can be particularly tough to track for multilocation employers.

changes than to fax multiple forms. Better yet, ask the broker whether employees can enroll directly on the Web. This can be accommodated through the plan's Web site or portal owned by the broker. Representatives should always be available to intervene in problems with billing and claims. They will know who to call or contact by e-mail, be able to create verbiage for letters when hard copy is required, and intervene on your behalf—or at least point you in the right direction.

Look for these additional services:

Customized Web Portals. The broker owns the product but creates access for each client and employee populations with customized benefits information and company logos. The best ones have the look and feel of the company culture and allow employees to research, link to claims information, and make changes where appropriate. Whatever level is provided by the broker, make certain that it uses language and directions appropriate for your own employee population; put it through a few test runs before anything is introduced live. Always ask about any additional up-front costs for this option.

Benefits Brochures. Providers will send out plenty of glossy material, but one brochure that summarizes all of the plans and eligibility can be very useful. Brokers often create this content, but pass printing costs on to the employer. A brochure is a great concept, but make certain that a large budget is not spent for beautiful booklets that describe a medical benefits plan that is

---

WORTH REPEATING

My Own Customized Benefits Web Site

Solid Benefits Guidance provides clients in its home state of New Jersey and across the United States with a customized Web site that includes benefit-specific information, interactivity, and general human resources forms. Employees get online benefits enrollment and have access to company news in one spot. The addition of dependent access makes the site even more valuable, increasing satisfaction and providing time-saving tools. Employers gain the impact of a complete site they can call their own, which is constantly updated, without start-up pains and costs.

---

likely to change in a year. Think flexibility in these designs and formats.

Enrollment Forms. Plans will provide forms, but the entire process for enrollment and changes can be made simpler with one universal form that includes information and choices for medical, dental, vision, life insurance, and disability. A broker should be able to design the format for you.

Compliance and Reporting. For health and welfare plans the broker should obtain or prepare ERISA-required annual IRS Form 5500 reports and any other government reporting. Retirement plan 5500 reports are very time-consuming and complex and more likely to be completed by accounting specialists, who will charge prevailing rates for this work. Though there will be an additional charge for retirement plan testing and compliance reporting, the health plan forms are relatively simple and should be prepared for your signature without an additional charge.

Benchmarking. This can encompass benefit comparison surveys by geographic area or industry. Benchmarking can be completed by the agency or they may purchase reports completed by a consulting firm.

Employee and Beneficiary Education. These benefits experts can be tapped into for meetings at open enrollment and throughout the year. Brokers may also provide ongoing information in the form of a newsletter, mailings to employees' homes, or via social media.

Employee Surveys and Focus Groups. Employee buy-in and satisfaction are often enhanced when they are part of the decision-making process. Brokers can use their product knowledge in creating surveys and facilitating conversations and interpreting the results.

Mergers and Acquisitions. A broker should be able to provide assistance in evaluating plan options, costs, locations, and the steps that need to be taken to enroll participants, merge content, or maintain separate offerings. There may be regulations that are triggered when workers are employed in different states or when ownership changes alter filing requirements.

COBRA Administration. This begins with the notice that needs to be sent when employees are first covered by the plan and continues with compliance requirements that can be triggered when an employee leaves, divorces a spouse, or dies. If the broker administers COBRA for you directly, ask how they keep up-to-date with the details and changes. They may work with a third-party vendor and pass the charges on to you.

WORTH REPEATING

Thanks, We Didn't Really Want to Change Plans

After receiving notification of a 20% rate increase, a small company contacted another broker to market the plan to other providers. The relationship with the previous broker had lasted many years with the operating principal being "because that's the way we've always done it." In conversations with the client the agent learned that the company preferred to stay with the same carrier but felt that they could not afford to do so. The broker approached the carrier and asked for alternatives that would save the client money. After some modifications the contract was renewed with a 7% increase.

Will I Get a Better Price by Using Two Brokers to Compete for My Business?

It is possible to ask two brokers to simultaneously seek bids for your health care coverage. Although it might seem that this would produce healthy competition, the strategy can backfire. Competing brokers might blanket the market with requests and, because no one is the broker of record, an insurer will receive bid requests from two or more different agents. Facing competing interests without any commitment makes it hard for the provider to have confidence that they will win the business, and the broker has little leverage other than their good relationship.

If a new broker is under consideration, the better approach is to allow the existing agent to seek a renewal with the current carrier while the competitor markets the business elsewhere. Ask for the names of carriers being approached for quotes and you can direct brokers to steer clear of specific providers; doing so can enable more concentration on fewer bids, allowing agents to leverage their relationships rather than spending time producing volume and hoping something is acceptable.

REMEMBER THESE ARE EMPLOYER-PROVIDED BENEFITS

Brokers have the tools, resources, and expertise to complete a needs analysis and assess current programs. They have the experience to advocate on behalf of your business and its employees, reducing the pain of managing employee benefits by taking it off your plate. You have to be comfortable with, understand, and agree on recommendations before they are adopted. Accepting high escalating costs as the price of doing business and maintaining the status quo are strategies that are not acceptable in managing a business—and should not be acceptable in designing and administering employee benefits plans.

CHAPTER 7

Benefits That Save Payroll Taxes

What's Involved in Flexible Spending Accounts, Transportation, and Tuition Assistance Plans?

EMPLOYERS CAN REALIZE TAX SAVINGS WHENEVER they offer a range of benefits. The costliest component, the amount paid towards health premiums, is generally not considered taxable income for the employee. Better yet, if the plan is fully insured, the amount contributed towards coverage is completely deductible by the employer as long as the premiums meet general standards for deductibility, which would include that they be of a reasonable amount. If the plan is self-insured it must meet nondiscrimination tests before an employer is allowed to take this tax deduction. The nondiscrimination testing ensures that highly compensated employees do not receive additional benefits and eligibility for the same coverage that is extended to a majority of the employee population. A table at the end of this chapter summarizes the employment tax treatment of various benefits.

HEALTH REFORM AND TAX ADVANTAGES

PPACA includes tax incentives to help small companies better afford health coverage.

What Do Tax Credits and Cafeterias Have to Do with PPACA?

The PPACA included some valuable tax components that are effective as of 2010. The first phase allows small businesses a tax credit of up to 35% of an employer's contribution toward providing health insurance for employees. Eligible employers will have no more than 25 employees with average annual wages of no more than $50,000 per person.

Cafeteria or Section 125 plans create tax savings for both employers and employees. They allow employers to set up a plan that includes employee contributions towards health benefits as pretax dollars. Employees must sign an acknowledgment of this contribution before enrollment and at the beginning of each plan year. There is no ERISA requirement to file a plan document for a Section 125 plan. The cafeteria plan rules are relaxed under the PPACA to encourage more small employers to offer tax-free benefits to employees. The rules cover employers with 100 or fewer employees and plans including those related to health and certain plans offered through a cafeteria plan, such as group term life insurance, self-insured medical, and dependent care assistance benefits. Your benefits broker or tax professional will be able to identify your eligibility to allow contributions in a form that saves payroll taxes for you and your employees.

Flexible Spending Accounts

Flexible Spending Accounts (FSAs) are designed with tax savings features for both employers and participating employees. FSAs are individual accounts that allow employees and employers to deposit pretax dollars that can be used for eligible expenses. There are two distinct types of FSAs covering different expenditure categories: health care and dependent care.

Where Do Health Care Flexible Spending Accounts Fit into the Health Benefits Picture?

Flexible Spending Accounts (FSAs) provide employees the opportunity to make voluntary contributions of pretax dollars into an account to be used for reimbursement of qualified medical and dental expenses. Employers may also contribute to FSAs, and these contributions are not considered taxable income. Though FSAs may sound similar to HSAs they are really quite different.

Key points about FSAs include:

- Employers have a great deal of flexibility in the combination of benefits that include FSAs; participants do not have to be covered under any other health plan.

- The plan sponsor, the employer, identifies the maximum annual contribution allowed into the plan as a total dollar amount or maximum percentage of earnings. There are currently no limits, but effective 2013 PPACA limits the amount of FSA contributions that cover health expenditures to $2,500 per year, which can be indexed for later years by the cost of living.

- Before the beginning of the plan year employees designate the total amount they wish to contribute into the plan, and the voluntary deduction is deposited from pay in equal amounts throughout the plan year. This is sometimes referred to as a salary reduction agreement.

- Employees request reimbursement for qualified medical and dental expenses or may be able to use a debit card to access these funds.

- FSAs cannot be used to pay for health insurance premiums, long-term care, or any item paid by another health plan.

- The FSA must reimburse up to the maximum amount allocated for the account, whether or not the funds have already been deposited. If the plan year begins in January of 2011 and an employee has chosen to contribute $4,000 for the year to an FSA, a $1,500 claim for braces in January will be eligible for reimbursement even though only less than $350 is in the account at the end of the month.

- Qualified medical and dental expenses must be incurred during the plan year in order to be eligible for reimbursement.

- An employer may choose to extend the claims period up to 2.5 months after the plan year ends. For example, if an employer with a calendar year plan chooses to extend the claims period to March 15th, an employee can receive payment for new glasses in January from funds left over in the plan from the previous calendar year.

- FSA accounts are "use it or lose it." At the end of the plan year, or after any grace period, employees cannot receive any distributions of funds.

- Participants can only make changes in voluntary contributions during the plan year if they experience a change of status, such as marriage or the birth of a child. They may then be eligible for a new annual maximum and increase their funding.

- Employees with access to an HSA are not eligible to participate in a FSA.

FSAs provide great value for employees in reducing taxable income to pay for routine expenses incurred by copays and for such items as glasses and contact lenses. FSAs can also be used to pay for over-the-counter medications through December 31, 2010; PPACA eliminated these as allowable FSA and HRA expenses as of January 1, 2011.

Can an Employee Use a Dependent Care FSA to Pay All of Their Day-Care Bills?

Dependent Care Accounts can be established to enable eligible employees to pay for child-care and elder-care expenses with pretax dollars from an FSA. The funds in these accounts can be used to reimburse expenses incurred to care for a qualified dependent while an individual is working, or looking for work. A qualified dependent is defined as a child under the age of 13 or any dependent who is mentally or physically incapable of caring for him- or herself. Because these accounts are meant to subsidize the ability to work, or seek employment, an employee cannot take advantage of this benefit if he or she has a spouse who is not in the workforce or searching for a job. As with health care FSAs, employees identify an annual contribution amount, within employer-defined limits, to be contributed from their pay at regular intervals and the funds are "use it or lose it" for expenses incurred during the plan year. Unlike health care accounts, the IRS imposes a maximum annual contribution and employees cannot receive a reimbursement from a dependent care account until the funds have been deposited. The employee who chooses to deposit

$3,000 into a dependent care account at the beginning of the calendar year will have $250 available at the end of each calendar month. If he submits a claim for $1,500 on February 1st, the employee will be reimbursed for $250, or the plan may hold the claim until the entire $1,500 is accumulated in the account. Employees can never receive reimbursement for payments made in advance of services. When summer day camp fees are paid in April or May, the employee will have to wait until a session ends for payment of the claim.

The following chart includes a list of child- and elder-care expenses and indicates whether they would be covered under an FSA:

CHILDCARE EXPENSES	ELIGIBLE
Activity fees	No
Before- or after-school program, extended care	Yes
Au pair or nanny	Yes
Babysitting (work-related, in employee's home or someone else's home)	Yes
Babysitting (not work-related, for other purpose)	No
Babysitting by employee's relative who is not a tax dependent (work-related)	Yes
Babysitting by a tax dependent (work-related or for other purpose)	No
Child care	Yes
Dance or music lessons	No
Dependent care (while employee works; while looking for work)	Yes
Educational, tutoring, learning, or study skills services	No
Field trips	No
Household services (housekeeper, maid, cook, and so on)	No
Housekeeper who cares for child (only portion of payment attributable to work-related child care)	Yes
Kindergarten preschool or private school tuition	No
Language classes	No
Late-payment fees	No
Meals, food, or snacks	No
Medical care	No
Payroll taxes related to eligible care	Yes

(Continued)

(Continued)

CHILDCARE EXPENSES	ELIGIBLE
Registration fees (required for eligible care, after actual services are received)	Yes
Registration fees (required for eligible care, prior to actual services received)	No
School tuition	No
Sick-child care	Yes
Sleepaway camp	No
Summer day camp	Yes

ELDER CARE EXPENSES	ELIGIBLE
Adult day-care center	Yes
Custodial elder care (not work-related, for other purpose)	No
Custodial elder care (work-related)	Yes
Day nursing care	No
Elder care (while employee works; while looking for work)	Yes
Elder care (in employee's home or someone else's)	Yes
Medical care	No
Nursing home care	No
Senior day care	Yes
Expenses for a housekeeper whose duties include caring for an eligible dependent	Yes

Can I Use the FSA to Pay My High School Senior to Watch Our Sixth-Grader After School?

No, FSAs cannot be used to reimburse anyone you claim as a dependent. The IRS also requires that the caregiver be someone who declares wages paid as taxable income. The paperwork required for claims will ask for the provider's Social Security number or the taxpayer ID from a licensed day care. If an individual refuses to give you a Social Security number, employees can still request the payment from their account by writing and signing a letter that includes the babysitter's or housekeeper's name and address. Dependent care account administration does not require verification of preemployment paperwork, such as an I-9, or payment of employment taxes; those are household employer issues.

Can Employees Take Advantage of a Dependent Care FSA and the Dependent Care Tax Credit?

Employees must choose between the FSA and Dependent Care Tax Credit; they cannot reap the tax savings from both. In order to identify the most favorable option, employees will need to compare the maximum available under each choice; a tax professional can answer this question. Employees who are single, or married and filing a joint tax return, can contribute up to $5,000 each year to a Dependent Care FSA. For married employees, the limit covers combined contributions of both spouses. Married employees who file separate tax returns can each contribute up to a maximum of $2,500 into a Dependent Care Flexible Spending Account.

Are These Plans Really Worth the Hassle?

Unfortunately, FSAs have been perceived as cumbersome by both employers and employees. Though roughly half of all employers who offer benefits—including 90% of the largest employers—also offer FSAs, the number drops below 20% for employers with fewer than 100 employees. Even with offerings concentrated in the largest employers, fewer than 20% of eligible employees take advantage of the benefit. The "use it or lose it" feature tends to scare off employees who think they will not be able to spend all of the funds. It's easy to provide models showing how deposits will be spent, and you can create examples for single employees and families to illustrate the tax savings. It only takes a list of copayments for a few doctor and dentist visits combined with allergy medication, one monthly prescription, and a pair of glasses to show an employee where $500, less than $10 per week, of eligible expenses is spent. Solid explanations will create the difference between a valued benefit and a perceived extra headache.

Participation in these plans is also encouraged by the simplest reimbursement vehicle possible. This is typically a debit card, which looks like a standard credit card, that can be used for all eligible expenses. Employees are encouraged to keep receipts, but in most cases no longer have to when visiting nationwide chains. Providers should supply easy-to-use lists and explanations of eligible expenses for which the card can be used. The debit card option is now routinely available for small employers. If the administrative costs and funding do not make sense, speak to another vendor; it's a very competitive market.

Employers may shy away from the plans due to the potential risk involved in funding FSA reimbursements when an employee leaves before the plan year, and full allocations have already been spent. Yes, an employee can be reimbursed $1,000 for braces in January from a $3,000 allocation for a health care FSA when no more than $250 will be in the account at the end of the month. If the employee resigns in February, the employer will be responsible for the unfunded amount that was already paid out. But employers can use money left over in any other health care FSAs to cover these amounts; they should review a model of potential payroll tax savings generated by the plan before turning down the concept. Plans can also be started with low annual maximum employee contributions to encourage participation, facilitate communication, and gain a track record to calculate financial exposure. Effective brokers and vendors will be partners in this effort.

TRANSPORTATION BENEFITS

Transportation benefits that allow employees to subsidize commuting costs with pretax dollars are very popular, whether or not an employer subsidizes the program. The components can be most valuable in metropolitan areas but have applicability in many commuting scenarios.

Will the Government Really Pay Me to Ride My Bicycle to Work?

The 2008 economic stimulus legislation extended its reach from financial institutions to two-wheeled commuters. New employer-provided tax savings benefits were tucked into complex legislation to allow employers to provide a monthly reimbursement of up to $20 for employees who cycle to work during a qualified bicycle commuting month. A qualified bicycle month is any month the employee regularly uses a bicycle for a substantial portion of travel between work and home and does not receive any transit pass or qualified parking benefits. Though the terms "regularly uses" and "substantial portion" are not clear, the list of reimbursable expenses is very specific. It includes "purchase of a bicycle and bicycle improvements, repair and storage." The $20 per month maximum and employer tax savings make the benefit more affordable even in the unlikely event that all eligible employees opt to receive a bicycle commuting reimbursement. This modest expenditure certainly sends a message that reinforces healthy and green habits. Employees can receive the benefit for individual months—it does not have to cover an entire year—but they cannot be paid the bicycle commuting benefit and any other qualified transportation benefits within the same month. For example, the employee who rides her bike to the train won't be reimbursed for bike expenses and train tickets.

If you are already providing any kind of transportation benefits, your provider should be able to help with set-up and administration. A new plan should not be complicated to establish; there is no requirement for a written plan document. Plan start dates can be any time during a year. A January 1st start date can be the perfect way to accompany New Year's resolutions, as long as your workplace is not in a snow belt. If flakes are flying, the bicycle commuting benefit can be introduced in the spring.

Where Does Travel by Train, Bus, or Ferry Fit in?

Beginning in 1993, the IRS allowed employers to provide pretax transportation benefits for commuters. As of 2010 these allow contributions of up to $230 per month for van pool, bus, ferry, rail, or any form of public transportation and an additional $230 per month for qualified parking that is required for an employee's commute to work. Employees who get to their desk using a combination of public transportation and parking, such as driving to a bus or train station, can access a combined benefit of $460 per month.

Though employers can contribute towards qualified transportation benefits, they are more commonly offered as a voluntary benefit, paid for by the employee. If an employer does choose to contribute, the total amount must remain within the maximum of $230 per month for each type of expense. Plans can be set up to utilize a debit card that is only accepted for transportation, or to use a card that creates stored value for this benefit and FSAs. Employers may also choose to provide checks in exchange for the employee's completing a form acknowledging that the funds are used for qualified transportation or to purchase bus or train passes for local systems.

Transportation benefits should not be viewed as another payroll headache. In this extremely competitive market, employers of all sizes should be able to find a vendor that will minimize administration and ensure employee satisfaction. In locations where the plans make sense, qualified transportation benefits are extremely popular, as employees realize a tangible payback each month from a scheduled outlay for a regularly recurring expense. The tax savings on the plan contributions effectively pay for the plan.

TUITION ASSISTANCE

Employers can implement a huge range of options to provide education assistance, from reimbursing $150 for a licensing course to full payment for master's and doctoral programs. The most effective choices will fit with a benefits strategy focusing on workforce demographics and the skills, knowledge, and succession needed to meet organizational goals. New technologies will demand expanded levels of expertise, whereas a team that focuses on providing routine retail service does not require the same level of investment for growth.

The following questions will help make decisions, whether you are exploring the potential of education assistance or reviewing a plan already in place:

1. What's the purpose of the plan?

    Tuition assistance can be a strong component of an employee retention strategy in that it has the capacity to influence loyalty and develop individuals for internal promotions. It can be a necessary strategy for a small employer competing for talent with large companies that offer generous programs with few strings attached. This doesn't mean that a 75-person company must reimburse $8,000 a year to attract a candidate who is contemplating an offer from a national telecommunications giant. A plan that targets classes tied to growth in positions, with a payback requirement in the event of turnover, can be presented as extremely attractive.

2. Who will be eligible for education assistance?

Eligibility criteria include length of service and employment status. Tuition assistance is likely to require a longer waiting period, frequently at least a year, to reward longevity, and plans often include a payback requirement for employees who leave within a specified period after the class has been reimbursed. Some employers choose to provide a prorated benefit for part-time employees as an incentive to continue while in school and graduate into full-time roles. This would not make sense in a workplace where part-timers typically work a year or less.

3. What types of classes will be covered?

The parameters for types of classes to be covered must describe the format in which appropriate education is delivered and the relationship between course content and the employee's work. Educational opportunities are available in myriad ways through public sources and private vendors, in-person, and through an explosion of online tools. A plan can identify accreditations or acceptable educational institutions, or take a broader approach and allow approvals upon review of course content. The broader approach makes sense for most employers. A neighborhood high school continuing education Excel class can introduce necessary spreadsheet skills for less than $200, whereas a college course on the subject will be much costlier and take more time to present content that is beyond the knowledge required for the job. Establish criteria and a common approval path when discretion is allowed. If developing writing skills is important, one VP may say yes to an online class while another turns it down with the explanation that "Proper English can only be taught in person." The criteria should also take into account employee schedules and knowledge gaps. A blanket statement that denies reimbursement for any college coursework that is taken online can have the result of restricting the usefulness of the benefit.

The broadest views should be tailored to focus on courses that relate to an employee's ability to perform in the current job or to follow an established career path. Employers may allow eligibility for courses that lead to advancement; for example, an employer could contribute toward math classes for the receptionist who may have a future in accounting, but should not be expected to pay for a purchasing professional's interest in geology. Any policy should clearly define these criteria and apply them consistently.

4. When and how is payment made?

The total benefit will be determined by your budget, competitive climate, and the cost of classes that are most likely to be taken. Plans can begin with a modest benefit, covering costs as low as $250 a year to initiate the concept; this amount can always be increased in subsequent years. If you are starting with a relatively low benefit amount, don't publicize it as the answer to all employee personal educational costs; rather, describe it as a subsidy. Be specific about the types of expenses that will be eligible for reimbursement; many employers include books but not fees in their repayment arrangements. Employees should know whether or not your plan will pay for $300 in books before they open the first text.

Payment processes can be set up once a budget has been established that identifies maximum amounts allowed under the plan. Education assistance is most commonly paid as reimbursement after a course is completed. Employers typically require proof of successful completion, such as passing or earning a minimum grade. Plans can be written to include a scale for payment of tuition based on the grade that was earned:

100% for an A, 85% for a B, and 75% for a C. Employers can choose to deliver checks to employees or make arrangements to pay colleges and universities directly. Employees are discouraged from using tuition assistance to gain classroom knowledge that enables them to jump to a job at a new employer by instituting a payback requirement, in effect during the first few years after receipt of a payment. These might include an 80% payback for employees who leave within a year, 60% after two years, and 40% following three. In applying any payback requirement, make certain that any deductions from wages are allowed under applicable state wage and hour laws.

5. How are requests processed?

The internal processes for providing education assistance must be clearly laid out and communicated to all employees. The most logical starting point is to require a request for reimbursement before a class is taken through a written statement or application form that describes all approval steps. Ideally, employees should apply for the benefit before signing up for the class in order to avoid disappointment or misplaced expectations about payment. Include due dates for employees to use in planning and processing such as "Requests must be submitted at least two weeks before a class begins and both grades and proof of payment are due within thirty days of course completion."

An Example of One Company's Process of Distributing Benefits Through the Tuition Assistance Program

Step 1: Employees complete an application for reimbursement for appropriate classes.

Step 2: Within 120 days before the start date of their courses, employees submit the application to their manager for approval.

Step 3: The manager approves or denies the request within five days of receipt, in writing, and forwards the application to the Controller.

Step 4: The Controller verifies eligibility for funding and approves or denies the application within five business days of receipt and returns the response to the employee.

Step 5: If the request is approved, the employee must submit proof of payment and completion of the course, including any grade earned if necessary, within thirty days of the last day of class, in order to receive any eligible reimbursement.

With a clear policy in place that defines expectations, process, and outcomes, employers can measure results to determine effectiveness. Metrics to watch include turnover, internal promotions, job satisfaction surveys, and correlations between performance ratings and educational reimbursement. Use these tools to tweak a program to meet current and future needs.

Where's the Tax Savings?

The cost of providing education benefits may be considered nontaxable income to the employee. IRS guidelines allow employers to create an Educational Assistance Plan under which up to $5,250 of the amount paid for employee continuing education will be considered nontaxable income. This doesn't mean that a plan has to allow $5,250 in benefits. It does mean that the benefit must be detailed in a written plan document and must not favor highly compensated employees. Within the framework of an Educational Assistance Plan, an employer identifies the eligibility requirements for employees, types of classes, and the amounts that will be paid for tuition and other costs. Absent a plan document, benefits for education may still qualify as nontaxable income, particularly if payment is for courses required for certifications or licenses. A tax professional will be able to clarify the requirements in this area.

A well-rounded benefits package can include all or some of these items. With so much time, energy, and money spent on health coverage it's easy to avoid adopting other offerings that can be complex or can create administrative headaches. It takes time to disseminate the details about plans that may confuse, but the effort expended to create information targeted to your employee population will increase utilization and satisfaction. These are options that save employers and employees money for expenditures that participants can control and from which they can realize results on a regular basis.

IRS Special Rules for Various Types of Benefits

Treatment Under Employment Taxes

Type of Benefit	Income Tax Withholding	Social Security and Medicare	Federal Unemployment (FUTA)
Accident and health benefits	Exempt[1,2], except for long-term care benefits provided through a flexible spending or similar arrangement.	Exempt, except for certain payments to S corporation employees who are 2% shareholders.	Exempt
Achievement awards	Exempt[1] up to $1,600 for qualified plan awards ($400 for nonqualified awards)		
Adoption assistance	Exempt[1,3]	Taxable	Taxable
Athletic facilities	Exempt if most of the use is by employees, their spouses, and their dependent children, and the facility is operated by the employer on premises it owns or leases.		
De minimis (minimal) benefits such as occasional parties, use of company equipment, and non-cash gifts	Exempt	Exempt	Exempt
Dependent care assistance	Dependent care assistance exempt[3] up to certain limits, $5,000 ($2,500 for married employee filing separate return).		
Educational assistance	Exempt up to $5,250 of qualified benefits each year.		
Employee discounts	Employee discounts exempt[3] up to IRS limits.		

(Continued)

TREATMENT UNDER EMPLOYMENT TAXES (*Continued*)

TYPE OF BENEFIT	INCOME TAX WITHHOLDING	SOCIAL SECURITY AND MEDICARE	FEDERAL UNEMPLOYMENT (FUTA)
Group term life insurance coverage	Exempt	Exempt[1,4] up to cost of $50,000 of coverage. (Special rules apply to former employees.)	Exempt
Health savings accounts (HSAs)	Exempt for qualified individuals up to annual HAS contribution limits.		
Lodging on your business premises	Exempt[1] if furnished for your convenience as a condition of employment.		
Meals	Exempt if minimal or provided on your premises for your convenience.		
Moving expense reimburse-ments	Exempt[1] if expenses would be deductible if the employee had paid them.		
Retirement planning	Exempt[5]	Exempt[5]	Exempt[5]
Transportation (commuting) benefits	Exempt[1] up to certain limits if for rides in a commuter highway vehicle and/or transit passes ($230), qualified parking ($230), or qualified bicycle commuting reimbursement[6] ($20). Exempt if *de minimis.*		

[1] Exemption does not apply to S corporation employees who are 2% shareholders.

[2] Exemption does not apply to certain highly compensated employees under a self-insured plan that favors those employees.

[3] Exemption does not apply to certain highly compensated employees under a program that favors those employees.

[4] Exemption does not apply to certain key employees under a plan that favors those employees.

[5] Exemption does not apply to services for tax preparation, accounting, legal, or brokerage services.

[6] If the employee receives a qualified bicycle commuting reimbursement in a qualified bicycle commuting month.

CHAPTER 8

Retirement Plans

What Do I Need to Know About Pensions, 401(k) Plans, and Nonqualified Plans?

EMPLOYER-SPONSORED RETIREMENT CAN BE DIVIDED into three basic formats: defined benefit (DB), defined contribution (DC), or Individual Retirement Arrangements (IRAs). Defined benefit plans provide a specific dollar amount at retirement based on a formula that commonly takes into account years of service, age, and wages earned. These traditional pension plans are rapidly becoming the exception, offered by fewer than 20% of U.S. private sector employers. Defined contribution plans identify a method for depositing funds into a plan but do not guarantee a specific or regular long-term benefit; the actual retirement benefit depends on the contribution amount and gains and losses of the account and can be based on length of service. 401(k) plans are the most common type of DC plan. Employer-sponsored IRAs create retirement savings opportunities for even the smallest employers without extensive reporting requirements. DB, DC, and IRA options can be created using different formats, and all describe qualified plans that are governed by federal regulation that enables tax advantages. The money employees put into these plans is commonly called elective deferrals; that is, they have chosen to defer a certain amount of salary into the plan on a pretax basis. Employers may also establish nonqualified plans using a wide variety of arrangements without the scrutiny of ERISA requirements.

Benefits strategy should be the platform for decisions about retirement plans, but business owners and senior executives often view this benefit in very personal terms, initiating research and driving discussion directed to meet their own long-term financial goals. Designing plans that are purely self-serving will not support broad employee relations strategies and is likely to conflict with regulatory requirements for qualified tax-favored options. The adoption of a retirement plan also includes a fiduciary responsibility to act on behalf of all eligible employees. Review all the available options to find an offering that best fits the needs of the organization.

Defined Benefit Plans

Traditional retirement plans are commonly associated with public sector employers and less-fashionable paternalistic employers. There are options within this category that don't look like your grandfather's pension plan.

Pension Plans

Pension plans are not the norm but may fit well within certain employer benefits strategy.

Does Anyone Start a Pension Plan Today?

In 1985 there were approximately 114,000 defined benefit plans in the United States; by 2009 that number had shrunk to 38,000. Cost, complexity, and an increase in funding requirements have been the main drivers of the decline in popularity of employer-sponsored pensions. DB plans can be started by businesses of any size and will continue to be an appropriate alternative for some workplaces.

Employers may appreciate certain specific components allowed in defined benefit plans:

- Participant's annual retirement benefit is determined by the plan's benefit formula; employees appreciate a predictable benefit.

- Higher annual retirement benefits are possible as identified by the IRS, up to $195,000 per year for 2009.
- Greater design flexibility; employers can contribute more and realize a greater tax savings than with defined contribution plans.
- Plans may allow loans.
- Benefit amounts are not dependent on asset returns.
- DB can be offered alongside other retirement plans.
- Vesting can be immediate or spread out over seven years.

Employers shy away from the concept because:

- An actuary is required to determine employer's annual contributions to make certain that funding requirements are met.
- Plans must meet minimum coverage tests but can exclude some employees.
- Set-up and operation are costly and necessitate complex administration.
- Annual reporting in the form of a return is required.
- Yearly nondiscrimination testing is required.
- If minimum contribution levels are not satisfied an excise tax is applied.

Pensions are generally funded by employer contributions, but they can also include provisions for voluntary or required employee contributions and must meet criteria under specific formulas to ensure that the plan does not fall short in its ability to pay out the defined amount at the time of employee retirement. The Pension Protection Act (PPA) of 2006 imposed new tougher standards requiring employers to make sufficient contributions to meet 100% funding of pension liabilities and erase shortfalls by 2015.

How Do Pension Plans End?

Sponsors of defined benefit plans are required to pay insurance premiums to the Pension Benefits Guarantee Corporation (PBGC) established by ERISA legislation in 1974. These premiums are increased for employers with underfunded pension plans and

BETTER FORGOTTEN

Double-Check the Numbers

A multistate employer made the decision to end a defined benefit retirement plan that had been offered for many years by the
smaller manufacturing company they had recently purchased.
The decision was communicated to all affected employees,
including information on the formula that would be used to
calculate payouts. The parent company then sent individual letters to each covered employee. The calculations used for this
correspondence were incorrect so all of the dollar amounts were
wrong—they were too low. The employer scrambled to provide
updated information as soon as the error was spotted; the crisis
of confidence took much longer to overcome.

include a per-participant termination premium in certain situations.
The PBGC governs plan terminations identified as either a standard termination or distress termination. In a standard termination
the employer demonstrates to the PBGC that the plan has enough
money to pay all of the benefits owed to employees through annuities
or lump sum payments. Employers can apply for a distress termination if they are facing enough financial difficulty to prove that they
cannot remain in business unless they terminate the defined benefit
plan. If an application is approved the PBGC takes over the plan as
the trustee, including plan assets, and pays out benefits up to legal
limits.

What's a Cash Balance Plan?

Cash balance plans have been described as hybrids of defined
benefit and contribution options but they are classified as defined
benefit plans for regulatory purposes. Cash balance plans guarantee
a benefit amount to covered employees based upon a specific formula that provides benefit and interest credits. Benefit credits are
determined annually after each eligible year of service based upon
calculations that use earnings, years of service, or age and length

of service. Each employee has the ability to know the cash value of his or her individual account at any time. The plan sets retirement ages at which employees may receive a lump sum payout, based on a vesting schedule, if they leave the company before retirement. Traditional defined benefit plans define the pension amount as a series of lifelong monthly payments that begin at retirement; cash balance plans define the benefit in terms of a stated account balance. These accounts have also been described as hypothetical because they do not reflect actual contributions, gains, or losses; they are based on the defined credits. Employers assume all of the investment risk in a cash balance account, and they must deposit sufficient funds to make certain the plans can pay future benefits. Employers who convert a traditional defined benefit retirement plan to a cash balance plan must comply with an age discrimination standard and ensure that vested benefits are not reduced or cut. The rules for establishing a new cash balance plan or converting a regular defined benefit are very complex, but the result can be attractive to certain employers who may realize lower costs in both funding and administration, in addition to tax advantages. An actuary must be used to identify annual contributions; these professionals can create models that consider employee population demographics, investment options, and potential PBGC premiums to identify whether a cash balance plan is an option to be considered.

DB(k) Plans

Employers with fewer than 500 employees can take advantage of this new qualified retirement benefit format that combines features of DB and DC plans. The DB(k) was created as part of the 2006 Pension Protection Act to become available as of January 1, 2010.

These plans require:

- A defined benefit equal to a minimum of 1% of final average pay for each year of the employee's service, up to 20 years.
- Automatic enrollment into a 401(k) portion in the amount of 4% of pay, unless an employee specifically opts out or changes the contribution level.
- An employer match of at least 50% of employee 401(k) contributions, with a maximum required match of 2% of compensation.

The DB(k) allows small employers to minimize the paperwork burden of a retirement plan by exempting the plan from discrimination testing; in this case, employers only need to file a plan document and annual Form 5500. This new option was written into legislation to encourage employers to return to providing pensions, on a more manageable smaller scale, while also generating incentives for employee retirement savings.

Defined Contribution Plans

In October of 2009 the Bureau of Labor Statistics tallied more than 49 million U.S. employees enrolled in defined contribution plans; 85% of those were 401(k) plans. 401(k) plans, named for the section of the Internal Revenue Code (IRC) that includes the rules allowing this form of retirement savings, first became a permanent provision of the IRC in 1980. Since that time the addition of regulations and subsections that allow variations have created 401(k) choices to fit different employer situations.

401(k) Plans

A traditional, or original, 401(k) plan allows employees to choose to defer a portion of their earnings into an individual account. These salary, or elective, deferrals are considered pretax dollars and employees must have the ability to direct where they are invested. The IRS establishes annual maximums on the amount employees can contribute to their 401(k). This amount was published as $16,500 for both 2009 and 2010, with an additional savings allowance of $5,500 a year for employees who are at least 50 years old. 401(k) plans also allow employers to contribute pretax dollars to employee accounts but in 2009 and 2010 the combined contributions cannot exceed 100% of earnings or $49,000, whichever is less. The amount of compensation that can be considered in determining both employer and employee contributions is also limited each year; for 2009 and 2010 this number was set at $245,000.

How Does an Employer Start a 401(k)?

There are four basic steps required to adopt a tax-savings 401(k) plan.

1. Adopt a Written Plan

    Qualified plan provisions must be included in a written plan document that is communicated to employees, simply referring to the Internal Revenue Code is not sufficient. Most plans follow a standard form or prototype that providers use to create employer plans. IRS-approved prototype plans can be provided by banks, trade or professional organizations, insurance companies, or mutual fund companies. Plans may also be designed using a customized individually designed plan document; these will be costlier and may necessitate a lengthier IRS approval process.

2. Arrange a Trust for Plan Assets

    401(k) assets must be held in a designated trust to ensure that they are used only to benefit participants and their beneficiaries. At least one trustee must be designated to have the ultimate responsibility for handling contributions and to plan investments and distributions.

3. Develop a Record-Keeping System

    A plan administrator or the financial institution assisting with a plan will typically assist in maintaining required records. Details include tracking contributions, loans (if allowed), in-service withdrawals, rollovers, and statements to employees. An essential record-keeping task is preparation and filing the annual return or report mandated by the federal government.

4. Provide Plan Information to Eligible Employees

    Employers are required to provide eligible employees with a Summary Plan Description (SPD). Issuing an SPD will satisfy compliance but cannot be relied on as the sole source of information. Dense language, details, and fine print will not highlight the 401(k) advantages that encourage employee participation.

Are Employees Always Allowed to Contribute the IRS Maximum into a 401(K)?

Employers determine the allowable contributions that participants can make into their 401(k) account and these parameters are included in the plan document.

Consider the following questions when setting these guidelines or reviewing existing plans:

What formula is used to calculate employee salary deferrals?

Plans can set permissible salary deferrals based on a percentage of earnings or specific dollar amounts as long as they do not exceed designated IRS annual allowable maximums. Contributions indicated as percentages enable automatic increases and add to savings rates when wages rise. Flat dollar amounts may be easier for employees to use in visualizing their goals, and some plans allow both. Make certain that the selection is easily accommodated by your payroll system and record keeping.

What is the maximum allowable percentage deferral that the plan will allow?

Plans can allow deferral of any percentage amount up to the IRS maximum. Employers can set a maximum that allows employees to reach permissible limits by the end of the plan year or can facilitate a very high contribution that will reach limits as early as possible. It is not unusual for employers to limit the contributions of highly compensated employees into the 401(k) in order to ensure passage of annual compliance testing. The plan might state that employees can contribute up to 10% of their earnings, within IRS guidelines, with the exception of employees who earn $110,000 or more each year, who are allowed to put in up to 4%.

When can employees change the amount they contribute?

Employees must be allowed to stop their contributions at any time by following appropriate procedures. The ability to change the amount of the regular elective deferral or to restart contributions should be specified in the plan document. Some employers limit these changes to twice each year or quarterly, whereas others allow them at any time. It should be made clear to employees that 401(k) plans are designed to be long-term savings accounts and the parameters you choose must be compatible with payroll procedures and internal processes.

When can new employees sign up?

In order to identify the best initial eligibility date, employers must strike a balance between rewarding longevity and competitive forces. With a delayed enrollment there is really no way

---

WORTH REPEATING

Employees Make Videos to Spread the 401(k) Message

Electronics retailer Best Buy used a company social networking site to increase lagging plan participation. They ran a contest for employees to make and post videos describing the benefits of the 401(k). The winner earned a trip to the corporate office, runners-up were rewarded with gift certificates, and employees helped spread the word about the value of the 401(k).

---

to compensate a new hire moving from a large employer after 10 years of service where he enjoyed a generous contribution match. More than one-third of the smallest employers and up to 70% of large employers allow participation within the first month of service. A qualified plan must be offered to all employees who are at least 21 years old and who have worked at least 1,000 hours in the previous year within six months of the date they meet these criteria. Even if health benefits are offered only to employees working at least 35 hours a week, a 401(k) plan will have to be made available to those who work consistently 20 hours a week (1,040 hours a year). In establishing a 401(k) plan, employers identify the plan year; it does not have to be a calendar year. A review of turnover patterns and demographics will contribute to the decision about initial enrollment dates; establishing eligibility after three months of work will not make sense for a workplace where employees commonly cycle out after six to nine months. Plans also designate subsequent sign-up periods for employees who do not initially elect participation; these can be quarterly or monthly, though twice a year is very common, but should be set on a schedule that minimizes administrative burden and accommodates effective communication.

Can We Really Enroll Employees into the 401(k) Automatically?

Employers have found that 401(k) participation rates increase, particularly among younger and lower-wage staff, when savings is initiated through automatic enrollment as soon as employees become eligible. Automatic enrollment, encouraged by the Pension Protection Act of 2006, allows employers to begin salary deferrals into the plan at set default contribution rates and investment funds, unless employees explicitly choose to opt out. Plans can also adopt automatic escalation, increasing contribution rates at periodic intervals, absent employee action. For example, if the default contribution rate at enrollment is 3%, the plan sponsor can increase the employee savings rate by 1% per year with a maximum set at 5 or 6%. The PPA also provides a solution to decrease the potential for a large pool of stranded accounts created when employees stop contributions after the accumulation of only a few hundred dollars. Plan sponsors can choose to implement a 90-day window during which a participant who was automatically enrolled in a 401(k) can reverse the enrollment and receive a refund of the money deducted from her pay, including any gains or losses.

How Much Do Employers Contribute?

An employer match can be a significant incentive for employee participation and is often described as "free money." Employers have the ability to spend pretax dollars to match some portion of individual contributions into 401(k) accounts, deposit a fixed amount, combine set and variable, or make no contribution at all; there is no requirement to do so. Of the variety of formulas used to determine company contributions, the most common is $.50 per $1.00 up to the first 6% of earnings. Employers can then tout the benefits of

---

WORTH REPEATING

That Match Earns an A Plus

A midsize service company instituted a graded match of 401(k) contributions to encourage participation. The first 3% of earnings contributed were matched at 60% and the next 3% at 40%. Effective communications of the benefit spurred lower earners to become participants and thus more regular savers.

earning an extra 3% of pay deposited, tax free, into a 401(k) account just for saving money. Under a traditional 401(k) plan employers can retain the ability to change the amount they contribute into the plan each year, increasing, reducing, or stopping deposits, as long as this right is written into the plan document. Any changes of this nature must be made within plan document parameters and be clearly communicated to participants; employers cannot simply announce, "Due to reduced cash flow we won't be making our normal 401(k) contribution this week."

When Does the Money Have to Be Deposited into the Account?

The salary reductions from employee pay for contribution to the plan must be deposited in a timely fashion. The law expects this to be accomplished as soon as reasonably possible, but no later than the 15th business day of the month following the payday. If employers can reasonably make the deposits in a shorter time frame, they need to make deposits at that time. For any matching contributions made by an employer into traditional 401(k) accounts, employers determine the timetable; some deposit these along with employee contributions, others add the match monthly, quarterly, or annually. This too will be included in plan documents and employee communications.

Who Chooses Investment Options?

Selecting investment options is part of the fiduciary responsibilities of a plan sponsor; they may do this with the help of a committee within the company, an investment adviser, or both. If an investment committee is formed it should begin with a policy statement that is reviewed each year and maintain minutes of all meetings. Employers have an obligation under Department of Labor regulations to offer diversified plan investments with different risk levels, adequately communicate specifics of fund investments, and ensure opportunity for participants to change investments. Options that range from low to high risk might include a fixed income assets, money market fund, stock fund, or a balanced fund with domestic and international equity funds. Employers can incorporate company stock in the mix, but must be certain to offer a variety of other options and have a responsibility to provide adequate education and inform employees of the value of diversification. Building a list of funds to present 22 investment options does not necessarily meet the requirement to offer differentiated funds; the characteristics of each investment will make this determination. Lifestyle, age, or stage funds that bundle investments into categories based on a risk profile can be popular. These are composed of a group of the least risky investments for those closest to retirement and the highest for the young and newly employed. Plan sponsors can also include a choice for directed investments; participants check the box and their funds are deposited according to a predetermined formula. Whatever decisions are made, investment performance should be reviewed on a regular basis and employers should not be afraid to drop funds when necessary and add others as appropriate.

Investment Education or Investment Advice

Employers are discouraged from providing investment advice that steers employees towards any particular fund choices but are required to make investment education available. The PPA requires plan sponsors to provide regular statements with information about account balances and vested benefits. These must be available at least quarterly for participant-directed defined contribution plans; at least annually for non-participant-directed defined contribution plans; and at least every three years for defined benefit plans. Investment education from an independent source is a great way to help employees understand these statements and give general information, including modeling asset allocations tailored to the employer's plan. Investment education and, when appropriate, advice by independent sources, build a sense of the importance of the partnership involved in a 401(k) plan and encourages participation and appropriate allocations. When a plan sponsor sees that 80% of all employee contributions are directed into fixed income assets, it's time for an education or advice program. When employers offer advice it should be by using independent financial advisers without links to the company plan who are registered with the SEC. Participation in education and advice programs should be attractive but never mandatory.

The One-on-One Advice Was a Big Help

A Midwestern manufacturer of construction materials brought in an investment adviser to help employees manage their accounts and provided tailored one-on-one meetings. The company has achieved 100% participation in its 401(k) plan among the 240-plus eligible employees.

When Do We Accept Rollovers?

Rollovers allow employees to take the vested balance in a 401(k) account at a previous employer and deposit the funds into the plan for which they are newly eligible. Plans do not have to accept rollovers; they must be specified in the plan document and can only be transferred between qualified plans. For example, an employee cannot move money from an IRA into a 401(k) account. Rollover distributions take advantage of the portability of 401(k) accounts and give employees the ability to build a larger account as they change jobs. Plans can be set up to accept rollovers before an employee is eligible to make new contributions or after the enrollment date. Any money that is rolled over is always 100% vested. Rollovers today are typically accomplished through direct processing from one plan provider to another.

Distributions and Withdrawals

Today's mobile workforce will want to know how and when they can access 401(k) dollars.

When Employees Leave Do They Get the Whole Account?

Any money that an employee contributes into a 401(k) through salary deferral or rollover is always 100% vested. A vesting schedule is created for employer contributions and included in the plan document. Vesting arrangements of employer contributions can be immediate, graduated, or all at once after a specified period, also called cliff vesting. Graduated vesting is the most common. For example, employer contributions vest at 20% for each completed year of service and become fully vested after five years of service. The PPA amended the minimum vesting requirements; the longest allowable period for cliff vesting is three years of service and graduated vesting must begin no later than after completion of two years of service and be complete at six years. Employers can always be more generous than the regulatory mandates. The definition of a year of service should be included in the plan document and must allow any employee who works at least 1,000 hours during a plan year to be credited with service for that year.

Workers generally have four choices about distribution of 401(k) savings when they leave a job before retirement. They can leave money in a previous employer's 401(k) plan unless the employer requires a distribution, roll the money into an IRA, move the money into a new employer's plan if available, or take the money as a cash distribution. Before employees choose a distribution, they must be fully informed of the tax and penalty consequences of receiving 401(k) funds before age 59-1/2—they could pay a 10% federal penalty and an automatic 20% income tax, and departing employees will face federal, state, and possibly even local income taxes on these funds. Plans have the option, which must be included in the plan document, to begin making distributions within the year after an active employee turns 70-1/2. These funds are subject to income tax but there are no penalties associated with early withdrawal. Retirees can be given the option of a lump sum or rollover to an IRA or annuity that will pay out benefits over time.

Departing employees may also choose to maintain their accounts in a previous employer's 401(k), but plan sponsors are not required to keep up accounts for former employees with balances of less than $5,000. If these employees have at least $1,000 in an account, they must be given notice of the option of receiving a lump sum payment, rollover into a new employer's 401(k), or rollover into an IRA that is identified by the plan sponsor and set up for direct rollovers. Employers can automatically distribute any vested account balances that are less than $1,000. Unvested funds forfeited by departing plan participants can be used to cover future liabilities as long as a mechanism for this is written into the plan document. Former employees with at least $5,000 in the plan can remain as inactive participants with the ability to change investment elections, but they cannot make additional contributions or take loans or hardship withdrawals.

What Is a Hardship Withdrawal?

Plans can allow what are described as in-service distributions in the event of immediate and heavy financial need under the following circumstances identified by the IRS:

1. Unreimbursed medical expenses for an employee, spouse, or dependents

2. Purchase of an employee's principal residence

3. Payment of college tuition and related educational costs such as room and board for the next 12 months for an employee, spouse, dependents, or children who are no longer dependents

4. Payments necessary to prevent eviction or foreclosure on the mortgage of an employee's principal residence

5. Funeral expenses

6. Certain expenses for the repair of damage to the employee's principal residence

Employees must exhaust all loans available under their 401(k) plan, can be subject to a maximum amount, and cannot make additional contributions for six months after the hardship withdrawal. Hardship withdrawals are subject to income tax and, for employees who are younger than 59-1/2 years old, to a 10% penalty. It's important for employers to understand that allowing hardship withdrawals is not mandatory; instructions and allowances should be included in plan documents. When hardship withdrawals are allowed, plan sponsors are responsible for requesting and reviewing necessary documentation to ensure against fraud.

Did That Employee Just Ask for a Loan?

Loan provisions are a common part of 401(k) plans. They are not required but are attractive for employees, even if they never use them, as they provide the knowledge that funds can be accessed before retirement. The specifics about loan requests and interest rates are outlined in plan documents, but the law does limit the amount that can be borrowed to 50% of vested account balances or $50,000, whichever is less. Although employees like the convenience of borrowing from themselves at attractive rates and repaying through payroll deduction, they should understand that unpaid balances become taxable income within a short period of time after termination of employment. Employers must also consider administrative requirements for loans; they can even request documentation for specific needs and establish minimum amounts to cut down on employees taking repeated or multiple loans for $1,000 to pay off bills. Loans can be a valuable benefit when used properly but education is essential about potential long-term consequences of misusing this plan feature.

What's a QDRO?

A qualified domestic relation order (QDRO, often pronounced "quadrow") is a specific type of court order used to divide pension rights between divorcing spouses or to collect alimony or child support from an employee benefit plan. The QDRO creates or recognizes the existence of an alternative payee, other than the employee, with rights to receive all or a portion of the benefits payable to a participant under a qualified retirement plan. QDROs can be mandated as part of divorce proceedings or separately after a divorce is completed. Plan sponsors should include QDRO procedures in plan documents, including specifics about beneficiary designations. When employees divorce and continue to designate a former spouse as a 401(k) beneficiary, conflict is almost inevitable. The advice of an attorney is often valuable in deciphering court orders, timetables, and plan activity that causes significant confusion in addressing QDRO issues. Employers may be able to recoup the cost of review as long as this is specified in the plan document.

Beneficiaries

At enrollment employees are asked to designate a beneficiary for their account assets in the event of death. For married participants this beneficiary must be the spouse unless they provide a notarized form that clearly states that the spouse knows that he or she has not been named as the beneficiary, or is a partial beneficiary. It's a good idea to request beneficiary updates for 401(k) plans whenever a participant marries or divorces.

Choosing a Plan Provider

Choosing a provider is an important decision irrespective of the format your plan takes, whether the search is spurred by poor performance by an existing administrator or as part of the creation of a new plan. The market for 401(k) plan administration is competitive; firms have consolidated and must differentiate themselves, as most new business is found from employers disgruntled with their current providers. A well-planned process is likely to take up to six months from the time the decision is made to seek a vendor to the initiation of a new plan or completed conversion.

Incorporate the following steps into your vendor identification:

- Document the process thoroughly; the selection of a provider is part of a plan sponsor's fiduciary responsibility.

- Create a cross-functional team or committee that includes individuals who represent ownership, human resources, legal, accounting, payroll, finance, and operations. The committee may be internal or include external experts.

- Identify the needs and expectations of the company, plan participants, and the provider including, if applicable, needs that are not being met by the current administrator.

- Set priorities that include elements that are must-haves and those that the plan sponsor can live without. For example, materials and meetings must be available in multiple languages, but the availability of information about every one of the existing funds is not essential.

- Target vendors that fit the company. The market is divided by plan size; small plans have up to 100 participants, medium include 100 to 1,000, large plans are those with 1,000 to 10,000 participants, and jumbo plans cover more than 10,000.

- Consider present needs and those projected within the next five years.

- Seek out others who have been through the process before, not just providers, and compare notes and experiences.

- Identify six to eight vendors to send a Request for Proposal (RFP) that identifies needs and expect to receive at least five responses.

- Review proposals received in response to RFP and select two to three meetings with the potential vendor to review expectations and discuss plan details, including the transition process.

- Don't back down in seeking answers to questions from vendors, including fees, transparency, and service details. Have a clear understanding of who is paying for what and which services you can expect to receive as a client.

- Check references, focusing on organizations that are similar to your size and employee population.

When checking references for a potential 401(k) vendor it is important to gain information about customer service, record keeping, and systems integration. If you are contemplating changing plan administrators, make certain that you speak to a client who had a transition with the same team. A difficult transition experience reflects poorly on the employer and can result in a drop in plan participation by employees who lose faith in the product. Any transition is likely to result in a blackout period, a set time during which participants cannot make account changes, including investment choices. An employer is required to give 30 days' advance notice of a blackout period that will last more than three consecutive business days. Poor communication about a blackout period, or a lengthy time frame, will frustrate participants if there are market changes or they were planning to request a loan or rollover.

Vendor selection may be facilitated through a broker, or employers may interact directly with providers. If a broker is involved it is essential that the potential provider provides information and answers questions directly. Effective retirement plan administration requires a good relationship with a responsive provider; relying on a broker for all transactions can delay processes. The responsibility for administration of salary deferrals, employer contributions, and record keeping rests with the employer, who coordinates these tasks with any payroll provider and 401(k) vendor. Brokers will be helpful when questions arise relating to interpretation and understanding of the 401(k) as outlined in the plan document.

SIMPLE 401(k) Plans

Regulations allow small employers to take advantage of the 401(k) concept. When specific criteria are met employers can skip the most complex plan reporting and testing.

What Makes a Simple 401(k) Plan Easier?

Employers with fewer than 100 employees who each earned at least $5,000 during the previous calendar year can establish a Savings Investment Match Plan, or SIMPLE 401(k). Employers who offer a SIMPLE 401(k) cannot have any other retirement plans.

Under a SIMPLE 401(k) employees can choose to make salary deferrals into the plan but the employer must make a contribution using one of two formats:

1. A matching contribution up to 3% of each employee's pay.

2. A nonelective contribution of 2% of each eligible employee's pay.

The limits on employee contributions are lower than those for a traditional 401(k) plan; for 2010 the maximum is $11,900 with a catch-up contribution of up to $2,500 for employees age 50 or older. All deposits into employee accounts are automatically 100% vested. SIMPLE 401(k) plans can allow for hardship withdrawals and loans within the same guidelines as a traditional 401(k) plan. These are qualified plans that can also accept and distribute rollovers to other qualified plans.

The SIMPLE 401(k) plan requirement for a contribution comes with employer benefits, particularly in reporting and testing. The ability to use a model IRS form for plan documents and the availability of only two options for employer contributions facilitates setup and administration. The plan sponsor is required to file a Form 5500 each year for a SIMPLE 401(k) but is exempt from complex discrimination testing. This saves time, fees, and the potential for the necessity of corrections to contributions to ensure plan compliance.

Safe Harbor 401(k)

A Safe Harbor 401(k) can be the option that meets a broad range of retirements goals and plans.

Isn't a SIMPLE 401(k) the Same as a Safe Harbor 401(k)?

There are similarities, but SIMPLE and Safe Harbor 401(k) plans are distinct types of qualified retirement plan options. Safe Harbor 401(k) plans can be offered by any size employer, can be combined with other retirement plans, and though they ease administrative burden by eliminating the requirement for discrimination testing, they must be set up using a plan document, most likely with assistance from a financial institution. These options allow the same high level of employee salary deferrals, including catch-up contributions, as traditional 401(k) plans.

Employers make the Safe Harbor plan contribution in one of three ways:

1. An automatic contribution of 3% of earnings for all participants, whether or not they make elective deferrals. Once an employee becomes eligible, there is no hours or earnings requirement to trigger employer contributions in subsequent plan years.

2. Employers match 100% of employee elective deferrals up to 3% of earnings and 50% of elective deferrals on the next 2% of compensation.

3. Employers may choose to match additional compensation up to 6% of earnings.

Employers may identify a different formula as long as they meet the minimum for an automatic nonelective deferral or, if they are using a match, as long as the match does not increase as elective deferral rates rise and does not exceed 6% of earnings. Employers may, for example, decide to contribute 3.5% as a nonelective contribution or match up to 4% of employee elective deferrals. Employers are required to provide notice of plan contributions before the end of each plan year at least 30 days but not more than 90 days before the beginning of a new plan year. If during a plan year an employer decides not to make the required Safe Harbor contribution he can do this by providing a required notice 30 days before the change. The employer will have to make any Safe Harbor contributions up until the time the modification takes effect and will be subject to regular 401(k) plan discrimination testing for the plan year. Employers may also add a Safe Harbor contribution during a plan year as long as it is done no later than three months before the end of the plan year. The Safe Harbor contribution can be added retroactively but is only required for the period in which the provisions are effective. This is likely to trigger the necessity of a plan amendment and applicable notices to employees. Employer contributions that meet the minimum Safe Harbor requirements are always 100% vested. Any additional contributions above these can be vested according to a schedule included in the plan document as with a traditional 401(k) plan. If an employer match is 100% of all elective deferrals up to 6% of earnings, a different vesting schedule can be applied to the 50% match on 3 to 5% of earnings and on 100% of the match from 5 to 6% of earnings. In choosing this type of formula for vesting, make certain that communications regarding the different rates are designed to meet the needs of your employee population; specific examples that use relevant salaries, without any identifying names or even positions, will create the clearest picture.

Roth 401(k)

A Roth 401(k) is a traditional 401(k) plan that includes a feature that allows employees to designate all or part of their elective deferrals as Roth contributions to be included in gross income and not considered to be pretax elective contributions. Employees cannot simply make this decision; it must be an element included in a plan document which allows employees to make this designation at least once during each plan year. Employees may allocate contributions to be divided between the designated Roth account and traditional 401(k) account, but the total amount of elective deferrals, including catch-up contributions, cannot exceed annual maximums designated for regular 401(k) plans by the IRS. Once employee contributions are made they cannot be switched between Roth and traditional portions of a 401(k). Under a Roth 401(k), employer contributions always go into the pretax account. The structure of a Roth 401(k) is most attractive to highly compensated employees who anticipate that their income tax rate will not drop in retirement; thus, they prefer to pay the taxes when they have the additional income. These plans also provide the opportunity for employees to contribute to a Roth account who would not be eligible for a Roth IRA due to income ceilings.

Nondiscrimination Testing

Each year plans are required to undergo rigorous compliance testing in order to make certain that employers do not offer 401(k) benefits that only add wealth to the highest-paid executives.

When Does Having a 401(k) Plan Become Discriminatory?

All benefits, including retirement plans, are prohibited from discriminating against employees of employers covered by federal equal opportunity laws based on race, color, religion, gender (including pregnancy), national origin, age, disability, or genetic information. The discrimination testing for qualified retirement plans refers to a requirement that plans benefit not only highly compensated employees but also rank-and-file employees. Traditional 401(k) plans are subject to two types of annual testing to ensure nondiscrimination; the Actual Deferral Percentage (ADP) and Average Contribution Percentage (ACP) test. Both must be passed in order to maintain tax advantages under qualified plans, and plans that do not pass are referred to as top-heavy. Highly compensated employees are defined as anyone who owns more than 5% of the company during the plan year or who earned more than the threshold designated by the IRS ($110,000 for 2009 and 2010) during this same period. All eligible employees, whether or not they participate in the plan, are included in testing calculations. These nondiscrimination tests are extremely complicated and should be conducted by external experts with the skill and knowledge to perform them accurately. Identification of these resources and the cost of the process should be completed before a 401(k) plan is launched. If a plan fails these tests, employers are required to refund deferrals that exceed allowable amounts. This must be completed within 2-1/2 months after the end of the plan year. Managers are rarely happy to see these checks that result in additional taxes and reporting. Employers can take steps to avoid test failure by capping the amount that highly compensated employees can contribute into the plan or by selecting a plan that does not require testing, with the implementation of a required employer contribution. The correct balance of contributions can be modeled using pretests and hypothetical data before and during a plan year. If employee demographics or other changes make it clear that a plan will not pass testing, the contributions of highly compensated employees can be stopped during a plan year to avoid negative testing results.

How Is All of This Paid for?

The costs involved in operating 401(k) plans are paid through a variety of sources and can fluctuate between providers, types of investment offering, and plan design. The increase in investment options, account balance changes due to market performance, employer financial difficulties, and litigation about excessive fees have brought a greater scrutiny to these charges. Plan sponsors have a fiduciary responsibility to consider the fees and expenses. The key here is to increase transparency and information about fees that meet participants' level of sophistication.

Fees incurred to manage and administer 401(k) plans include:

- **Asset-Based Fees** are assessed as a percentage of plan assets and expressed as a percentage or basis points. These can represent a large part of overall plan expenses and can vary based on the size of plan assets.
- **Per Person Charges** are determined by either the number of participants in the plan or total employees eligible for the benefit.
- **Transaction Based** costs for the execution of particular transactions or services such as distribution checks, loan administration, or rollovers.
- **Flat Rate Fees** do not change with the size of the plan assets or number of participants. One-time fees are more common for plan start-ups, conversion to a new provider, or terminations.

When per-participant fees are minimal or nonexistent, greater scrutiny of asset-based fees will be necessary. There will certainly be a cost to the services and there is no expectation that the employer will assume all investment fees; ERISA does require that fees be "reasonable."

Ask vendors for a breakdown of all of the fees, including examples that assume plan growth over five and ten years. Fees should be an important factor variable in investment selection, but not the only factor; fund performance or other management factors may make up for the cost. If a plan provider can't explain the fee structure in a way that you understand, keep asking questions until you do—of the same vendor or another. Additional services will likely add higher costs but there may also be ways to structure the product to meet company and participant needs. Ask for a review of fees on a regular basis or if there are any significant changes in participant population.

IRA-Based Plans

Employers also have the ability to set up plans that are based around the use of IRAs. This option does not result in a qualified DB or DC plan but it does create an employer-based plan to save for retirement with minimal paperwork and filing requirements.

These can be broken into three types.

1. **Payroll Deduction IRAs** allow employees to contribute to an IRA by designating money to come out of their pay. Employees make the decisions about when and how much to contribute up to IRS maximums for IRAs, $5,000 for employees under 50 years of age in 2010 and $6,000 each year for those 50 and older.

2. **SEP** plans build individual accounts funded only by employer contributions in the annual amount of up to 25% of compensation with a maximum of $49,000 for 2010. Employers can decide each year whether or not to make the contribution, but plans must be offered to all employees who are at least 21 years old, were employed for three of the previous five years, and earn a minimum amount of compensation. Contributions are immediately 100% vested.

3. **SIMPLE IRA Plan** can be created by an organization with 100 or fewer employees that does not maintain any other retirement plan and can combine employee and employer contributions. For 2009 and 2010 employees can contribute up to $11,500 each year into the plan and an additional $2,500 if they are 50 or older. Employers must either match employee contributions up to 3% of earnings or 2% of each eligible employee's

compensation, whether or not they participate in the plan. A SIMPLE IRA plan must be offered to all employees who have earned at least $5,000 in any prior two years and are expected to continue earning at least that much. Employer contributions are immediately vested at 100%.

Nonqualified Plans

Nonqualified plans are retirement or deferred compensation arrangements that do not meet ERISA or IRS requirements for favorable tax treatment, but they do provide a long-term investment vehicle for senior executives or owners. Nonqualified plans allow highly compensated employees to defer and invest greater amounts than they are able to under a 401(k), particularly if the plan has been determined to be top-heavy. Nonqualified plans can take numerous forms and include potential risk for both participants and the employer. When investigating these options, retain a reputable investment adviser to design the plan and obtain an opinion from an external accountant before beginning any benefit. It is most important to understand how contributions are made and invested and to be aware of the availability of any early withdrawals.

With So Many Choices, How Does an Employer Choose?

Retirement plans are considerable investments that can be an important source of stability and retention. Unlike other benefits, they cannot be created and easily changed each year. Employers should consider and model more than one plan design and type before selecting one. A good comparison includes projections that compare with company growth, both in income and employee population, in the next five and ten years. Although plans cannot be changed within a month or two, it is possible to create plan amendments to meet needs, for example, taking a traditional 401(k) and turning it into a Safe Harbor 401(k). Questions about the ability to move between designs should also be asked during the research stage. The proliferation of types of plans also affords plan sponsors the opportunity to investigate new options as needs change.

CHAPTER 9

Benefits That Provide Economic Security

Do Employees Expect Life Insurance and Disability?

Life insurance and disability are often described as benefits that provide economic security for employees and their families in the event of unforeseen events. More than 60% of all U.S. employers offer group term life insurance and, where it is available, more than 95% of eligible employees take advantage of the benefit. U.S. employees rely on workplace plans for these benefits, and for most this is their only life insurance. Employer policies commonly include Accidental Death and Dismemberment coverage, and many programs provide the opportunity for employees to purchase increased policy amounts and dependent coverage. Short-term disability (STD) may be mandated by state law as described in Chapter One or included in a separate plan to augment a sick leave benefit. Long-Term Disability (LTD) plans are designed to be employer paid or as voluntary benefits to provide partial income replacement when an injury or illness necessitates a lengthy absence.

GROUP TERM LIFE INSURANCE

Group term life insurance refers to policies that are purchased for a specific period, generally a year, and employers renew them without difficulty for the next plan year. Term life insurance has no savings features or accumulation of cash value; it is basic insurance protection that pays a benefit only after death. Group term life can be an unsung hero of benefits plans that employers quietly offer the plans year after year without much fanfare; costs and benefit levels do not rise dramatically.

How Much Does Group Term Life Cost?

Group term life insurance rates are quoted per month for each $1,000 of the benefit amount and range from $.05 per $1,000 to $2.00 based on the size of the group and the age of participants. The premium can also be charged at a flat rate for the entire group without consideration of employee age. Group term life policies are experience rated, meaning that the cost can rise for the policy year after claims occur.

Eligibility

Employers are most likely to provide group term life benefits for full-time employees, and though for many coverage is effective on the first day of work, waiting periods of thirty to ninety days are common. Administration is facilitated when life insurance eligibility coincides with entry into health insurance plans. Group term life insurance is guaranteed issue; employees do not have to complete forms to determine whether they will be covered. Under most plans employees are not required to complete paper enrollment forms for the insurance company. The employer maintains eligibility records and beneficiary forms with invoices calculated based on the eligible population using a self-billing format that should be available using a secure Web site.

Amount of Insurance Benefit

The most common formula used for determining basic life insurance coverage amounts uses a multiplier of earnings with a maximum amount for the benefit. Employers frequently provide coverage at one times salary and benefit amounts are always rounded to the nearest thousand. Employers also offer two and three times base salary but should keep in mind that the employer's cost of any group term life insurance in excess of $50,000 is considered taxable income using a formula published by the IRS identifying the fair market value of the policy. If a 38-year-old employee is eligible for $75,000 of life insurance and the IRS considers the value to be $.09 per thousand dollars of coverage per month, the calculated cost of the additional insurance, $27 will be added to income at the end of the year for tax purposes. Group term life amounts take into account base salary, excluding bonuses and incentives. When employees derive most of their earnings from incentives or commissions, a standard base rate can be set for the first year of employment and a different formula used at a subsequent open enrollment when 12 months of actual earnings are available. As raises occur rates should be adjusted effective the month after the increase. Age-rated policies should be set up to allow for any change to be made in age groupings once each year, at the beginning of the plan year. About a third of employer plans provide a fixed life insurance benefit, referred to as a flat dollar amount, in amounts ranging from $10,000 to $25,000. The amount you identify should be consistent with your benefits strategy and reflect the weight put on long-term economic security.

Accidental Death and Dismemberment Insurance

Group term life plans are commonly paired with Accidental Death and Dismemberment (AD&D) insurance that pays an extra amount if an employee dies in an accident or suffers the loss of a limb or eye. The AD&D benefit is likely to be equal to the amount of basic insurance in the event of death and paid as a portion as the result of a dismemberment. AD&D insurance is purchased at low group rates and does not require proof of good health. Employers may also offer supplemental AD&D coverage, paid for by employees, to increase available benefit amounts using a wide variety of formulas.

Supplemental and Dependent Life Insurance

Employees appreciate the availability of supplemental life insurance that allows them to add to the benefit purchased by their employer at attractive group rates. Additional available coverage can be represented as multiples of base salary or flat dollar amounts up to a maximum stated benefit. Employees pay for these plans through payroll deductions, and they are most likely to be age rated. The plan determines whether the coverage will be guaranteed issue or require a health questionnaire or physical exam. Insurers may offer a specific amount as guarantee issue and request further information before approving a policy for the total coverage level requested. Supplemental coverage is more prevalent in plans that determine basic insurance as a multiple of earnings. Illustrations of the cost and value of these plans using actual pay and insurance rates including age brackets, without identifying employee information, enhance employee understanding and participation. When employees who earn $75,000 a year see that they can double their life insurance for a few dollars a month, a nominal amount from each paycheck, the illustration makes the benefit manageable and even more valuable.

Dependent life insurance, paid for by employees, usually provides a flat dollar benefit for a spouse and smaller amount for children. Formulas vary but can be a percentage of employee coverage or $5,000 or more for a spouse and from $1,000 to $6,000 for each child. Employees can select the additional coverage that best suits their needs and add coverage, within a specified period, after marriage or the birth of a child, and may be allowed to increase coverage at open enrollment. Make certain that these deadlines are clearly communicated, including the potential requirement for evidence of insurability, a physical or questionnaire, if requests are made at open enrollment after initial eligibility.

Beneficiary Designations

Employers are responsible for obtaining and maintaining beneficiary designations. It's a good idea to keep these in a safe, secure location in the event of a worksite fire or other incident that damages files and data. Beneficiary forms must be signed by the employee in order to be valid. Any new valid beneficiary designation supersedes previous records; at the time of a claim the most recent designated beneficiary is the one who will receive the payout. Employees have the option of naming multiple beneficiaries; if this is done, make certain the allocation makes sense. An employee cannot give 60% of a benefit to one child, 30% to another and 40% to the spouse.

BETTER FORGOTTEN

Sorry Mom, My Wife Is the Beneficiary Now

The HR director at a property management company was reviewing benefits files when he noticed that the life insurance beneficiary for the company president was his mother. The 40-year-old executive had not changed the beneficiary in the five years since his marriage. It's a good idea to request updated beneficiaries on an annual basis.

Administration

Carriers should make group term life as easy to administer as possible. Insurers supply notebooks with information and explanations for every step of the enrollment, billing, and claims process. When an employee dies it can be traumatic for the workplace and processing life insurance benefits is never pleasant; knowing where the resources are and which steps to take will ease the situation and provide an important payment to the beneficiary.

BETTER FORGOTTEN

Please Don't Deny the Claim

A hospitality employer was not surprised to learn of the death of an employee who had been out of work on an extended disability. HR was shocked to learn that the life insurance claim was denied. The employer had not notified the insurer when the employee went on disability. After pleading, persistence, and with the help of a broker, the claim was ultimately paid; family members never knew about the question. Avoid problems by clarifying any requirements for notification when employees are out; there may even be a premium reduction.

Is a Group Term Life Benefit Tax Free?

The premiums paid by employers for group term life are tax deductible and any claims paid to beneficiaries are exempt from federal income tax up to IRS-defined limits. As stated earlier, employees can receive up to $50,000 of employer-provided life insurance without paying income tax on the expenditure and are taxed on the cost of any insurance above this amount. Payments that employees make for supplemental and dependent coverage are made from post-tax dollars as long as the employee is covered by at least $50,000 of employer-purchased basic life insurance. When the plan is paid for entirely by employees or the employer-provided benefit amount is below $50,000, the IRS rules for imputing taxable income are complicated; a tax professional or your payroll provider should be able to decipher these regulations, as they have experience with this situation.

DISABILITY COVERAGE

A key component of economic security is replacement income available in the event of an accident or illness that results in an extended period away from work.

Short-Term Disability

Employers in five states and Puerto Rico are required to provide and pay for short-term disability (STD) for all employees, whereas employers in other states extend the benefit as a way to replace part of the income lost due to a temporary non-work-related illness or injury. Almost 40% of all employees in private sector employment participate in an STD plan. STD plans feature short waiting periods for benefits during which employees can use any available sick days or other leave time. Plans pay a percentage of base wages, typically 60 to 75%, up to a maximum salary level. State plans designate benefit amounts, but employers may choose to pay for more generous coverage. If an employee is also eligible for workers' compensation, STD benefits will be reduced to ensure that payment does not exceed 100% of base pay. Most STD plans provide the benefit for a period of 90 to 180 days. Employers set initial eligibility dates and employee categories in states where coverage is not mandated.

When employers pay for STD coverage, any benefit received under the plan is considered taxable income; conversely, if the employee pays the premium, any resulting benefit is not subject to federal income tax. Short-term disability policies must balance needs for employee attendance with employer compassion. The policies should not be so generous or lacking in monitoring that employees are essentially encouraged to linger out of work while collecting a disability check.

Long-Term Disability

Long-Term Disability (LTD) provides replacement income in the event of a lengthy absence due to injury or illness. It is a popular but often misunderstood benefit provided by almost a third of private sector employers and is more likely to be a voluntary benefit, paid for by employees using payroll deduction. LTD benefits generally begin after any STD is exhausted or after a three- or six-month waiting period. Most plans provide benefits for the length of the disability up to a specified age, such as 65, when Social Security benefits usually begin. Plans must pay benefits to employees who become disabled at age 65 or older, but these can extend for a shorter duration or at a lower rate, as long as the employer costs are equal to those paid for benefits for younger employees. Typical LTD polices pay benefits amounting to 60% of an individual's predisability base pay. Some plans pay up to 70%, but all plans should set a maximum monthly benefit, generally between $6,000 and $10,000. Disability income is taxable if the premium is employer paid and tax free when employees foot the bill. Effective LTD programs encourage employees to return to work and not linger at home collecting fat checks. They replace only a portion of regular earnings and may include the requirement that the individual accept a similar position if one is available. When an employee is out of work on LTD, consistent contact from the company can help to speed up a return to work. Phone calls to check in will keep the employer in mind and demonstrate concern. If appropriate and available, reduced schedules may facilitate the transition back to the workplace after an extended absence. Make certain that you understand the definition of a disability under the policy and that this is clarified for employees; for

> ### WORTH REPEATING
>
> ### *Same Benefit, Half the Price?*
>
> An LTD carrier brought clear and convincing examples to the managers at a regional financial institution that showed how a plan that would pay 50% of income in the event of a qualifying disability would cost only $20 to $25 per month through the employer's group coverage. If employees purchased the same plan through an individual plan, from the very carrier offering the group coverage, the premium would range from $52 to $160 per month. Enrollment increased by 20%.

example, the plan may pay only if an employee cannot perform any job, a similar occupation, or specific job categories. Long-Term Disability could be a positive addition to benefits that provide economic security. Investigate the options and think about whether they fit into your benefits offerings and if they could be good news during the open enrollment offered as a midyear enhancement.

Communication and Information Are Key

The value of voluntary disability can get lost amid the volume of benefits information. Use plenty of examples and frequently asked questions (FAQs) to get the message across before an employee faces an extended absence without pay.

Why Don't More Employees Take Advantage of Voluntary Disability Plans?

Employees are frequently unaware of or not focused on many aspects of disability coverage. Employers can play a key role in disseminating information using assistance from carriers.

These actions should boost participation and satisfaction:

- Host employee education sessions or enrollment meetings. The carrier can take an active role in these and provide materials translated into other languages when appropriate. A good meeting starts with the basics of how disability insurance works and does not assume employee familiarity.

- Use self-running or Web-based presentations that can be made available by carriers. Monitors can be set up in the workplace.

- Distribute educational materials at work, by mail to employees' homes, or through a variety of communications channels including any company intranet.

- Target communications to specific needs; young singles, baby boomers, and families are more likely to appreciate information that is focused on their situation.

- Be clear about costs of coverage and expected benefits; income-needs calculators will help model budget costs and help decision making.

- Effective communication is a year-round process, not limited to open enrollment time.

Disability Plans and FMLA

Employees eligible for FMLA leave as the result of an injury or illness are likely to be eligible for available STD, but qualification for STD does not automatically create approval for FMLA leave. The employee may not have worked the requisite number of hours to qualify for FMLA or may have exhausted the 120 eligible days. Waiting periods for LTD are likely to be longer than available FMLA leave. Individuals who are eligible for LTD for an extended period of time do not retain any rights to reemployment beyond FMLA requirements just because they are receiving benefits under an employer-sponsored plan.

WE'RE READY FOR GROUP TERM LIFE AND DISABILITY—WHERE DO I START?

A broker can help set up or change group term life or disability benefits; advisers commonly handle both types of plans. The process typically requires submission of census data that includes dates of birth and salaries of the employee population to be covered. Take extra care to make certain that any census information is protected against the potential of identity theft. Ask about the path that any hard copy or electronic information will take. A lengthy detailed report left on top of a desk can be the start of a huge data breach. Brokers will be able to obtain more than one quote; it's a very competitive market, but price should not be the only determinant. Obtain the financial ratings and customer service data for any insurer under consideration. A change in carriers may or may not require updated documentation from employees; find out if new beneficiary or enrollment forms for any supplemental coverage will be requested and identify and track all due dates. Disability insurance is dominated by a few large carriers. Pricing for newly covered employers will be based upon typical claims volume in your industry and geographic area. This does not mean that quotes will not be competitive, and consistently good claims experience during multiple years should be reflected in reduced rates.

CHAPTER 10

Benefits Buffet

From EAP to Concierge Services, What Else Do Employees Want and What Should You Provide?

THE LIST OF OTHER BENEFITS THAT EMPLOYERS CAN provide is endless. In order to identify the most valued extras consider conducting an employee survey or forming focus groups and stay true to your benefits strategy. A benefit that sounds cool based on a vendor's description or the zeal of an employee championing the idea won't be worth the time and effort if employees don't sign up because they fail to see what's in it for them. This does not mean that every additional benefit has to appeal to the entire workforce. Other benefits are not necessarily designed as universal offerings like health coverage or retirement; one of the beauties of this category is that they can be introduced to meet the needs of a targeted population tailored to demographics and personal interests. Consider other benefits also as additions to enhance satisfaction when premium increases or financial constraints result in a reduction of existing offerings or an increase in employee contributions. Other benefits are undoubtedly driven by cost and include items that are commonly employer paid, employee paid voluntary benefits, savings facilitators, or deals and discounts that may not incur any expenses other than disseminating information, tickets, or forms.

Voluntary Benefits

Employees consistently give high marks to the availability of voluntary benefits that afford access to types of coverage through work, paid for with the convenience of payroll deduction, which would be much more expensive to purchase as an individual. When offering voluntary benefits employers can leave communications and enrollment up to the provider, scheduling information sessions, distributing print materials, or publicizing Web access. Employers are then responsible for payroll deductions, reconciling accounts, and bill payment. Employers should be vigilant about making certain that these voluntary benefits meet expectations and do not create excessive administrative burdens; it's a very competitive market with plenty of providers eager to enroll your employees. Enrollment for voluntary benefits does not necessarily need to coincide with health care open enrollment; you may set initial eligibility and election at times that meet your needs. Though it can be advantageous to have provider representatives handle the entire enrollment, you still want to publicize the option as an employer-offered component of your benefits strategy. You can ask for materials to be customized for the group with your logo and plan specifics. Though voluntary benefits can be arranged directly with individual providers, there are large insurers who can offer access to a whole range of products. The most common benefits offered in a voluntary format are life, dental, and vision coverage; these are described in other chapters.

WORTH REPEATING

I Voted for That

Natural and organic food retailer Whole Foods asks team members to vote every three years to help determine the benefit package they offer. The process creates an educational opportunity while obtaining employee input. Well-informed employees are always better consumers of benefits.

Cancer or Critical Illness Insurance

A clever marketing campaign has made AFLAC a well-known name and exhorted employees to ask their employers about the plan. The duck is quacking about cash and indemnity insurance to pay for expenses incurred as a result of treatment for cancer, heart attack, stroke, renal failure, and other serious medical conditions. The plans pay for medical expenses not typically covered under group health policies such as ambulance transport, and a list of costs that can mount as a result of these illnesses ranging from additional child care to assistance in rent payment. Plans can be offered in a choice of benefits and corresponding premiums. The elimination of regular health plan maximums, mandated by 2010 health reform, could reduce the appeal of some of this coverage; check plans to make certain employees are not signing up and paying for unneeded coverage. A long list of illnesses covered does not necessarily mean a better plan, as it may only trigger higher premiums. Cancer and critical illness plans should not be seen as replacements for health coverage or to be accessed for regular copayments for office visits and prescriptions; they are designed to step in when illness is severe and associated costs mount. Look for a simple plan that covers the whole family with clear explanations of claims and payouts. These plans are designed to be portable when employment ends.

Elder Care Consultation and Referral

Taking care of an elderly parent can consume more time and energy than child care. For employees shouldering both responsibilities, the potential for distraction and time off from work is even greater. Elder care consultation can be a subset of an EAP or a stand-alone service that is appropriate for the demographics of your employee population. This can be accomplished with classes, a consultant contracted on a fee-for-service basis, or the provision of educational materials. Research into providing elder care consultation as a benefit can be triggered when a senior manager faces a crisis with a parent and seeks to spare other employees some of the anxiety and help them get back to work.

Identity Theft Protection

Identity Theft Protection is a relatively new product; offering it as a group benefit is an even newer concept. If employees become victims of identity theft, and they have a protection policy in place, employers gain when the affected individuals spend less time, money, and energy restoring their identities. When offering this kind of protection, employers should make certain that materials and the opportunity to sign up are extended to all employees. If an employee declines and later becomes a victim of identity theft, the employer will want to be able to prove that the plan was offered—in case there are potential fines, fees, and lawsuits, particularly if the data breach is claimed to have been due to inaction by the employer. Consumer advocates question the value of these protection policies, stating that individuals can take the same steps for lower costs or that the benefits are not clear. Review any service carefully and check references specifically from other employers; you may find that the cost is worth the time savings and even offer to subsidize a portion of the fees.

Insurance to Cover Personal Property

Group discounts can be obtained for a number of types of personal insurance, including automobile, homeowners, renters, and even marine coverage. The convenience of getting information at work and making payments spread out via payroll deduction make these programs attractive, but discounts available through the group purchase increase the value. Make certain that the plan identified for employees in Indiana will also be able to provide auto insurance for regional offices in Kansas and Tennessee and is in compliance with any applicable state insurance regulations. Check references in multiple locations if necessary; don't just take a salesperson's word. Plans are written through brokers, directly with companies, or with specialists in the group auto and homeowners market who work with more than one insurer. Set up a system to ensure payment when employees are out of work due to a leave of absence, or if they terminate or retire. Good record keeping and transfer of status changes to the carrier are essential; they can take over billing when necessary.

Long-Term-Care Insurance

The combination of an aging workforce and the high cost of care for chronic illness and disability treated outside of a hospital make long-term-care insurance a valuable voluntary benefit. When offered, however, participation rates have been low due to the complexity of the product and the cost. Such coverage is expensive and employees don't like to think of the potential need for themselves or a loved one. Carrier selection is extremely important for this benefit; consider plan design, pricing, quality of operations, financial stability, and a track record of commitment to offering the coverage. The landscape of long-term-care coverage will be changed by PPACA that includes the Community Living Assistance Services and Supports (CLASS) Act that creates a federally structured employer option for automatic enrollment of employees into a long-term-care insurance program effective January 1, 2011. Employees will have the ability to opt out, but if they remain enrolled the premium will be based upon the age at enrollment and, after at least five years in the plan, they could receive assistance in the form of a cash benefit, for example, $50 per day for services in the community such as respite, home health aides, and accessible transportation and up to $75 per day for institutional care. The rates would increase with inflation but provide only a baseline benefit, particularly for care such as a nursing home that costs an average of $250 per day. Existing or new plans can combine with CLASS requirements to create a more robust benefit. Long-term-care coverage requires repeated, consistent communication to impart the value. The very nature of the communication and the existence of the new CLASS plan may generate more interest in group long-term-care insurance plans.

Pet Insurance

Americans spend billions of dollars a year caring for their pets. The employee who just paid $1,500 for treatment of a cat's kidney condition will be worried about a favorite feline and the expenses incurred. Employer-offered pet insurance that spreads out payments through payroll deduction and offers group rate discounts can provide plans that cover dogs, cats, birds, ferrets, hamsters, and exotic pets when they are ill or injured. Plans will have some similarities to the structure of human health insurance with deductibles, networks, copayments, preexisting conditions, hospitalization, x-rays, and prescriptions covered at varying levels. In many cases premiums are based on the age and type of pet and employees will be able to choose the level of coverage they prefer. Find out details about the insurer, including financial stability, claims servicing, and customer service experience. You don't want employees signed up with the insurer that the only vet in town refuses to deal with.

Prepaid Legal Services

Group legal plans have the ability to appeal across demographics offering some or all of services such as preparation of wills, trusts, and other estate planning documents; purchase, sale, or home refinancing; consumer protection matters; and adoption and guardianship. Employees commonly elect this benefit at open enrollment and pay less than $20 a month through payroll deduction. Participation in the group plan is likely to pay off the first time an employee uses it to resolve a legal issue. Employers find group legal plans easy to administer, with enrollment requiring minimal employee data and the added advantage of saving employee time in finding and using legal assistance. Compare at least two services before selecting the one that best meets your employee needs. These plans use a panel of attorneys in general practice, so make certain they have a good reputation and are well represented where employees live or work.

As There Are No Cash Outlays, Should We Offer All of These Voluntary Benefits?

It can be tempting to add on every voluntary benefit to pass along good rates and burnish your reputation as a caring employer. Diving into voluntary benefits with these six offerings or more, all at the same time, increases the potential for an overload of options and decreases the time available to study each one effectively. Employees who feel they just can't live without multiple voluntary insurances may also be surprised at the size of the reduction in take-home pay when all of the deductions for premiums are taken, as these plans are not paid for with pretax dollars. Check the appreciation for voluntary benefits by starting with the top one to three that have the broadest appeal to your employee population. Surveys, continued employee conversations, enrollment rates, and user feedback will identify successes and help make decisions about additional plans.

FACILITATING SAVINGS

Personal savings rates in the United States have notched up a bit from negative numbers but remain well below the thriftier habits of earlier generations and other countries. Facilitating savings through easy-to-use programs at work can help employees build nest eggs—other than retirement plans—through handy payroll deductions. These programs incur minimal administrative hassles; employees typically sign up directly with financial institutions and create what is often essentially another account for direct deposit, which will require reconciliation but no additional billing.

College Savings Through 529 Plans

Saving for college is rarely easy; payroll deductions into a tax-advantaged 529 plan can put the task on automatic to encourage accumulations for higher education for a child or grandchild. Withdrawals from 529 plans are not subject to federal income tax and many states provide similar tax savings. Employees contribute post-tax dollars into these plans, and there are typically no setup fees involved for state-run plans. These state 529 plans allow employees to begin with contributions as low as $10 or $15 each pay period. Investigate the track record of a plan before deciding to offer it to your employee population.

Credit Unions

Offering banking services through a credit union is very popular with employees who can realize slightly higher savings rates and comparably lower loan rates. Employers can sponsor credit unions and provide access through a Select Employee Group (SEG). To learn how to become a SEG in order to offer credit union membership to your employees, contact a nearby credit union. Investigate both customer service and financial performance and make certain that assets are protected by the National Credit Union Administration (NCUA), a federal agency that oversees the safety and soundness of credit unions.

Preferred Banking Arrangements

Setting up a preferred banking arrangement is probably the easiest employee benefit to initiate and will involve no out-of-pocket costs. The best place to start is the bank used for your payroll account. They will give employees preferential treatment for checking accounts, and they should be free. There are also many banks that will provide free checking for anyone who uses direct deposit. Banks do all the work for this benefit; there is no reason not to publicize the availability. Pick one that has convenient branches and ATMs. This is also an arrangement that is easy to change and you may be in a position to spread the word about perks for your employees available at more than one bank.

U.S. Savings Bonds and Treasury Securities

More than 40,000 employers participate in a Payroll Savings Plan that deducts funds used to buy U.S. Savings Bonds. The traditional paper format may be a nice add-on, but TreasuryDirect offers an electronic alternative. Employees establish their own TreasuryDirect accounts with direct deposit (payroll) deductions that are just like any other direct deposit deduction. TreasuryDirect is a Web-based system that allows individuals to buy, hold, and conduct online transactions in Treasury securities. Employees can use payroll deductions to purchase electronic Series EE and I savings bonds as well as Treasury bills, notes, bonds, and Treasury Inflation-Protected Securities (TIPS) through TreasuryDirect. There is no employer involvement in account administration beyond transmission of the funds, as is done with any payroll direct deposit.

OTHER EMPLOYER-PAID BENEFITS

The selection of these items that are paid for entirely, or heavily subsidized, by an employer will depend on the nature of the employee population and company benefits strategy. Some items, such as an

Employee Assistance Program, will be a must-have for many employers and seen as money well spent to promote an effective workforce, whereas others, such as a matching gift program, will be included for philosophical or competitive reasons.

Adoption Assistance

Adoption assistance can generate a great deal of goodwill for a relatively small expense. The availability of this benefit continues to grow; it can be found in more than 20% of U.S. workplaces. These programs announce workplaces as adoption-friendly and caring by subsidizing costs and providing information. Benefits can include paid leave and financial assistance in the form of reimbursement of expenses for agency fees, court costs, legal fees, medical costs, temporary foster care charges, and transportation for foreign adoptions. The most common employer reimbursements range from a few hundred dollars to $10,000, with the average set at $5,000.

Child Care

Subsidized on-site or nearby day-care centers are few and far between. The barriers to start-up from costs to regulatory requirements are prohibitive. Employers are more likely to choose Dependent Care Flexible Spending accounts as described in Chapter Seven and pay a portion of these funds. Child-care benefits could be arranged through an information and referral program, discounts, or subsidies at centers in the geographic area. This can be difficult with a dispersed workforce but made more doable by partnering with a child-care company that operates multiple centers nationally or regionally. Child-care benefits rate very high among items that strengthen recruitment and retention, particularly as the percentage of women who work continues to increase. A consortium of employers can work together to achieve greater success in identifying child-care resources and benefit from the greater buying power of a larger group.

Classes

Educational sessions, whether they are scheduled as lunch-and-learn, before or after work, can draw employees with convenience and interesting

---

WORTH REPEATING

Thanks for Letting Me Meet That Challenge

Outdoor equipment retailer REI offers a Challenge Grant program to provide employees with an opportunity to determine a personal outdoor challenge and apply for a special grant to achieve their goals. Employees have received funds for a variety of challenges, from a 50-mile bike ride to a Mount Everest expedition. Employees return to work with the pride of accomplishment, new experiences, and added outdoor knowledge to share with customers.

---

or important topics. A regular series can cover subjects as diverse as foreign language instruction, self-defense, or anything that employees have expressed interest in and would be valuable for individual growth. Lunch sessions are a good time to offer topics that might be covered in an hour, from local history to flower arranging. You may find employees or local experts who are interested in sharing knowledge for free. Employee interest groups can be asked to handle the entire experience from publicity to speaker selection and room setup.

College Counseling

The college admissions process today is exceedingly competitive and unlikely to change dramatically in the foreseeable future. College counselors can conduct sessions that take employees through research, tips and tools for the process and discussions of financial aid and decision making. The costs incurred will pay off in goodwill and stress reduction. In a small community a local high school or even college may help; in more populated locations check for individuals who have experience with both group and individual consulting.

Concierge Services

A hotel concierge caters to the needs of guests. Workplace concierges handle time-consuming tasks for employees that can

WORTH REPEATING

Just-in-Time College Counseling

A financial services company realized that the majority of its staff had teenage children a year or two away from applying for college. They contracted with a company that created a series of one-hour sessions for parents that covered every aspect of the college application process. The information reduced the collective stress level and continued to prove valuable as employees shared experiences. The minimal investment paid off over a number of years.

include dry cleaning, meal catering, child-care arrangements, auto servicing, event tickets, and ordering flowers. Employers reap benefits when employees spend less time taking care of these activities during the workday and are able to get more done. The concierge does not have to be sitting on-site at a desk graced with flowers; there are many services that cater to employers via toll-free numbers or a Web site. The company concierge can be a benefit for employers of any size. The cost will vary based on workforce size, ranging from $20 to $40 per employee per month, and is usually paid by the employer. Companies can expand the population covered and potentially lower the cost by putting together a group of nearby worksites, especially in the same building, to contract concierge services. Employees are expected to pay for all of the actual expenses incurred for the services rendered. When employers choose to also pay for the services, the value of the benefit becomes taxable income.

Emergency Back-Up Dependent Care

Personal illness or injury is not the only cause of employee absenteeism. A child with a bad cold or an elderly parent with a broken arm can trigger a sick call. Emergency Back-Up Dependent Care is designed to provide resources for these short-term situations to enable an employee to come to work with the peace of mind that a loved one is being taken care of. This arrangement is most likely to be made through a dependent care provider in a center designed specifically for emergency care, or in a larger facility. Back-up care is also valuable when a regular arrangement is interrupted or for school vacations and holidays. Family community centers such as YMCAs and Boys and Girls clubs can be partners for school vacation programs and, as with regular child care, a group of employers can work together to secure common back-up care spaces.

Employee Assistance Programs

Employee Assistance Programs (EAPs) provide valuable resources for employees and employers. While EAPs are most common in large companies, found in more than 80%, they are also available at employers of varying sizes. An effective EAP assists with a wide range of personal situations, referred to as broad brush programs, that all have the potential to negatively affect an individual's ability to perform on the job: substance abuse or alcohol abuse; divorce issues; economic issues; living situations; and marital, financial, or emotional problems. An EAP is not charged with treating these problems but rather to provide initial counseling and referral to experts. A good EAP becomes a trusted resource and coordinator of services, taking a burden off employers who can refer an employee without having to make determinations they are not qualified to make. Educated employers can call the EAP to help guide them through difficult conversations about employee potential and personal issues that are affecting attendance or performance. EAP services can be accessed from large providers or local counselors with expertise in this area. The most common fee structure for an EAP is a flat fee for each employee per month of coverage. Smaller employers may find a fee-for-service structure to be a better fit for their budget. EAPs should make education and information available to encourage usage; at the same time managers must be trained in the correct steps to spot potential problems and make appropriate EAP referrals. It is essential that all records of EAP usage be kept in the strictest confidence; don't be surprised when the only information you receive from a provider is the number of employees and dependents served and a very general breakdown of the type of issues.

BETTER FORGOTTEN

Call the EAP, They Helped Sue Stop Drinking

A start-up did a thorough job of employee education about their EAP beginning with new hires, updates, and management training. The EAP was well used and earned a reputation as a trusted and valuable partner. One day the director of human resources overheard one team member announce to another, "You should call the EAP about your drinking habits if you think they are getting out of control—you know Sue, she called and got the help she needed to get sober." Education and communications were reviewed and updated to make certain they clarified the importance of confidentiality.

Employee Referral Bonuses

Tough hiring climates gave rise to bonuses paid to employees who refer successful candidates. These can be quite generous, paying thousands of dollars, or be limited to a small check or even merchandise or a gift certificate; averages range from $150 to $350. Employee referral bonuses can also be limited to only hard-to-fill positions or staggered based on job category; chemical engineers are at a premium but human resources managers are easier to find, so the plan provides generous incentives for the engineers and a small sum for referral of successful HR candidates. An employee referral bonus plan must coincide with a system for proper handling of candidates who are submitted. These programs operate on the premise that great employees refer people just like them—but be prepared for questions as to why a best friend or relative was not hired and allow time for courtesy interviews. The payout for a successful referral is typically phased to promote retention, involving a small portion at the time of hire, and more at a later date of thirty days to six months after the first day on the job.

Matching Charitable Gifts

Employers use matching gift programs to generate goodwill and demonstrate corporate responsibility. Matching gifts are part of an overall strategy; they would not be a determinant for acceptance of a position or retention. As with other items included here, matching charitable gift programs can be scaled to fit within a benefits budget and should include a waiting period before eligibility begins. Employers may choose to contribute an amount equal to an employee's donation or match a percentage or portion. Companies often shift their matching gift programs in response to significant financial changes. These programs commonly require verification of the recipient, specifically the tax exempt status as a 501(C)(3), and may also request an annual report. Companies often choose to restrict matching gifts and will not donate to private foundations, political organizations, religious groups, or even athletic programs at colleges and universities. Any restrictions should be in line with company philosophy and profile in the community. Clarify all of the record-keeping requirements for tax-exempt status of donations before launching a matching gift program.

Mortgage Assistance

Whether employees are first-time buyers or seeking refinancing, assisting them in the mortgage process can be as simple as setting up an educational seminar at no cost using a local financial institution. Large employers and some business and trade associations have developed more comprehensive programs designed to facilitate the mortgage process and invest in employee longevity. These are particularly attractive in high-cost-of-living areas and can provide financial assistance to employees who meet a length of service requirement and

---

WORTH REPEATING

Support Energy Savings at Home

Seventh Generation, an earth-friendly product developer based in Burlington, Vermont, extends its world view to employees by offering $500 stipends toward energy savings purchases for employees' homes. The benefit demonstrates that the company mission goes beyond a marketing model.

have annual earnings below a maximum set by the plan. Mortgage assistance can be given in the form of a grant, forgivable loan, or matching funds deposited into a savings account designated for a home down payment, and is typically set within a range of $1,500 to $5,000 from the employer. Every detail must be understood when offering these benefits, which will be most appropriate for a stable work force of moderate income earners.

DEALS AND DISCOUNTS

Employers are often in a strong position to offer deals and discounts on products and services to employees. These can be reduced prices for company products or from suppliers, area retailers and service providers, and national chains.

Employee Product Discounts

Product is less likely to walk out the door without authorization if a procedure is in place to purchase with an employee discount. This includes goods and services. Whatever is offered, the policy should be clear about who is eligible. Some situations limit purchases only to employees; in others it is advantageous to extend the same offer to friends and family. If family members are included, define "family." You may also want to designate blackout periods when discounts are not available, such as during the busiest periods when customers can be depended on to pay full price.

Group Purchasing Power

Employers can negotiate good prices on big-ticket items and pass the savings on to employees. From computers to automobiles, discounted purchase plans can be a huge benefit. The most appreciated allow for repayment over time using payroll deduction. Others may provide a subsidy or one-time discount. There are national plans for these arrangements, but don't be shy about asking a local dealer for preferential treatment. Neighborhood retailers are often eager to extend individual discounts that drive traffic to their establishments. These can range from movie tickets to dry cleaning and tax

---

WORTH REPEATING

Thanks for the Gas Discount!

A Southwest-based communications company that provides out-sourced customer service in multiple locations partnered with a fuel price consultant to create a discount plan that provides employees with 60 cents off per gallon of gas for all grades of fuel at almost every gas station. Called "Miles of Smiles," the benefit has been used by more than 90% of employees, helped recruit from a larger geographic area, and gained positive publicity for the employer.

---

preparation. Don't be surprised if the dry cleaner is willing to pick up and deliver if 10 employees sign up, or that the tax expert will do the same. Other ideas to explore for convenience and savings are car washes, oil changes, travel planners, and even personal shoppers. Amusement parks and shows frequently provide discount coupons to employers to distribute to large groups.

Where's the Ping-Pong Table and Foosball?

The dot-com boom and Silicon Valley start-ups brought tales of work environments where employees did their best thinking over a game of foosball. If you have room for a ping-pong table, and it fits your image, have a good time, but don't feel forced to create a constant party in your workplace as the only way to attract recent college grads. Nap stations, massages, game rooms, hair styling, and manicures all have their place in certain worksites. Make sure it's a fit with yours before you invest in air hockey equipment.

Food Service

From morning coffee to three meals a day, some form of free food and beverage is pretty much a mainstay in American workplaces. Employers order in, brew their own, and contract services to fuel employees according to tastes and budgets. Every course may not be free, but it is frequently subsidized by employers who engage a food service company or stock vending machines priced without a profit margin. Whatever you do, make certain that the level of quality meets expectations. When the food service exceeds expectations, employers may use the opportunity to publicize the expense as part of the benefits strategy.

ERISA Considerations

When deciding whether to offer any new benefit, check with a tax professional to see whether the value qualifies as taxable income or whether contributions can be taken from payroll as pretax earnings. For any item that may be considered a health or welfare program, remember that you will be required to complete a plan document and Form 5500.

Don't be baffled by the array of other benefits; use them as an opportunity to meet employee needs, enhance packages, and provide good news at open enrollment and throughout the year.

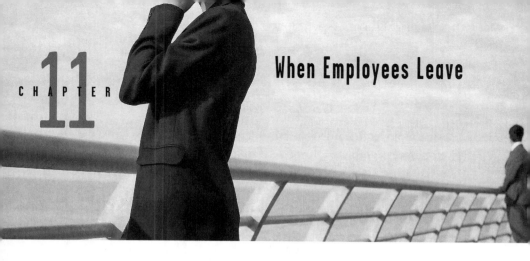

CHAPTER 11

When Employees Leave

How Does COBRA Work and What Else Do I Need to Do?

EMPLOYERS' BENEFITS RESPONSIBILITIES DO NOT end with the last day of work, whether an employee is permanently laid off, fired, resigns with notice, or walks off the job. If you offer health benefits, a 401(k) plan, or Flexible Spending Accounts, employees may be able to continue to participate in your plans. Other benefits frequently have provisions that allow for conversion to individual plans. Decisions have to be made about the disposition of benefits files and information about departing employees—whether to save, toss, or shred.

Organize this process by using an individual checklist for each person upon departure or a spreadsheet of all terminations with a list of available benefits. An effective record includes space for follow-up steps such as letters to be sent to the employee and notifications to send to providers. This list will be your trigger to notify all providers of the employee's last day of work. The spreadsheet will be helpful to track these steps, as changes may take place long after the employee is gone.

Step one when employees leave is to notify all applicable plans of the change in employee status. Don't delay notice to providers to end benefits even if an employee tells you that he or she plans to

---

WORTH REPEATING

Get the Correct Address

An employer included a reminder in their checklist to have employees complete a form verifying their correct address. This saved time tracking down people, especially when they were relocating.

---

continue coverage through COBRA. An individual who chooses to continue health benefits will be reinstated as a COBRA participant in the plan. Late notifications of terminations can result in billing problems and overpayments.

COBRA Basics

COBRA, the Consolidated Omnibus Budget Reconciliation Act, was enacted in 1986 to help employees avoid a lack of benefits coverage by allowing those who participate in employer-sponsored health plans to continue their coverage after employment ends or when dependents are no longer eligible. COBRA administration, with its long list of deadlines and required notices, can be a nightmare. Employers of all sizes will avoid headaches by outsourcing the process or using software-specific solutions for COBRA administration. Basic understanding of COBRA compliance deadlines and notifications is still important for both internal administration and outsourcing.

In addition to federal COBRA rules, each state, with the exception of Alabama and Delaware, has some type of COBRA legislation. State laws commonly extend coverage requirements to all employers, regardless of size, or add types of plans to the list of options that need to be offered. Your state department of labor will be a good source for information about these laws.

If I Have Fewer Than 20 Employees, Am I Exempt from COBRA?

COBRA covers all group health plans maintained by employers who had 20 or more employees at least half the time during the previous calendar year. If you had 22 full-time employees last year and you lay off 10 this year, you are still covered by COBRA. When calculating the number of employees to determine COBRA coverage, part-time employees must be included on a prorated basis, even if they are not eligible for benefits. An employee who worked 10 hours per week, when you require a 30-hour work week for benefits eligibility, will be considered a third of an employee in calculating the size of your staff. This doesn't mean that part-time employees are eligible for COBRA benefits if they leave, but that other employees covered by the plan could be eligible. Most states also require COBRA coverage for smaller employers.

We Have Very Low Turnover—Can't I Wait Until Someone Leaves to Worry About COBRA?

Employers are required to tell employees and their spouses about rights available under COBRA within 90 days of the date they are initially covered by a health plan. This "General Notice of COBRA Rights" describes employee and beneficiary eligibility to continue coverage when employment ends and the requirement that they notify the employer of a qualifying event. Employers can send a separate notice or include this with a Summary Plan Description (SPD) given to employees.

Sending a separate letter is the best way to satisfy this requirement because spouses need to be addressed and the SPD is probably much longer. The Department of Labor's Employee Benefits Security Administration (EBSA) publishes a four-page model General Notice

---

WORTH REPEATING

Tell Them What the General Notice Means

A multilocation employer included a simple statement in sign-up materials to inform employees about the General Notice of COBRA benefits before it was sent home. When newly eligible employees read it quickly it can sound like coverage is ending and they are being offered COBRA!

with directions for including the employer-specific information that is required for good faith compliance. This General Notice must be addressed to the employee and his or her spouse. This requirement can be met by a letter addressed to "Jane Doe and John Doe" or "Jane Doe and Spouse."

What Is a Qualifying Event?

Qualifying events are circumstances that cause health benefit coverage to end for an employee or eligible dependents.

Qualified events for employees include:

- Death
- Termination of employment
- A reduction of hours that results in an employee no longer being eligible for health plan coverage
- An employee or spouse becoming eligible for Medicare benefits
- Divorce
- A dependent child having reached the maximum coverage age under the plan

Employees are responsible for notifying the company plan administrator within 60 days of qualifying event that affects dependents. Employers should have a reasonable written procedure for employees to follow when qualifying events occur that is described in the General Notice and included in information about company health plans.

How Does an Employee Sign Up for Coverage Through COBRA?

The qualifying event triggers the requirement for a COBRA Election Notice to be sent to the employee or dependent. The guidelines for the timing of this notice are confusing. If the qualifying event is termination or death and the employer is also the plan administrator, they have up to 44 days from the date of the qualifying event to send the Election Notice. When employees are required to notify the employer of a qualifying event like divorce, employers have 14 days after being informed or told directly to send out the Election Notice. When employers are not the plan administrator, they have up to 30 days to tell the plan administrator about the qualifying event and the plan administrator has up to 14 days to send the notice. A Model COBRA Continuation Coverage Election Notice is available from EBSA.

The COBRA notification form must contain specific information and instructions for employees or dependents to choose or elect coverage. Individuals can continue under the identical plans they had as employees or only parts of the coverage. For example, if an employee had family medical, dental, and vision offerings, he or she can choose to continue only dependent dental coverage. Participants can't switch to new plans when they elect COBRA but they do not have to retain coverage in every plan.

The length of time that coverage can be continued varies based upon the specifics of the situation as described in this chart:

QUALIFIED BENEFICIARY	QUALIFYING EVENT	MAXIMUM LENGTH OF COBRA COVERAGE
Employee, Spouse, Dependent Child	Termination or loss of coverage due to reduction in hours	18 months—can be extended to 29 months due to disability or 36 months if a second qualifying event occurs
Spouse, Dependent Child	Medicare eligibility, divorce or separation, death of employee	36 months
Dependent Child	Loss of dependent child status (aging out of benefit plan)	36 months

Employees, or their dependents, have 60 days from the date the notice is sent or the date coverage ends, whichever is later, to make a decision about whether they want to continue these benefits. During this same period of time, the employee and beneficiary can also change their minds. A form included in the Election Notice must be completed in order to continue or decline coverage under COBRA.

Do I Have to Include the Dental Plan When COBRA Is Offered?

COBRA defines a group health plan as one that provides medical care. Plans that cover inpatient and outpatient hospital care, physician care, surgery or other major medical, prescription drugs, health care flexible spending accounts, dental and vision care are all considered to provide medical care. Life insurance, disability plans, long-term care, and dependent care flexible spending accounts are not considered medical care and do not have to be offered for COBRA continuation.

When Does COBRA Start If Former Employees Receive a Severance Package?

Employers may continue to provide coverage under a group health plan as part of a severance package. Whether the separation was due to a permanent layoff or termination, the last day of any extended coverage—not the last day worked—is used as the last date of coverage for COBRA purposes. For example, if an employee was laid off on December 15, 2008, and the employer agrees to maintain coverage by the group health plan for three full calendar months, March 30, 2009, is the date when coverage under the plan ends and COBRA eligibility begins. A severance agreement can state that any extended coverage will end when the former employee becomes eligible for a new employer's group health plan. This coverage end date is then used to trigger COBRA eligibility.

Who Pays for Coverage?

Employees can be charged the entire cost of coverage plus a 2% administration fee; the premium charged is commonly 102% of the regular rate. If a beneficiary becomes disabled, and therefore eligible for an extension of coverage through COBRA of up to 29 months, he or she can be charged 150% of the cost of coverage. Whenever plan rates go up, charges to COBRA participants can be increased accordingly.

In order to continue coverage under COBRA, individuals do not have to send a check with the Election Notice; they have 45 days after they return the form to pay for the coverage. COBRA coverage and billing is always retroactive so effectively there is no period of time when benefits would not be in force. If an employee's coverage ends on July 31st and she doesn't elect continuation until September 10th, she will be covered and required to pay for the cost of the plan as of August 1st.

Employers can set due dates and allow COBRA payments at any interval—quarterly, weekly, and so on—but must grant a request by a former employee or qualified beneficiary to pay monthly. Invoices or reminders of payment schedules are not required. After an employee chooses coverage and pays for the first period there must be a 30-day grace period after the due date for any subsequent payments. If premiums are not paid by the end of the grace period, coverage can be ended. A Notice of Early Termination of COBRA including the reason why coverage was terminated and the end date and any individual rights to other coverage must be sent to the individual(s) who had elected to continue benefits. This notice has to be sent "as soon as practicable." The DOL has not been specific about the language for this notice and has not published a template to guide employers in writing this type of correspondence. These guidelines create plenty of work in tracking dates, notices, and payments. Employees who leave to accept a new job can delay sending back the Election Notice and any payment until they are covered by benefits at their new employer. Former employees may wait to see if they need coverage and elect COBRA any time during the notice period; if and when the need arises, benefits will be reinstated and payment required retroactive to the date coverage ended.

Who Gets a COBRA Subsidy?

Economic stimulus legislation enacted in 2009 granted a subsidy for COBRA participants who had been laid off or terminated, beginning in September 2008. The subsidy provided for government funding to reduce the required payments for COBRA continuation to 35% of premium for up to 15 months, or as long as a former employee is eligible, whichever is less. Subsidies are subject to income ceilings during the year that the 65% is granted. If employees earn more than the allowable amount, they correct the overpayment on their tax return. The initial plan was extended a few times to cover employees who lost their jobs through May 2010. There is no similar subsidy in PPACA but this does not mean that the existing additional coverage is not extended via other legislation.

What Happens If We Don't Comply with COBRA?

COBRA violations can be investigated by the IRS or the Department of Labor (DOL) who may conduct an audit of processes and records. Violations for noncompliance include penalties of $100 per employee per day from the IRS and $110 per employee per day (more for dependents) by the DOL. Though these penalties can add up, the DOL and IRS are not particularly aggressive in this area; the real potential cost is in subsequent court claims over errors in COBRA processes. Lawsuits by individuals over mistakes in COBRA administration can lead to high attorney fees and judgments that require payment of huge medical bills. An angry ex-employee with mounting hospital expenses may feel there is little to lose in pursuing a claim.

How Do I Outsource COBRA Administration?

There are plenty of options for outsourcing COBRA administration. These range from independent third-party administrators (TPAs) to health plan providers and payroll processors. Begin a search for a COBRA administrator by making a list of potential providers. If you outsource payroll this is a logical place to begin. Payroll providers already have demographic information and records of coverage based on employee contributions. The service could be provided by a payroll processor other than the one you use, and even if you do not use one at all, they will be eager for the business.

Your benefits broker, health plan provider, and colleagues in similar businesses will have recommendations that can be added to a list of resources created from a simple Web search. The size of your organization should not affect the quality of the service because the process follows standard guidelines.

This list of questions and guidelines will help in interviewing and selecting a COBRA administrator:

- Is communication Web-based? Authorized staff should be able to start the COBRA Notice process by inputting information and changes online. Can you test drive the process?
- What kind of training is available for users?
- What do references say about the ease of use, service to COBRA participants, and customer service response?
- How long has the provider been in business and what are their plans for the future?
- What is involved in the implementation process?
- What is the process for distribution of premium payments collected from COBRA participants?
- What liability will they assume for mistakes that they make?

Increased competition has resulted in very competitive rates for outsourcing COBRA administration with two basic methods for determining the price: a fee for each qualifying event or monthly fees per benefits-eligible employee. Costs for qualifying events could range from $10 to $20, whereas per-employee, per-month fees range from 50 cents to $2.00. In order to select the most cost-effective option for your organization, review turnover and COBRA activity. You should be able to negotiate any setup charges and may save some money by retaining specific functions, such as mailing out the General Notice when employees become eligible for health benefits.

Don't rush implementation and risk creating errors that will take more time to fix. Once you have outsourced COBRA don't neglect the steps that keep the process running smoothly. It is essential that the COBRA administrator receive timely notification of qualifying events. Don't forget to communicate all terminations and changes to benefits providers, and update the COBRA administrator when plan changes occur and costs increase. During your annual open enrollment, COBRA participants are still eligible to make plan changes; an administrator should be able to help you with this communication.

BETTER FORGOTTEN

The COBRA Administrator Stopped Servicing the Account

An employer with locations across the United States used a subsidiary of their health care provider to administer COBRA. Three months before the end of the year a decision was made to change health care providers. The broker assured the company that the subsidiary would continue the COBRA administration; the service was billed and handled separately. In mid-December the employer learned that the administrator had stopped servicing the account after individuals covered by COBRA received letters notifying them that service was being discontinued. When plans or payroll providers change, ask if COBRA administration can continue, and check the contract.

FLEXIBLE SPENDING ACCOUNTS

Flexible Spending Accounts are not portable, but former employees may be able to request claims payment for eligible expenditures that predated the last day worked.

How Can Former Employees Submit Claims for Reimbursement from a Flexible Spending Account?

For both health care and dependent care Flexible Spending Accounts (FSAs), departing employees can receive reimbursements for expenses that were incurred while they were actively employed. Dependent care accounts will only reimburse up to the actual amount in the account. If an individual who quit effective August 1st with $1,000 in a dependent care FSA submits a claim for $1,200 for the month of July, he will only receive $1,000.

Health care FSAs must pay reimbursements up to the total annual amount the employee elected to put into the plan as long as the expenses were incurred while the employee was covered by the plan. For example, the same employee who quit effective August 1st elected to put $4,500 into his health care FSA for the calendar year, and when he left he had contributed $2,625 into the plan and received reimbursements for $2,000. In August he finds the bill for the new glasses bought in June and the July installment for a child's braces, and submits claims for $1,400. The plan must pay this entire amount because the $4,500 account election has not yet been spent. The employee cannot receive reimbursement for eligible expenses incurred after August 1st. FSAs are "use it or lose it" for both departing and active employees. Funds that are left over in accounts after the plan year and claims period ends cannot be used by participants to cover future reimbursements.

Employees who elect COBRA for a health care FSA can continue to receive reimbursements as active employees, as long as they keep up the agreed-on contributions.

401(k) Distributions

Departing employees can have options for actions on their 401(k) account depending on the size of the vested balance and plan parameters.

How Complicated Is 401(k) Administration When an Employee Leaves?

401(k) administration after an employee leaves is, fortunately, much less complicated than the steps required for COBRA. Individuals may receive a payout, stay in the plan, or transfer their funds to an IRA or to a new employer's qualified plan that accepts rollovers.

If an employee's account balance, including any vested employer contributions, is more than $5,000 she must have the option to continue as a participant in the plan. You need the employee's permission, and depending on your plan, permission from a spouse, to initiate a distribution.

When a former employee who has not retired stays in your 401(k) plan, notify the plan provider so the status will be changed to inactive participant. An inactive participant can typically not make contributions, unless repaying a loan, or take any partial distributions such as a loan or hardship withdrawal. If an employee remains in the plan as an inactive participant he will receive statements and can continue to make changes in the way his money is invested. Inactive participants should be instructed to access their accounts directly with the plan provider, either online or via a toll-free phone number.

If an employee has $5,000 or less in a 401(k) account, including the vested portion of any employer contribution, you can require a distribution. If a former employee does not make an election to receive the funds or a rollover and the amount in her account is between $1,000 and $5,000, the employer can transfer the distribution to an individual retirement plan (IRA) of a designated trustee or issuer as long as the holder of the account is notified in writing of the transfer. When the vested amount in the account is $1,000 or less, the distribution can be made automatically to the former employee.

Departing employees often ask how much of the employer 401(k) contribution is vested. Check with the provider for the most recent records to answer this question correctly. If you guess and give the wrong information you are not required to give the employee the larger amount, but you could create a disgruntled former employee.

The instructions for any distribution should clearly state the significant tax and IRS penalty implications of a direct payment to an individual before retirement age. Send a letter describing options and instructions to the employee's home, as a spouse or other family member may help interpret the information and be involved in decision making. Plan providers will have templates for this type of communication. Accommodating a former employee's needs will make the process smoother and gain goodwill.

BETTER FORGOTTEN

What Signatures Are Required for a Distribution?

Five years after a senior employee left the company, he requested a speedy distribution of his 401(k). After submitting necessary paperwork he was told about additional signatures, forms, and notary requirements because the account balance was more than $100,000. He was already frustrated and this delay made him angrier. Identify all requirements before processing a distribution.

It may seem easier to let employees stay as plan participants; it's one less letter to send. Allowing former employees to stay in the plan can increase costs if you pay any direct fees, specifically per participant; it also adds to record keeping with account statements and might make it hard to locate people at a later date. Whatever decision you make about the 401(k) for departing employees, it's important that you follow plan rules and apply them consistently; don't make individual deals.

TRACKING OTHER BENEFITS

Health and retirement benefits may be top of mind, but other plans potentially require notifications and all should be communicated and tracked for a smooth transition.

Can Employees Keep Their Life Insurance and Supplemental Disability When They Leave?

Other benefits such as life insurance, supplemental disability, and long-term care may all allow the option to continue coverage through an individual policy. The best way to handle this conversion is to understand the process and give the forms or information from the provider to employees when they leave. Some providers will send conversion packets directly to the individual. Make sure the information is timely and you can stay out of the middle of these transactions.

If you offer discount programs or similar perks, you may need to complete additional notifications when an employee leaves. You don't want to jeopardize a discount benefit or relationship if the provider finds out that they are giving a special deal to a growing number of former employees.

EMPLOYEE BENEFITS FILES

Some employers save every scrap of paper generated by the employment relationship. Others decide to shred all when an employee departs. There is a middle ground for retention of information that may be needed in the future.

When They Leave Can I Throw Out the Employee Benefits File?

After an employee leaves, don't toss out the separate benefit files that you maintain. These files are full of Social Security numbers, dates of birth, addresses, and dependent information that can be a target for identity theft. During the period when paperwork is being completed and notices are being sent, make sure the file is kept in a secure location and not easily accessible to contractors and night cleaning crews.

After the employee leaves use the following guidelines to decide what to save, toss, or shred:

Type of Document	Save	Toss	Shred
Medical/Dental/Vision plan enrollment forms for previous years			X
Medical/Dental/Vision Plan enrollment form for current plan year	X		
Descriptions of benefit plans without any employee identifying information		X	
COBRA documentation	X		
Life insurance beneficiaries			X
401(k) enrollment	X		
401(k) beneficiary	X		
401(k) loan information for loans paid off			X
401(k) information for outstanding loans	X		
FSA information for fully completed plan years			X
FSA information for the current plan year or during the active claims period for the previous year	X		

Make certain that the information that you may need to access more often, such as dates for COBRA, is accessible and secure.

How Does a Company Closure Affect Benefits Plans?

Whether a company closes, files for bankruptcy, or is sold, the details about benefits plans will be part of the transaction. Health plan benefits under COBRA can only be provided within an existing group health plan. When a business closure results in the end of a group health plan, the option of continued coverage under the plan through COBRA is no longer available. Former employees who are already covered under the plan through COBRA would also lose these benefits.

When a 401(k) plan is discontinued, participants are eligible to receive the vested assets in their individual accounts. In certain bankruptcy situations employer contributions may automatically be 100% vested regardless of employee length of service. Employee contributions are always 100% vested. 401(k) plans may be frozen, meaning that participants cannot make changes or receive distributions while the details and record keeping required to close the plan are completed.

Other benefits can be administered by providers, as they are in any termination. The payout of vacation and other benefit days will be guided by company policy, the details of the closure, and any applicable state laws.

What Happens to Benefits When an Employee Dies?

The death of an active employee is always tough on the workplace. Health benefits continuation for beneficiaries will be handled by the regular COBRA process. Distributions from the 401(k) are described in your plan. If the employee had flexible spending accounts, contact the plan administrator to determine whether beneficiaries can file claims for any eligible expenses.

After an employee dies, be prepared to send the paperwork and answer questions about the timing of life insurance and 401(k) payouts and any salary, sick, or vacation that is due to be paid. Maintain a secure, accessible location for up-to-date beneficiary information to expedite the process and minimize disputes.

When an employee is terminally ill it can be helpful to provide instructions and information to the employee or a family member before a death occurs. When appropriate, prepare a summary of the cost of COBRA coverage for any dependents on the plan, including up-to-date account information for a 401(k) and life insurance benefits. It will also be helpful to tell the employee or family member what kind of documentation will be needed and provide the necessary forms to submit any claim for life insurance or a 401(k) distribution.

Why Should I Be Nice to Employees Who Leave on Bad Terms?

It can be tempting to give former employees a hard time when they quit without notice, go to work for a competitor, or are fired for misconduct. Avoid interactions that have the potential to aggravate the person. They need information and you need certain paperwork and signatures to complete transactions. A hostile former employee is more likely to spread nasty comments about you as an employer and company or take his or her "case" to an attorney or government agency to initiate some kind of charge or claim. A professional approach to benefits transitions when an employee leaves will save time and money and guard your reputation.

CHAPTER 12

Cost Control

What Can Employers Do to Rein in Benefits Costs?

CONTROLLING BENEFITS COSTS, PARTICULARLY health insurance expenditures, is an urgent topic for employers of all sizes. The most common employer response to escalating medical premiums is to increase employee cost sharing. Though these changes can produce immediate results, they also increase dissatisfaction and create the potential for benefit plans that employees may not be able to afford. Health reform is scheduled to create some employee options in the long term, but is not designed to reduce employer premiums. Employers can take the creative steps of offering education and wellness and disease management programs to create better consumers and healthier plan participants—toward the implicit goal that better health will equate to less usage of costly services, resulting in lower costs. Planning and administration also create opportunities for savings, some of which are pretty much immediate. Last-minute purchases of coverage can be more expensive, given less time for research and shopping for the best plan, leading to administrative errors and oversights that routinely cost employers large sums of money.

EMPLOYEE COST SHARING

It has been many years since the majority of employees enjoyed first-dollar coverage in plans paid for entirely by the employer. Cost sharing can take many forms and should be considered carefully before implementation and changes.

Contributions Toward Premiums

Employee contributions toward premiums should be viewed as a cost savings and an educational tool. This is the starting point for the conversation about the total benefits investment made by employers.

How Much Should Employees Contribute for Coverage?

In 2009 the average annual health care insurance premium for employer-sponsored family coverage topped $13,000. The increase in rates over 2008 was not precipitous, but the longer view is much more dramatic: the average premium ballooned a whopping 131% since 1999. The average annual premium for single coverage rose a statistically insignificant amount over 2008. It now stands at more than $4,800, a startling increase of 119% since 1999. Premiums range between 80 and 120% of these averages due to the type of plan, size of employer, and geographic factors. Though employee contributions also range, it's helpful to start by looking at the average employee contribution of almost 20% of the total premium for single coverage and more than 25% for family coverage.

Sounds Like We Should Set Employee Contributions at 20%, Right?

Use a variety of factors to identify the best employee contribution. The first consideration is your budget; calculate projected annual premiums and develop a model that includes the amount you are prepared to pay. Setting employee contributions at a flat percentage may not be the best approach, especially if you offer employees choices between plans that come with different premium levels. When an employer pays 80% of the premium, costs will be much higher for the employee who chooses the most expensive plan. Consider setting employer contributions at a set dollar amount using the least expensive plan as the baseline; employees then make the decision as to whether or not they want to pay the difference for more expensive coverage. Employers can choose different rates based on the level of coverage, whether single, family, or any class offered by the plan.

With your budget in mind, research all of the available information about employee contribution levels among your competitors and in your region and industry. The Bureau of Labor Statistics compiles information divided regionally and by type of industry in its annual National Compensation Survey. Local business associations or industry organizations can also be good sources for benchmarking. When you match your employee contribution rates to applicable data, don't forget how other out-of-pocket costs add into the equation regarding contributions for your employee population. If the company across the street is paying 50% of the family medical premium, that plan will seem less generous if it also requires $50 doctor visit copayments and out-of-pocket costs of $75 per prescription, after a hefty deductible.

Should We Tell Employees How Much This Costs?

Beginning in 2012, employers will be required by PPACA to include the value of the health benefits they provide for each employee on the covered individual's annual Form W-2. This mandate will show up on the form to be completed that reflects 2011 earnings. There is no need to wait for this initiative to discuss costs. Too many employers miss an opportunity to share information about the huge sums of money they spend to purchase employee benefits. Give employees the big picture by taking advantage of this wealth of information during open enrollment and in regular communications. Use percentages, actual costs, and premium increase rates to explain changes in the employees' share of the financial burden. Health care costs may be headline news, but many employees have no idea that the $293 average that they pay each month for family health coverage only buys a plan because their employer foots the bill for the remaining $850 or more. With a workforce of only 10 covered employees at these levels, employers are paying more than $100,000 a year for family health benefits. It doesn't take sophisticated math and spreadsheets to give employees a view of expenses they may have never seen or contemplated.

We Are Very Generous and Pay for Everything; Isn't That Great?

If you pay the entire premium for family coverage you are in the minority; more than 90% of U.S. employers require employees to pay for a portion of this health benefit. Full premium payment for single employee coverage is more prevalent; about 75% of employees pay a required contribution. Paying the entire premium sounds generous, but it does nothing to encourage employees to be good consumers and increases the likelihood of employees signing on to a plan when they have coverage elsewhere, most commonly through a spouse. The expected contribution can be small and introduced with all of the comparison data and explanation of total costs.

Should I Give a Bonus to Employees Who Don't Sign Up?

Employers find it beneficial to provide some type of incentive to employees who decline employer health coverage because they receive benefits elsewhere. This can be a few hundred dollars over the year or each month but will certainly cost less than premium payments for family plans. When implementing this policy, ask that employees sign a waiver of coverage and provide some type of proof of the health benefits they receive through their spouse or another source.

Increasing Copayments and Deductibles

Plan design changes can be made to modify premium increases. Health plans will offer different rates according to the schedule of copayments for doctor visits and prescriptions and deductibles. Deductibles have become common even for in-network and HMO plans, particularly for prescription plans, where it is not unusual to ask employees to pay for the first $50 of covered drugs each year. Plans can encourage the use of generic drugs by waiving the deductible, making copayments very low, or automatically covering certain prescriptions at 100%. The choices may be reduced for some covered services, because PPACA requires qualified benefit plans to provide minimum coverage, without cost sharing, for preventive services to be identified by a federal task force.

Before selecting a plan you should be able to make a side-by-side comparison of cost sharing that shows how it affects premiums. With so many ways to change the structure, don't be afraid to ask for other choices, such as increasing the copayment for emergency room visits or creating a separate tier of the highest-cost prescription medications, requiring employees to pay $100 for a one-month supply month when a less costly drug is available. These are not easy decisions and you should be prepared to explain them to employees and respond to their questions.

Wellness Programs

A healthy workforce means reduced expenditures, and wellness programs keep popping up like weeds. Such programs include support for smoking cessation and weight loss, and a range of efforts to improve lifestyle habits through better eating habits and exercise. There are almost as many opinions about the effectiveness of wellness initiatives as there are options. The return on investment has not been consistently established and some employees may be suspicious of the big-brother overtones in plans that seek to guide personal habits. As waistlines expand, it's tough to say no to at least some help and most employees appreciate the gesture and ease of access through work. Whether you have a wellness component or are considering one, look at the idea from all sides to begin or improve participation. What are the benefits for the company and for employees? Clearly articulating these goals will help you decide whether you need incentives for participation or prefer to penalize employees who do not sign on. Incentives range from reduced employee contributions for premiums to subsidized health club membership, nutrition counseling, and in-house exercise classes or equipment. The penalties can be increased contributions for smokers or requirements for a return of program costs for employees who regain significant weight lost through a company-sponsored program. Rewards for participation can also include cash, premium reductions, gift cards, and merchandise; sometimes the concept of receiving any gift is more valuable than the actual cost. Don't overlook Web-based resources that make traditionally high-touch services, such as nutrition education and coaching, more affordable.

Employee decisions about wellness participation can be based on a number of factors.

Reasons Employees Participate in Wellness Programs

I want good health.	73%
Financial incentives or rewards through my employer.	48%
I want to minimize medical expenses.	38%
Financial penalties imposed by my employer.	17%

How Does Health Reform Affect Wellness Plans?

Health reform legislation gives a potential boost to wellness programs. Beginning in 2011, PPACA will provide grants for up to five years for employers with fewer than 100 employees who do not already have wellness initiatives, to establish comprehensive wellness programs. Health reform also increases the amount of reward or penalty that employers can impose to 30% of the wellness plan premium, with some leeway for federal agencies to increase this amount after completing a study on wellness programs.

What About Weight Loss?

Workplace weight-loss programs can be an easy way to begin a wellness initiative. The costs of obesity have been well documented as a contributor to health care expenses and employee absenteeism. Small cash payments for completion of health questionnaires, discounts at health clubs, and premium reductions for full participation in a weight-loss program can help. Employees can create "biggest loser" contests modeled after reality TV, or an employer can host Weight Watchers meetings in a conference room.

The federal Centers for Disease Control and Prevention (CDC) offers employer tips, strategies, and a wealth of ready-to-use information with the following recommendations for launching a company weight-reduction program:

- Involve employees throughout the development process.
- Offer programs at convenient places and times for employees.
- Reward participants for achieving program goals.
- Offer a variety of programs to meet different employee needs.
- Change the workplace environment to support healthy lifestyles, replace sugared beverages in vending machines, offer healthy foods, and encourage walking during the work day.

Have You Told Your Employees to Take a Hike?

A campaign to encourage walking is simple to start. Get a good price on pedometers, have employees pick striding partners, and find the route, indoors or out. An eager committee can create maps and recommended directions. Rewards can be simple water bottles, T-shirts, energy bars, and gift certificates to sporting goods stores.

Can Wellness Programs Create Legal Issues?

When you've made the decision to offer wellness initiatives, pay special attention to the information you collect about personal health habits or conditions. Avoid HIPAA violations and the potential for questions about discrimination by filing this data correctly, keeping information secure, and allowing access only to those with a need to know. Wellness initiatives can also run afoul of ERISA and the ADA if they are not offered across the board and end up favoring employees in one specific group.

Don't invest in a program that can't be changed to be a better fit for your organization. Three years of expensive health club memberships may just end up being a three-year expense. It looks like corporate-sponsored wellness is here to stay, and employers should ask for ways to measure the return on their investment.

Disease Management

Disease management products have grown in an effort to control the costs inherent in common conditions. From diabetes to high blood pressure, participant treatment and care are monitored and tracked for consistency and improved outcomes.

WORTH REPEATING

I Saw the Nurse at Work!

Advertising and marketing company 4imprint with 400 employees based in Oshkosh, Wisconsin, utilizes the services of an on-site nurse and wellness coordinator and realizes cost savings and reduced time away from work. It does not take a jumbo employer to afford these services. Investigate a solution that can fit your budget or be shared with a nearby company.

Is the Diabetic Employee Taking Care of Herself?

Disease management applies standards of care and oversight to employees and dependents affected by chronic conditions. Disease management can be offered by a health care carrier or purchased as a separate service. When interviewing vendors look for realistic returns on the investment, and plenty of opportunity for personalized health coaching. Not every person with heart disease is the same. Disease management should provide communications tailored to the employee demographic, including translated materials if needed, and take creative approaches using a variety of media. Programs that are well designed and implemented consistently have the potential to save money by preventing costly care, improving health, and connecting resources to avoid errors and complications.

PLAN FOR RENEWALS

Employers should begin planning for renewals as soon as a plan year begins. The process starts by requesting and reviewing as much information as is available. Ask for standard reports and see if they provide the information you need. Insurers and vendors may charge for specific detailed requests that identify utilization, but you should be able to negotiate any fees. A broker can help apply pressure for this information, analyze data, and create action plans. Pharmacy data helps track the use of specific prescriptions and develop a pricing strategy;

WORTH REPEATING

Cut Down on Emergency Room Visits to Cut Costs

A call center with 350 employees, based in Fort Worth, Texas, learned through data analysis that emergency room utilization was unusually high. The company launched an educational campaign promoting alternatives to emergency room visits and gave T-shirts to employees who had annual physicals. The number of physicals rose by more than 30% and emergency room usage dropped dramatically.

primary and specialty care usage can help target information and set copayments. Don't worry that you are tapping into sensitive health information protected by HIPAA, as reports should be created without employee identifiers.

When Does Renewal Season Start?

The following questions for your broker or provider can get the process started:

- When can I expect renewal information?
- What trends are you seeing in renewals?
- What information do you need for the process?
- Is it time to look at other plan providers?

Work with your broker to establish a timetable for renewal that includes plans and requirements for any employee data updates. If census information is needed, you should know in advance to make certain it is prepared properly. The calendar should be agreed on six months before the renewal, with activity to begin within a month. Ideally all negotiations should be completed and contracts set three months before the end of the plan year, but no later than two. If your broker or provider repeatedly says, "Let's wait until we have more data," you can reply, "Sure, I'll wait for more information, but give me what you can now." If they respond with outrageous figures, it may be time to look for a new broker. Too often small and even midsize employers wait until the last minute, which delays the potential for good communication to employees about any changes, adds to confusion, and can limit leverage. Choose a date by which you want to make a decision and tell the broker and providers. The date should not be December 1st, or you will still be scrambling on the 20th. Identify the steps you have to take for open enrollment and work backwards to allow enough time for meetings, mailings, and processing. Review all of the components of the plan. For example, if dental coverage is quoted with a nominal increase, you may want to make some changes to balance increases in health care; don't save dental for last because you know it will not be a difficult renewal. The pharmacy benefit should always be closely scrutinized to make certain the pharmacy benefits manager is taking all the steps available to control costs.

Check the Bills All Year Long

Benefits bills contain so much information and so many variables based on plan choices and coverage tiers that they inevitably include errors that can go unnoticed.

Are Those Rates Correct?

Employers routinely pay too much for health benefits. These overpayments have nothing to do with high premiums for medical and dental coverage. Unnecessary charges are common due to mistakes in enrollments, changes, and termination of coverage. An audit of benefits bills that compares enrollment data with statements can catch errors and save significant sums.

Pay special attention to the following items:

1. *Are the billed rates correct?*

   Take out up-to-date contracts for all the plans and check each rate and category. If you have more than one offering from the same provider, check each one. Are rates for single, family, and any other tiers of coverage accurate? Discrepancies can be found in favor of the employer.

2. *Are employees in the right bucket?*

Using a list of eligible employees and the coverage they selected, make certain that you are being billed for the right plan. When there is more than one option, employees can be enrolled by the carrier in the PPO when they chose the HMO. Similarly, employees with coverage for a parent plus children can be categorized as having family coverage if your plan rates include multiple tiers.

3. *Are terminated employees still listed as active?*

The most common mistake is employees remaining on the bill long after they have left the job. If a departing employee chooses to continue coverage under COBRA he or she should be listed separately on a bill under this category. When former employees are included in a long list of employees, it makes it difficult to check when their coverage does end. When you are still being billed for terminated employees or employees who dropped coverage, notify the plan immediately of the coverage end date. Many plans will not give full credit if the termination was many months earlier.

4. *Let the provider make the adjustments.*

When you correctly terminate employee coverage, the change may not show up on the subsequent invoice. Keep track of changes and let the provider make the adjustments. It's too easy to make errors when you try to apply credits yourself. When the invoice never matches the payments made, there are continuing arguments about correct payments and it is only harder to track.

These tips are the basics for those who are not financially oriented. Complete the steps on a regular basis to catch discrepancies before they pile up into hefty charges.

DEPENDENT ELIGIBILITY AUDIT

Why conduct a dependent eligibility audit? Pretty simple, it is very likely that you are paying for health care for people listed as spouses or children who are not really eligible dependents. Your plan has a definition of who is eligible for coverage. Start by taking out the definition and making sure you understand it. You may say, "But I know my employees, they are not cheating me." Or, "I don't want to add to the list of Americans without health insurance." No one wants to increase the rolls of the uninsured, but there is no reason for an employer to create a benefits plan that allows employees to cover anyone they want to sign up. An employee just came to you and said, "I really need to put my nephews on the plan. I'll say they are my kids, we have the same last name. My brother just got laid off and he can't afford COBRA." Would you hand over the forms and add the nephews to the plan? What about in-laws, cousins, boyfriends, and girlfriends? If you would not allow coverage initially, why should you keep someone on the plan if there has been some subterfuge?

This doesn't mean you walk out and start asking employees for proof of marriage or birth certificates for children, and fire those who have been getting away with something. Begin by identifying the documentation you will require. Don't just ask a certain group of employees; if you require proof, everyone will have to comply. If you don't want to be the bad guy, you can hire an external expert to perform the audit. Using a third party, you can announce the program, let employees know what's coming, specify the documentation that will be required, and then have the vendor review the information that employees provide. Some documentation can be tricky, such as divorce decrees, which require specific knowledge and experience to decipher who is eligible to be covered under a plan. If one employee has someone signed up who is not really an eligible spouse, the company can realize savings of $7,000 a year. That money goes right to the bottom line. It can pay for other coverage or go toward saving a job in tough times. Employers should not use an audit as a tactic to ferret out employees to fire and should provide amnesty from discipline for employees who comply with the audit. The advent of PPACA with the new requirement for coverage for dependents up to age 26 will make this type of audit even more valuable.

COMMUNICATE TO EMPLOYEES

In order to be truly effective, communications about employee benefits must be an ongoing effort.

Isn't Sending Out Provider Booklets Enough?

Good communication that makes employees better consumers is one of the best ways to control costs. Comprehensive, expensive benefits plans can be sabotaged by ineffective communication. Employees don't understand them, don't use them properly, don't make the best decisions for their needs, or are simply frustrated by the process. Before employees say, "Oh no, it's open enrollment—another pile of complicated paperwork," take steps to improve the communication. Start by sending a letter home to describe plan changes and the process. In many households a spouse or even a child takes much of the responsibility for personal benefits administration. Before any letter is sent out, show it to someone who is not familiar with benefit plans, such as a trusted manager or administrative assistant. If the employee who is not benefits savvy understands the letter, other people will too. Don't automatically send out a letter that the broker or provider writes just because they are the experts. Expertise does not guarantee readability. Additional communication steps include meetings, e-mails, and visits by provider representatives. You should not have to pay for provider or broker representative visits to explain benefits. Make certain that changes and any options that could save employees out-of-pocket expenses are explained completely and clearly. If a prescription plan has a mail-order option that cuts costs, create examples that highlight the savings, showing that this is a perfect way to save money for both employees and the company.

Where Do I Start with These Cost-Control Ideas?

Whatever steps you choose, doing nothing should not be an option. It is unlikely that you will be able to implement all of the ideas included in this chapter. Make it a priority to review billing and gain control over the renewal process; taking steps to make decisions will change the paradigm and spur additional questions, research, and action. When prioritizing other ideas, look for the return on investment or best use of existing resources. If you have an employee who is an avid hiker, you can turn the walking initiative over to him or her. Taking steps to control costs will help make you a better purchaser of employee benefits and increase the potential impact on your bottom line.

RESOURCE GUIDE FOR CHAPTER ONE

U.S. Chamber of Commerce Annual Survey of Employee Benefits
This tool for employers is available for purchase.
www.uschamber.com/research/benefits.htm

The Bureau of Labor Statistics
National Compensation Survey—Benefits
www.bls.gov/ncs/ebs

Annual Employee Benefits Survey, published each year in June and specific surveys on current topics throughout the year
Society of Human Resource Management (SHRM)
www.shrm.org

The Kaiser Family Foundation and the Health Research & Education Trust (HRET) *Annual Health Benefits Survey,* released each year in the fall, includes slides
www.ehbs.kff.org

MetLife's *Study of Employee Benefits Trends*, released annually, includes slides and a Benefits Benchmarking tool
www.whymetlife.com/trends/

International Foundation of Employee Benefits Employer Benefits Survey; United States and Canada 2009
www.ifeb.org

Data compiled by The Employee Benefits Research Association
www.ebri.org

RESOURCE GUIDE FOR CHAPTER THREE

Bureau of Labor Statistics National Compensation Survey, March 2009
Seventh Annual MetLife Study of Employee Benefits Trends, May 2009

RESOURCE GUIDE FOR CHAPTER FOUR

Quality Assurance Evaluations and Accreditations:
National Committee for Quality Assurance
111-13th St., NW, Suite 1000
Washington, DC 20005
(888) 275-7585
www.ncqua.org

Prudential's *Group Insurance Study of Employee Benefits*; 2009 and Beyond

PricewaterhouseCoopers' *Health Research Institute Behind the Numbers Medical cost trends for 2010*

Medical and Dental Expenses (Including the Health Coverage Tax Credit)
Publication 502
Department of the Treasury
Internal Revenue Service

EEOC Compliance Manual
The U.S. Equal Employment Opportunity Commission

Medical Tourism; Update and Implications
Deloitte Center for Health Solutions

Consumer Reports Best Buy Drugs
www.crbestbuydrugs.org

Resource Guide for Chapter Five

MetLife Evaluating the Value of Dental Benefits
Available through **National Association of Dental Plans**
12700 Park Central Drive, Ste. 400
Dallas, TX 75251
(972) 458-6998
info@nadp.org
Employee Communications, 2009
National Association of Dental Plans: www.nadp.org

RESOURCE GUIDE FOR
CHAPTER SEVEN

For information, forms, and so forth about bicycle commuter transportation benefits:

League of American Bicyclists

1612 K Street NW, Suite 800

Washington, DC 20006

(202) 822-1333

www.bikeleague.org

Employer's Tax Guide to Fringe Benefits

Publication 15-B

Cat. No. 29744N

Department of The Treasury

Internal Revenue Service

RESOURCE GUIDE FOR CHAPTER EIGHT

IRS Retirement Plans Navigator

www.retirementplans.irs.gov/

BrightScope, 401(k) analytics firm provides fee comparisons for plans

www.brightscope.com

Choosing a Retirement Plan for Your Small Business

Reference publication #3998. Available online from www.irs.gov/pub/irs-pdf/p3998.pdf or call the IRS at (800) 829-3676.

Testimony Before the Special Committee on Aging, U.S. Senate

401(k) Plans: Several Factors Can Diminish Retirement Savings, but Automatic Enrollment Shows Promise for Increasing Participation and Savings, Statement of Barbara D. Bovbjerg, Director Education, Workforce and Income Security, October 29, 2009

Annual Survey of Profit Sharing and 401(k) Plans by the Profit Sharing/401(k) Council of America

Model Investment Policy Statement

Profit Sharing/401k Council of America

20 North Wacker Drive, Suite 3700

Chicago, IL 60606

(312) 419-1863

Fax: (312) 419-1864

psca@psca.org

RESOURCE GUIDE FOR CHAPTER NINE

Employee Benefits: The Employer-Insurer Partnership for Financial Security

American Council of Life Insurers, 2009

101 Constitution Ave., NW, Suite 700

Washington, DC 20001-2133

www.acli.com

United States Department of Labor

Bureau of Labor Statistics

Employee Benefits in the U.S., March 2009

www.bls.gov/ebs

RESOURCE GUIDE FOR
CHAPTER TEN

College Savings Plan Network

www.collegesavings.org

Privacy Rights Clearinghouse

www.privacyrights.org

To Catch a Thief; Are Identity Theft Services Worth the Cost?
Consumer Federation of America, March 2009

Identity Theft Resource Center

(858) 693-7935

Monday-Friday, 8 AM to 4:30 PM Pacific Time

itrc@idtheftcenter.org

www.idtheftcenter.org

Kaiser Public Opinion Spotlight; The Public's Views on Long-Term Care, December 2007

National Credit Union Administration

1775 Duke St.

Alexandria, VA 22314-3428

(703) 518-6300

www.ncua.gov

Credit Union National Association, Inc.

601 Pennsylvania Ave. NW

Washington, DC 20004-2601

(202) 638-5777

www.cuna.org

Understanding Employer Assisted Mortgage Programs: A Primer for National Banks, August 2007

Controller of the Currency

Administration of National Banks

U.S. Department of The Treasury

U.S. Savings Bonds Treasury Direct

www.treasurydirect.gov

National Association for College Admissions Counseling

1050 N Highland St. Suite 400

Arlington, VA 22201

(703) 836-2222

www.nacacnet.org

Dave Thomas Foundation for Adoption

525 Metro Place West

Dublin, OH 43017

(800) 275-3832

---

100 Best Adoption-Friendly Workplaces

www.davethomasfoundation.org

RESOURCE GUIDE FOR CHAPTER TWELVE

The Wellness Imperative; Creating More Effective Organizations

World Economic Forum in partnership with Right Management (A Manpower Company) 2010

Global Corporate Challenge

www.gettheworldmoving.com

7th Annual MetLife Study of Employee Benefits Trends

Behind the Numbers; Medical Cost Trends for 2009

PricewaterhouseCoopers' Health Research Institute

The Healthcare Blue Book is a free online consumer tool to help find the best prices for practitioners, procedures, and prescriptions; organized by zip code. The book offers free access and customized enhancements for employers at reasonable costs.

www.healthcarebluebook.com

CDC Lean Works!—A Workplace Obesity Prevention Program

Centers for Disease Control

www.cdc.gov/leanworks

Resource Guide for Health Reform

Department of Health and Human Services:
www.healthreform.gov
Questions can be sent to healthreform@hhs.gov

IRS Guidelines for Small Business Health Reform Tax Credit
www.irs.gov
Telephone assistance for businesses:
(800) 829-4933
Monday–Friday, 7:00 AM to 10:00 PM your local time (Alaska and Hawaii follow Pacific Time)

For research and explanatory information:
The Kaiser Family Foundation
http://healthreform.kff.org/
Headquarters
2400 Sand Hill Road
Menlo Park, CA 94025
(650) 854-9400

Washington, DC Office/Public Affairs Center

1330 G Street, NW

Washington, DC 20005

(202) 347-5270

Tools and Templates

1. Suggested Employee Benefits Language for Employee Handbook
2. Sample Benefits Overview—Including Health Plan Comparison Chart
3. Sample Broker of Record Letter
4. Sample Participant Health Plan Benefits Waiver
5. Sample 401(k) Automatic Enrollment Election—New Hires
6. Typical Request for Proposal Content for a 401(k)
7. Employee Survey—Wellness Programs
8. COBRA Administration Checklist

SUGGESTED EMPLOYEE BENEFITS LANGUAGE FOR EMPLOYEE HANDBOOK

Your Benefits

[Company Name] offers a number of benefits plans to eligible employees such as:

- Medical Coverage
- Dental Coverage
- Vision Coverage
- Short- and Long-Term Disability
- 401(k) plan
- Life Insurance

The provisions of the plans, including eligibility and benefit provisions, are found in the Summary Plan Descriptions (SPD), which may be revised from time to time. The official plan documents are available for your review through the Company [include title of position or department name]. In the determination of benefits or other matters under the plans, the terms of the official plan documents shall govern over the language of any descriptions thereof, including that of the SPDs.

[Company Name] may add to, modify, or rescind any benefits provided after notice to you.

Sample Benefits Overview

Hourly Employees

We are pleased to provide [Company Name] employees with a comprehensive benefit plan. *[This is a good place to insert a summary of benefits philosophy.]* This Benefits Overview is designed to introduce these benefits and provide general information and instructions for enrollment and changes. Detailed information is available for each plan from the carriers or from the company office.

Benefits plans can seem complicated and confusing. Using this overview and other sources listed here will help you understand your benefits. Becoming comfortable with finding answers to your questions is the best way to obtain the information and services that you need to meet your own individual needs.

This overview contains information about the following benefits:

Health Insurance

- Medical Plan

Benefits That Provide Economic Security

- Group Life Insurance
- AD & D coverage
- Disability Insurance

Benefit Days

- Holidays
- Sick Days

Retirement

- 401(k) Plan

This Overview includes plan highlights only and is not intended as a comprehensive guide to your benefit plans. The actual delivery of benefits under these plans is controlled by the Summary Plan Descriptions (SPDs) for each benefit plan. You can request copies of SPDs from the company. This information applies to the 2011 Benefits Plan. [Company Name] may change the Benefits Plan from time to time.

Health Insurance

When am I eligible?

You are eligible to be covered by health insurance effective the first day of the month after 60 days of full-time employment. If you start working on September 9, 2010, you can enroll in health insurance coverage effective December 1, 2010.

Is there a choice of health insurance plans?

You may choose to enroll in medical coverage in one of two plan options provided by ABC Health Plan or you can waive coverage in this plan.

Do I have to pay for this coverage?

[Company Name] pays for a significant portion of the cost of these benefits. Your contributions, listed on the health plan comparison chart, are determined by the coverage you choose.

What if I pick a plan and want to make changes?

Once a year on January 1st you can make changes in your health care coverage. You can change plans or add eligible dependants, who had not already been enrolled. At other times, if you get married or add a child to your family, you can enroll the new dependent within 31 days of the marriage, birth, or adoption. If you wish to add a newly eligible dependent contact the [Company Name or designated Department] for the necessary forms and complete them within the time required.

How do I decide which plan is best for me?

The ABC HMO plan features the lowest out-of-pocket costs for participants but does not cover expenses from doctors or other providers who are not members of the ABC HMO Network. The ABC PPO balances higher in-network costs for coverage with lower deductibles and comparable coinsurance for participants who use providers outside of the ABC PPO Network.

The Health Plan Comparison chart has an outline of frequently used benefits and lists the employee contributions. Think about your health care needs and review the information on the chart. In order to decide between these plans, make a list of typical expenses and compare your level of use both in and out of network.

How do I find out if my doctor is in the network? How do I find an ABC Health provider?

The most up to-date-list is on the ABC Health Plan Web site www.abchealthplan.info:

- Click on "search for an ABC doctor" in the bottom left corner of the home page.
- Follow the directions to search by location, specialty, or name of doctor; make sure you choose the ABC Midwest Network.

You can also look in the hard copy ABC Health Network Roster. Or call ABC Health at (800) 333-0000.

Where do I sign up?

In the ABC Health envelope you will find enrollment forms and more information about the plans and ABC Health services. Complete the enrollment form and submit it to the [Company Name or Department]. You can complete these as soon as you make a decision, but they must be submitted no later than 31 days after the date you become eligible for these benefits.

Complete the Employee and Dependent Information Sections of the enrollment form. Whichever plan you choose, you must write down a primary care physician. You can change this doctor at any time. If you choose the ABC PPO plan, you do not have to access care through this or any in-network doctor.

On the top of the form write the name of the plan you are selecting: ABC HMO or ABC PPO. Return the completed form to the [Company Name or Department].

[Company Name] enrolls you. ABC Health will send benefit cards to your home.

You can also submit enrollment information online. Go to www.abchealthplan.info, click on "New Enrollment" and follow the instructions. If you choose online enrollment, be prepared with a list of the names and provider numbers of primary care doctors, and dependent dates of birth and Social Security numbers before you log on to fill out the forms.

What about prescription benefits?

The prescription benefit is the same no matter which plan you choose. This benefit is only available at participating pharmacies. Coverage is described on the chart below:

PRESCRIPTION DRUG	PARTICIPATING PHARMACY
All rates are in effect after a $50 deductible is satisfied.	
Tier 1—Retail Generic	$10 for a 30-day supply
Tier 2	$30 for a 30-day supply
Tier 3	$50 for a 30-day supply

ABC HEALTH PLAN COMPARISON

	ABC HMO	ABC PPO	
COVERED SERVICE		**IN NETWORK**	**OUT OF NETWORK**
Primary Care Office Visit Copay	$15	$15	Deductible and Coinsurance
Specialist Office Visit Copay	$30	$30	Deductible and Coinsurance
Routine Adult Preventive Care	No Charge	No Charge	No Charge
Well Child Care (up to age 19)	No Charge	No Charge	No Charge
DXL/Lab Fees	No Charge at Participating Lab	No Charge Participating Lab	Deductible and Coinsurance
Annual Deductible– Individual	None	$500	$1,000
Annual Deductible – Family	None	$1,000	$2,000
Coinsurance	None	90%	70%
Hospital Stays pre-approved or ABC Health contacted within 48 hrs for emergency	$150 Copay Per Incident	Deductible and Coinsurance	Deductible and Coinsurance

Emergency Room	$100 Copay	$100 Copay	$100 Copay
Outpatient Mental Health	50% Copay; 30 visits per calendar year	50% Copay; 30 visits per calendar year	50% Copay; $25 max 30 visits covered per calendar year
Chiropractic Care	$30 Copay	$30 Copay	Deductible and Coinsurance

EMPLOYEE CONTRIBUTION	ABC HMO	ABC PPO
Employee Only	$46.59 per pay period	$65.77 per pay period
Employee Plus Spouse	$272.11 per pay period	$289.22 per pay period
Employee Only	$46.59 per pay period	$65.77 per pay period

BENEFITS THAT PROVIDE ECONOMIC SECURITY

The [Company Name] Life Insurance plan is another cornerstone of you and your family's financial health. ABC Life administers our Group Life, AD & D, and Long-Term Disability coverage.

When do I become eligible for life insurance?

Hourly employees are eligible for life insurance and long-term disability benefits one year after their date of hire. Eligibility for short-term disability begins immediately after your date of hire.

Who pays for these benefits?

The company pays the premiums for all of these benefits.

Do I have to complete enrollment forms for these benefits?

No, you are automatically enrolled in these benefits when you become eligible. You do have to complete a beneficiary form for the life insurance plans.

How do I change my beneficiary?

You can change your beneficiary at any time by completing and submitting a new form to the [Company Name or Department]. Once each year during open enrollment you will be asked to submit an updated form.

Group Life Insurance

The [Company Name] life insurance plan provides a benefit in the event of your death equal to 100% of your annual earnings rounded up to the nearest $1,000. The maximum life insurance benefit under this plan is $75,000.

AD & D Coverage

The Accidental Death and Dismemberment (AD & D) insurance plan provides financial protection for your beneficiary(ies) by paying an additional benefit in the event of your death due to an accident. This benefit is equal to the group life insurance benefit amount.

Disability Insurance

Your short-term disability plan is guided by [California, Hawaii, New Jersey, New York, Puerto Rico, and/or Rhode Island] state requirements. You are eligible to receive [include state criteria] of your earnings up to a maximum of [include state amount] per week after a [include number of days] day waiting period for a disability due to an off-the-job injury or illness.

Under the [Name of State] Law this disability is payable for a maximum of [benefit period, for example 26 weeks—during any 52 consecutive week period].

Once you have been employed by [Company Name] at least one year you are eligible for long-term disability coverage. When an illness or injury causes you to be out of work for more than 90 days you are eligible to receive long-term disability (LTD). This benefit pays for 60% of your earnings with a maximum benefit of $5,000 per month.

How do I apply for disability benefits?

Contact the [Company Name or Department] for the necessary forms. There are portions that you will need to complete, sections for your doctor, and sections that the company completes.

Benefit Days

Are there holidays and holiday pay?

All full-time employees are eligible for paid holidays on the first day of the month after 60 days of employment. An employee will receive one day of compensation at their regular rate of pay for each of the holidays listed below. An employee who works on a holiday will receive holiday pay in addition to his or her regular rate of pay for the day.

List of Holidays:

New Year's Day

Martin Luther King Jr. Day

Presidents' Day

Memorial Day

Labor Day

July 4th

Columbus Day

Thanksgiving

Day after Thanksgiving

Christmas Day

If an employee does not come to work as scheduled the day before, or after, a designated holiday he or she will not be entitled to receive holiday pay. Holiday pay will not be paid to employees who are out of work due to an approved leave of absence.

What about sick days?

All full-time employees are eligible for sick days on the first day of the month after 60 days of employment.

During the first year of employment, full time employees are eligible for sick days according to the following schedule:

Sick Days During the First Year of Service	
After 60 days of employment	1 Day
6 full months after date of hire	2 Days
9 full months after date of hire	2 Days

During the second year of employment, and every year thereafter, employees are eligible for six (6) sick days after their anniversary date.

If an employee is going to be out of work due to illness, he or she is expected to contact the manager of the location where he or she works no later than 7:00 AM. If the illness causes more than one day of absence, employees are expected to call their managers each day unless a leave of absence has been approved. Employees should call the manager themselves. If they are not able to call due to the nature of the illness, an immediate family member should do so.

Unused sick days cannot be carried over after the end of the anniversary year.

Employees who leave the company for any reason will not receive pay for any unused sick days. [Check for applicable requirements to pay unused sick days upon termination.]

How does vacation pay work?

Full-time [Company Name] hourly paid employees begin to earn vacation days after they complete 120 days of employment.

Vacation days are earned according to the following schedule:

Years of Employment	Vacation Earned
0–1	6 days at the rate of 1/2 day per month
2–5	10 days at the rate of 5/6 days per month
6–10	15 days at the rate of 1 1/4 days per month
10 or more years	20 days per year, at the rate of 1 2/3 days per month

An employee who leaves the company after one year of service or more will be paid for any earned unused vacation days. [Check state laws for requirements to pay out unused vacation.]

401(k) Savings Plan

The habit of lifetime savings is an essential, yet often overlooked, component of planning for retirement. [Company Name] encourages employees to save for retirement not only by offering a way for you to put money aside on a pretax basis, but also by making actual contributions to your retirement nest egg.

When am I eligible to participate in the 401(k) Plan?

After you have worked for [Company Name] for one year, and at least 1,000 hours, you can enroll in the plan on the following January 1st or July 1st as long as you are at least 21 years old on the date you enroll. If you decide not to enroll when you are initially eligible, you can enroll on any subsequent January 1st or July 1st.

How much can I contribute into the plan?

The annual maximum contribution is determined by the IRS. For 2010 you may contribute up to $16,500, $22,000 if you are fifty years old or older.

Is there a company match?

Yes the company matches 50% of every dollar of regular contributions into the plan up to 6% of your earnings. For example, if you contribute 3% of your earnings, [Company Name] contributes a matching amount of 1.5% of your earnings.

How is my money vested?

The term vesting refers to the amount of the company contributions that you are eligible to receive if you leave the company. You are always 100% vested in any money that you contribute into the Plan and all of the matching contributions made into the Plan by [Company Name].

How do I enroll?

Complete the enrollment forms provided by [Company Name]. Make sure your investment options add up to 100%.

You must also complete the beneficiary information and sign and date the form. If you need to update your beneficiary, contact the [Company Name or Department] for a form to update this information.

How do I change the percentage of my contribution?

You can always stop your contributions. If you decide to stop your contributions you can begin contributing to the plan again effective any subsequent January 1st or July 1st. Contact the [Company Name or Department] to do this. If you wish to change the percentage of your contribution, you can do this at any time by contacting the [Company Name or Department] for the appropriate form.

I have another 401(k) from a previous employer; can I put this money into my new 401(k) account?

Yes, this is a qualified plan that accepts rollovers from qualified plans. Contact the [Company Name or Department] for the necessary paperwork.

How do I get information after I enroll in the 401(k)?

You will receive regular statements about your account. You can also obtain information by calling ABC at 1–800–111–0000. You will need your PIN number, which you will receive in the mail, and the plan contract number that is located on your statement. Information will also be available at www.abc401(k). info. You will need your PIN and contract number to register to use the Web site.

This Overview includes plan highlights only and is not intended as a comprehensive guide to your benefit plans. The actual delivery of benefits under these plans is controlled by the Summary Plan Descriptions (SPDs) for each benefit plan. You can request copies of SPDs from the company. This information applies to the 2011 Benefits Plan. [Company Name] may change the benefits plan from time to time.

SAMPLE BROKER OF RECORD LETTER

[On Company Letterhead]
[Current Date]
ABC Insurance Carrier
Street Address
City, State, Zip Code

Re: ABC Policy # 1234567

Dear [Name of Contact or to Whom It May Concern]:

This will notify you that effective [date}, our company has appointed [Name of Brokerage] as our Broker of Record for the above named policy. Please copy [Name of Brokerage, with individual and contact details] on all information relating to our contract.

This designation of Broker of Record will remain in effect until we notify you in writing to the contrary. This replaces any previously appointed broker.

Sincerely,

[Signature]

[Company Official Title]

SAMPLE PARTICIPANT HEALTH PLAN BENEFITS WAIVER

[On Company Letterhead]

Employee Name: _____

Date Eligible for Coverage: _____

Date: _____

Department: _____

Position: _____

I hereby waive the right to all medical benefits provided under any [Name of Company] plan. The advantages of the medical benefits have been explained to me, and I willingly decline enrollment because I have coverage from another source.

Signature of Employee: _____

Date: _____

SAMPLE 401(K) AUTOMATIC ENROLLMENT ELECTION—NEW HIRES

To: [Employee Name]

From: Human Resources

Re: Automatic Enrollment in the Employer 401(k) Plan—Notice of Authorization

At [Company Name], we are interested in helping employees save for retirement.

To help our employees save more, our plan:

1. Allows all employees to participate after they have worked for [Company Name] for a year.
2. Has an automatic 401(k) election feature.

Under the plan provisions:

- You will be automatically enrolled in the plan on [enrollment date].

- [Company Name] assumes that you have authorized the company to withhold for each pay period on a pre-tax basis an amount equal to 2% of pay.

- This withholding percentage will remain in effect until the date that you make an election to increase, decrease, or stop your contributions to the plan.

- As a participant, you may make such a change in contributions at any time to be effective beginning on the payroll date after your election notice is received in Human Resources.

- If you are satisfied with the election percentage, sign and date this acknowledgment and return it to Human Resources.

You have the following options:

1. Increase contributions in any amount up to 10% of pay, or
2. Decrease contributions to 1% of pay, or
3. Stop contributions effective _____, or
4. Continue contributions as stated above.

Fill out the attached 401(k) change form if you wish to choose option 1, 2, or 3.

All withheld pay deferrals (and company matching contributions) will be invested in the (name of the fund or investment vehicle) until otherwise instructed. For 20__, the company match is 20% of employee contributions up to 5% of pay and is subject to a vesting schedule.

I certify that I have received and read this automatic enrollment notification and understand that I have the right to make alternative contributions and investment fund selections within one payroll period of my providing such notice to Human Resources.

_____ Signature

_____ Date

Typical Request for Proposal Content for a 401(k)

A cover letter outlining project schedule—include a high-level timetable for review, conversion, and implementation.

Response time—one week to let you know if they intend to respond, but allow three to four weeks for them to complete the full RFP.

Specific information about your company—complexity of account, size of assets, number of employees, locations, systems, such as multiple, integrated, or stand-alone.

A request for vendor information:

- Types of investments they handle
- Range of fund selection.
- Your company stock—assure the vendor can properly handle.
- Self-directed brokerage accounts—some employees want to access more than one family of funds.
- Lifestyle funds—tailored mutual funds based on the risk tolerance of the investor. (These funds have increasing popularity as they reduce the amount of decision making the investor must make.)
- Bundled (one vendor does everything) or unbundled (different vendors handle various aspects of the account)

The trustee arrangement—who they use, how it is handled.

System capabilities and hardware requirements—this can be a major expense in time and money if not assessed properly.

Blackout period—this is the time when accounts are reconciled and assets are transferred. Try to minimize the amount of this blackout period as this is also when employees cannot access their accounts.

Recordkeeping and reporting cycles:

- Is there daily processing of transactions, which allows for quickest handling of loans, withdrawals, terminations, fund exchange confirmations?

- Do they provide full participant transaction services?
- 24/7 coverage.
- Web-based, Internet.
- Voice response system (VRS—review the vendor's standard VRS, as tailoring a script can be costly.
- Multilingual capability—for customer service as well as other written communications.
- Participant statements—request samples and compare these to what you have now or want in the future.
- Management reporting—state desired frequency and ask for samples.
- Fund performance—request vendor history against industry indices.

Communication—How much will the vendor provide and at which locations, during the introduction? This expense should be part of the implementation project cost.

Education—How much, and how often, will the vendor provide written or live communication/education regarding the plan? Ask for samples of the written material they have available. Writing your own communication is time-consuming, expensive, and potentially increases your legal liability if not done properly.

Performance Guarantees—Establish a few that you want a vendor to agree to in the RFP such as:

- Transaction confirmation time
- Statement mailing schedule
- Processing of withdrawals and loans within specific amount of time

Fees and Charges—You cannot ask enough questions on this subject.

- What will be charged for the conversion and implementation?
- How are the administrative charges imposed—basis points, per capita, fixed dollar?

Size of Account

- Find out whether you will be a small, medium, or large account for the vendor. If you are small, your service requests may suffer. If you are a large account, your vendor may not be able to keep up with your requests.

Compliance—What is included in the administration fee and what is an extra cost?

- Nondiscrimination testing
- Government reporting
- Plan documents—initial draft, ongoing changes

References—This is a worthwhile and often enlightening activity. Ask for:

- A couple of new customers—discuss their conversions experience.
- A couple of ongoing customers—discuss what is working well.
- Ask for the name of a client they recently lost.

Client Retention—What is their retention rate?

Customer Satisfaction—Do they conduct customer satisfaction surveys? If so, how were their services rated? What was their poorest score and what have they done to correct it?

Employee Survey—Wellness Program

[Company Name] is planning to implement a wellness initiative to respond to the needs of our employees. Please answer the following questions by checking the box next to your preferred answer to help us design our wellness program.

1. I would buy healthy snacks at work if they are available. Instead of candy, chips, cookies, and cupcakes, I would appreciate low-fat yogurt, dried fruit, nuts, fresh fruit, and pretzels.

   ☐ Definitely

   ☐ Sometimes

   ☐ Once in a while

   ☐ Never

2. If healthy snacks were available in a bowl or basket with low prices to be paid for on an honor system charging between 50 cents and $1, would you . . .

   ☐ Be more likely to buy healthy snacks?

   ☐ Continue to use the vending machine or go to a nearby convenience store for snacks?

   ☐ Keep bringing snacks from home?

   ☐ I don't snack at work.

3. Which of the following activities or groups would you participate in with coworkers if they were offered before the day, during lunch, or after work? (Check all that apply.)

   ☐ Walking   ☐ Meditation

   ☐ Volleyball   ☐ Cycling

   ☐ Stretching   ☐ Nutrition

   ☐ Running   ☐ Weight/resistance training

   ☐ Weight loss

☐ Hiking   ☐ Cooking

☐ Yoga   ☐ None of these

4. What's the best way to reach you with wellness information? (check one)

    ☐ A dedicated wellness bulletin board

    ☐ Weekly email tips

    ☐ Flyers distributed on payday

    ☐ On the company intranet

    ☐ At staff meetings

5. Do you feel that you get enough exercise to stay healthy?

    ☐ Yes

    ☐ No

    ☐ Don't know

6. Do you eat as well as you can to maintain optimum nutrition and health?

    ☐ Yes

    ☐ No

    ☐ Don't know

7. During the past year did you decide to make a significant lifestyle change related to better health such as weight loss, smoking cessation, or increasing exercise?

    ☐ Yes, but I did not carry through and have not been successful.

    ☐ I tried but only stuck to it for six months.

    ☐ I started my plan and am still carrying through and reaching my goals.

    ☐ No, I did not embark on any plan for change.

8. Do you think that good nutrition and regular exercise can help you be more productive at work?

    ☐ Yes

    ☐ No

(Continued)

9. If you were trying to make a healthy lifestyle change would you be more likely to embark on a routine by yourself or in a group?

   ☐ I'm more likely to be successful with a group, friends, or coworkers.

   ☐ I'm better at a program all by myself.

   ☐ I'm not sure.

   ☐ I don't need to make any lifestyle changes.

10. Would you be more likely to participate in a wellness program if there are incentives or you have a chance to win prizes?

    ☐ Most likely yes

    ☐ Probably not

11. Do you have any expertise in wellness-related activities that you could share?

    ☐ Yes

    ☐ No

    If yes, please describe _____

12. What items would you like to see in a workplace wellness information center? (Check all that apply.)

    ☐ Books

    ☐ Cookbooks or recipes

    ☐ Videos

    ☐ I would not access any of these things.

13. Would you be willing to join the company wellness committee?

    ☐ Yes

    ☐ No

Please add any additional recommendations for our wellness activities.

COBRA Administration Checklist

Employee Name _____

Type of Qualifying Event _____

Qualifying Event Date _____

COBRA Start Date _____

COBRA End Date _____

COBRA Administrative Task	Date	Completed by
1 Mail initial notification letter		
2 Mail spouse/dependent initial notification letter		
3 Notify all insurers of cancellation of coverage		
4 Advise providers of qualifying event		
5 Mail COBRA Qualifying Event Notice and Election Form to former employee *and* to former employee's dependents (spouse, children)		
6 Receive signed COBRA Election Form		
7 Receive initial COBRA premium (within 45 days from date of election)		
8 Reactivate qualified former employee and/or beneficiaries coverage with insurer(s)		
9 Terminate COBRA coverage		

It is recommended that:

1. This form be completed and kept in the employee benefit file.
2. Copies of all letters, forms, and related documentation be attached to this checklist.
3. First-class mail sent certified with a return receipt requested be used to mail notification (returned certified mail can be used to verify nonreceipt of notification).
4. Retain all COBRA correspondence in a separate COBRA folder or employee benefits file; do not include in personnel file.

RECRUIT RIGHT With more than twenty years of expertise **Rebecca Mazin** formed Recruit Right to create usable solutions for employers to meet increasingly complicated human resources challenges. Rebecca's clients benefit from clear guidance, tools, and techniques that quickly cut through fads, jargon, and complex regulatory issues. Recruit Right's consulting, training, and written materials produce measurable results in a range of businesses impacting organizations from small start-ups to industry giants.

Rebecca is the coauthor of *The HR Answer Book: An Indispensable Guide for Managers and Human Resources Professionals* published by AMACOM. Her advice and commentary appear in business publications, industry and trade journals, and is featured in *The HR Answer Blog* on the award-winning www.AllBusiness.com Web site. Follow Rebecca on Twitter at @thehranswer.

Prior to founding Recruit Right, Rebecca held key management positions at major organizations. Experience with Millennium Hotels and Hyatt Hotels Corporation built on work at Owens Corning and for the federal government at the National Labor Relations Board.

Rebecca is a graduate of Cornell University with a degree in labor relations. She is a certified facilitator of Achieve Global training programs. Rebecca is active in the community, using her skills and talents to enhance organizational effectiveness and outcomes.

Index

A

AARP's Best Employers for Workers Over 50, 2

Accidental Death and Dismemberment (AD&D) insurance, 139

Actual Deferral Percentage (ADP) test, 132

Adoption assistance, 155

AFLAC plan, 149

Americans with Disabilities Act (ADA), 44, 187

ASO (administrative services), 70

Asset-based fees [401(k) plans], 133

Average Contribution Percentage (ACP) test, 132

B

Beneficiaries: 401(k) plans, 126–127; group term life insurance, 140–141

Benefit education: broker-provided, 92–93; on ER visits alternatives, 189; HDHP (high-deductible health plans), 64–66; on increased costs or plan changes, 48–49; scheduling meetings for overnight shift employees, 51; taking enough time for effective, 65; throughout the year, 50–51. *See also* Employees

Benefits: additional types of employer-paid, 154–161; calculating your, 5–6; company closure and, 178–179; comparing competitive employers,' 3–5; deals/discounts on products and services, 161–162; death of employee and, 179; eligibility for, 6–10; facilitating savings, 153–154; food services, 162–163; group life insurance and disability, 137–146; planning for

renewals, 188–190; recruitment and retention role of, 2–3; surveys and focus groups on, 72, 93; tax credits for, 95–110; tuition assistance programs, 104–108; understanding how to spend your, 5–6; voluntary, 148–153. *See also* Employee benefits brokers; Health benefits; Retirement plans

Benefits costs: checking the bills to control, 190–191; communication to employees to control, 192–193; dependent eligibility audit to control, 191–192; employee cost sharing to control, 182–185; how to begin controlling, 193; increasing interest in controlling, 181; planning for renewals to control, 188–190; wellness programs to control, 185–188

Benefits eligibility: auditing dependents,' 191–192; benefits philosophy written statement on, 9–10; changes in status that trigger changes in, 52–53; for employee's domestic partner, 8–9; of extended family, 9; for federal holiday benefits, 28; group term life insurance, 138; of part-time employees, 6–7; PPACA on full-time employee, 6; sick days, 30–31; start time for coverage, 7–8; triggering COBRA, 168, 169, 170; tuition assistance, 105; unemployment insurance (UI), 13; vacation policies, 18–19, 21; waiting periods for health coverage, 8

Benefits enrollment: adding dependent, 45; benefits handbook provided after, 42–43; broker-provided forms for, 92; for COBRA coverage, 168–170; components

Benefits enrollment (*Continued*)
of an effective, 40–41; efficient processing of, 43–44; employee handbooks
provided during, 41–42; 401(k) plan
and automatic, 119–120; life cycle events
impacting, 45–46; management of
records, 44; open window of opportunity
for, 46–52; sign ups, 39–41

Benefits enrollment components: Benefits
Overview, 40; PPACA requirements
adhered to, 41; provide detailed
information and contracts, 40; schedule
introductory meetings, 40; use variety of
communications methods, 40

Benefits handbook: description and functions
of, 42–43; FAQs (Frequently Asked Questions) in, 42. *See also* Employee handbooks

Benefits philosophy, 9–10

Benefits strategy: functions of a, 1–2; three
questions to ask about your, 2–6

Benefits strategy questions: 1: what role do
benefits ply in recruitment and retention?,
2–3; 2: what benefits are offered by
employers in same industry or geographic
area?, 3–5; 3: how much can you spend
now and in the future?, 5–6

Bereavement leave, 34

Best Small & Medium Companies to Work
for in America, 2

Better forgotten tips: approving non-
routine dental procedures, 77; benefits
documents with wrong employee name,
43; clarifying life insurance notification requirements, 141; COBRA
administrator failure to service account,
174; confusing renewal dates, 50;
defining full- or part-time employees, 7;
double-checking information sent out to
employees, 114; EAP confidentiality, 159;
identifying all requirements for 401(k)
distribution, 176; inadequate broker
service, 85; new baby not enrolled with
HMO, 45; providing clear information
on benefits, 41; up-to-date life insurance
beneficiaries, 141; vacation accumulation
policies, 25; weekend warriors workers' compensation injuries, 12; written
acknowledgement of vacation, 22.
See also Worth repeating tips

Bicycle commute tax credit, 102–103

Birthdays, 35

BLS (Bureau of Labor Statistics): on
average vacation days, 18; comparative
information on medical plans costs, 48;
on employee benefits/wages percentages, 5–6; 401(k) plan statistics by, 116;
National Compensation Survey by, 183

C

Cafeteria (Section 125) tax credits, 96

Cancer or critical illness insurance, 194

Cash balance plans, 114–115

Child-care benefits, 155

CHIP (Child Health Insurance Program),
72

CLASS (Community Living Assistance
Services and Supports) Act, 151

COBRA: broker administration of, 93,
172–174; company closure and eligibility
for, 178–179; for dependents of deceased
employee, 179; description of, 166; health
care premium of, 48; HSA payments
for premiums of, 62; offered to laid-off
employees, 52; offering reimbursement of
expenses of, 8; providing employees information on, 43. *See also* Federal legislation;
Former employees; Health benefits

COBRA basics: dental plan and, 170;
eligibility for subsidy, 171–172; employer
exemption from, 166–167; Model
COBRA Continuation Coverage Election
Notice, 169; Notice of Early Termination
of COBRA, 171; outsourcing administration, 93, 172–174; payment responsibility,
170–171; qualifying events, 168, 169;
required "General Notice of COBRA
Rights," 167–168; severance package and
start of COBRA, 170; signing up for
coverage through, 168–170; violations
of, 172

College counseling programs, 156, 157

Communication: benefits education on
HDHPs, 64–66; benefits education
throughout year, 50–51; benefits
enrollment using different modes of, 40;
clarifying medical plan coverage, 80;
double-checking information sent out
to employees, 114; example of creative
benefits, 47; on Health costs value to
employees, 183; helping to control benefit
costs through, 192–193; importance
of clear paid time off, 38; on increased
costs or plan changes, 48–49; providing clear information on COBRA, 167;
providing disability coverage information
and, 144–145; scheduling meetings for
overnight shift employees, 51. *See also*
Information

Community Living Assistance Services and
Supports (CLASS) Act, 151

Concierge services, 156–157

Confidentiality, 159

Consumer-directed health care: description of, 58–59; FSA (Flexible Spending
Account), 63; HDHP combined with

HSAs (health savings accounts), 59–60; HDHP (high-deductible health plans), 59; HRAs (Health Reimbursement Arrangements), 63–64, 65, 78; HSAs (health savings accounts), 59–63, 64, 65, 78
Consumer-driven health plans (CDHP), 59
Copayments (medical plan), 184
Cost sharing: contributing toward premiums, 182–184; increasing copayments and deductibles, 184–185
Credit unions, 153–154

D
DB (defined benefit) plans: cash balance plan, 114–115; DB(k) plans, 115–116; pension plans, 112–114
DB(k) plans, 115–116
Deals/discounts programs, 161–162
Death of employee, 179
Deductibles (medical plan), 184
Defined contribution plans, 116. *See also* 401(k) plans
Dental discount programs, 78
Dental plan components: best practices in oral health coverage, 76; major restorative care, 75–76; orthodontia, 76; preventive care, 75; restorative care, 75
Dental plan types: DHMO or DMOs, 74, 76, 77; hybrid DMO and PPO, 74–75; PPOs (Preferred Provider Organizations), 74, 76
Dental plans: COBRA and inclusion of, 170; components of, 75–78; eligibility of laid-off employees, 52; tips on selecting, 77; types of, 73–75; UCR (usual, customary, and reasonable) coverage, 75. *See also* Medical plans
Department of Labor: COBRA violations investigated by, 172; Employee Benefits Security Administration (EBSA), 167–168
Dependent care tax credit: FSA Dependent Care Accounts versus, 98–102; selecting either FSA tax credit or, 101
Dependents: adding new, 45, 46; auditing eligibility of, 191–192; child-care benefits, 155; COBRA and 401(k) distributions to deceased employee, 179; domestic partners, 8–9; elder care consultation and referral benefit, 149; Emergency Back-up Dependent Care, 157–158; extended family members, 9; HSA payment for medical expenses of, 62; life insurance coverage for, 139–140; PPACA provision for coverage to age 26 of, 192. *See also* Employees
Diabetic employees, 188

Disability coverage: FMLA and, 145; LTD (Long-Term Disability), 143–144; providing employees information on, 144–145; setting up, 145–146; STD (Short-Term Disability), 14, 142–143
Discrimination: against same-sex domestic partners, 9; nondiscrimination testing of 401(k) plans, 132–133; vacation policies and risk of, 19; wellness programs potential for, 187
Disease management programs, 187–188
Dixon Schwabl, 2
Documentation: broker of record letter, 89; broker-provided enrollment forms, 92; controlling costs by checking the bills, 190–191; employee benefits files of former employee, 177–178; federal legislation on medical information, 44; 5500 Form, 16, 92, 163; SPDs (Summary Plan Descriptions), 15–16, 42, 43, 53, 167–168
Domestic partners: avoiding discrimination against same-sex, 9; benefits eligibility of, 8–9

E
Economic stimulus legislation (2009), 102, 171–172
Educational classes programs, 155–156
Elder care consultation and referral, 149
Elective deferral, 51–52
Eligibility. *See* Benefits eligibility
Emergency Back-up Dependent Care, 157–158
Employee Assistance Programs (EAPs), 155, 158–159
Employee benefits broker relationship: broker of record letter designating, 89; communication frequency during, 89–90; when to rotate, 90
Employee benefits broker services: benchmarking, 92; benefits brochures, 91–92; COBRA administration, 93, 172–174; compliance and reporting, 92; customized Web portals, 91, 92; employee and beneficiary education, 92–93; employee surveys and focus groups, 93; enrollment forms, 92; mergers and acquisitions, 93; renegotiating benefits costs, 93; setting up group term life and disability coverage, 145–146; tasks included in, 90–91
Employee benefits brokers: checking references, 87–88; description of, 83; finding a, 84–88; getting competing bids from, 94; inadequate service by, 85; obtaining coverage without a, 83–84; planning renewal process with your, 188–190; questions to ask a potential, 86–87; when to change, 90. *See also* Benefits

Employee Benefits Security Administration (EBSA), 167–168

Employee cost sharing: contributing toward premiums, 182–184; increasing copayments and deductibles, 184–185

Employee handbooks: limitations of, 41; types of information found in, 42. *See also* Benefits handbooks

Employee Pension Benefit Plans, 15

Employee product discounts, 161

Employee referral bonuses, 159

Employee Welfare Benefit Plan, 15

Employee-sponsored retirement plans. *See* Retirement plans

Employees: average vacation days for full-time, 18; benefits enrollment of new, 39–44; benefits for part-time, 6–7; benefits strategy role in engaging, 2–3; bonus paid for declining health benefits, 184; cost sharing by, 182–185; coverage under spouse's plan or Medicare, 46; death of active, 179; diabetic, 188; exempt from overtime, 23; paid time off for, 17–38; PPACA's definition of full-time, 6; required COBRA notification to, 167–168; responsibilities for notification of life events, 45, 46; retired, 62–63, 123–125; scheduling meetings for overnight shift, 51; survey on benefits requested by, 72. *See also* Benefit education; Dependents; Former employees

Employers: caution against matching benefits of competitive, 4; comparing benefits of competitive, 3–5; controlling benefits costs, 181–193; exempt from COBRA, 166–167; 401(k) plan contributions by, 120–121; percentage of premium made for by, 184; worker's compensation cost savings to, 11

EPOs (Exclusive Provider Organizations), 56

ERISA (Employee Retirement Income Security Act): confirming benefit compliance with, 163; description of, 14; Employee Pension Benefit Plans under, 15; Employee Welfare Benefit Plan under, 15; 5500 Form required by, 16, 92, 163; on 401(k) plan fees, 133; nonqualified retirement plan not in compliance with, 135; Pension Benefits Guarantee Corporation (PBGC) established by, 113–114; SPDs (Summary Plan Descriptions) required by, 15–16, 42, 43, 53, 167–168; vacation policies and discrimination violations under, 19; wellness programs violations of, 187. *See also* Federal legislation

Extended family coverage, 9

F

Facilitating savings programs: college savings through 529 plans, 153; credit unions, 153–154; Payroll Savings Plan to buy U.S. Savings Bonds, 154; preferred banking arrangements, 154

Fair Labor Standards Act (FLSA), 23

Family events, 35

Family Medical Leave Act (FMLA), 31, 44, 52, 145

Federal holiday policies, 27–29

Federal legislation: Americans with Disabilities Act (ADA), 44, 187; Community Living Assistance Services and Supports (CLASS) Act, 151; economic stimulus, 102, 171–172; on employees exempt from overtime, 23; Family Medical Leave Act (FMLA), 31, 44, 52, 145; Genetic Information Nondiscrimination Act (GINA), 44; health reform changes to, 10–11; HIPAA (Health Insurance Portability and Accountability Act), 187, 189; Pension Protection Act (PPA), 113, 115, 122; sick days and lack of, 14; unemployment insurance (UI), 12–13; workers' compensation, 11–12. *See also* COBRA; ERISA (Employee Retirement Income Security Act); PPACA (Patient Protection and Affordable Care Act); State requirements

5500 Form, 16, 92, 163

501(C)(3) tax exempt status, 160

529 plans, 153

Flat rate fees [401(k) plans], 133

Flu shots, 61, 71

Focus groups, 93

Food services, 162–163

Foosball, 162

Former employees: COBRA eligibility and severance package of, 170; converting other benefits available to, 177; dental plan eligibility of, 52; 401(k) plan rollovers and distributions to, 123–125, 175–177; FSAs (Flexible Spending Accounts) claims by, 174–175; maintaining cordial relationship with, 180; maintaining employee benefits files of, 177–178; portability of HSAs for, 62–63. *See also* COBRA; Employees; Retired employees

Fortune 100 Best Companies to Work For, 2

401(k) plans: allowable employee contributions to, 117–119; automatic enrollment into, 119–120; beneficiaries of, 126–127; choosing a provider for, 127–129; company closure and, 179; description of, 116; distribution to dependents of deceased employee, 179; elective deferral enrollment in, 51–52; employer contributions to, 120–121; as exception to employee eligibility, 7; fees associated with, 133–134; four basic steps required to adopt, 116–117; hardship withdrawal from, 125; investment education provided for, 122–123; investment options for, 121–122; loan provisions of, 125–126; management of information on, 44; nondiscrimination testing of, 132–133; open enrollment for, 51–52; QDRO (qualified domestic relation order) to divide, 126; rollovers, distributions, and withdrawals of, 123–125, 175–177; Roth 401(k), 131–132; Safe Harbor, 130–131; SIMPLE (Savings Investment Match Plan), 129, 130; timing of deposits to, 121; video communication about, 119. *See also* Defined contribution plans

401(k) vendors: choosing a, 127–129; operating fees of, 133–134

FSA Dependent Care Accounts: assessing value of participation in, 101–102; child-and elder-care expenses coverage by, 99–100; claims submitted by former employees, 174–175; Dependent Care Tax Credit versus, 101; description of, 98–99; limitations to, 100–101

FSA (Flexible Spending Account): Dependent Care Accounts, 98–102; description of, 96; health care expenditure category of, 96–98; HRAs offered alongside a, 63

FSA health benefits: description of, 96–97; key points of, 97–98; PPACA elimination of over-the-counter medications payments using, 98; PPACA limits to contributions to, 97

Full-time employees: average vacation days for, 18; importance of defining, 7; paid time off for, 17–37; PPACA definition of, 6

FUTA (Federal Unemployment) payroll tax, 109–110

G

"General Notice of COBRA Rights," 167–168

Genetic Information Nondiscrimination Act (GINA), 44

Great Place to Work Institute, 2

Group purchasing power, 161–162

Group term life insurance: AD&D insurance paired with, 139; administration of, 141; beneficiary designations, 140–141; description, cost, eligibility for, 137–138; distributions to deceased employee dependents, 179; formula for determining coverage amounts, 138–139; setting up, 145–146; supplemental and dependent life insurance, 139–140. *See also* Voluntary benefits

H

HDHP (high-deductible health plans): description of, 59; employee education on, 64–66; HSAs paired with, 59–60; preventative care covered by, 62

Health advocates, 68–69

Health benefits: bonus paid to employees declining, 184; coordinating spouse's plan or Medicare with, 46; dental plans, 52, 73–78, 170; for employee's domestic partner, 8–9; enrolling new dependent, 45; for extended family members, 9; Form W-2 inclusion of value, 183; FSA (Flexible Spending Account), 63, 96–98; PPACA coverage changes due to health care reform, 10–11; vision plans, 78–81; waiting periods for, 8. *See also* Benefits; COBRA; Medical plans

Health care reform: Essential Health Benefits under, 71; impacting health benefits, 10–11. *See also* PPACA (Patient Protection and Affordable Care Act)

HIPAA (Health Insurance Portability and Accountability Act), 187, 189

HMO (Health Maintenance Organizations), 56–57

Holiday closure policies, 27–29

Holiday pay rates, 28–29

HRAs (Health Reimbursement Arrangements): description of, 63; end of year rollover of, 64; how medical payments are covered by, 63; HSA compared to, 64

HSAs (health savings accounts): contributions made to, 60; dental expenses paid from, 78; end of year rollover of, 62; HDHP combined with, 59–60; how medical expenses are paid, 61–62; HRA compared to, 64; making withdrawals for nonmedical expenses, 63; portability of, 62–63; set up as interest-bearing, 60; tax advantages of, 61

I

Identity Theft Protection, 150

Income tax withholding, 109–110

Indemnity plans, 55–56

Information: benefit education providing, 48–51, 64–66; double-checking what is sent out to employees, 114; federal legislation on medical, 44; PHI (protected health information), 71; providing clear COBRA, 167; providing employees with disability coverage, 144–145. *See also* Communication

Insurance: disability coverage, 142–146; group term life insurance, 137–142, 145–146, 179; UI (unemployment insurance), 6, 11, 12–13

International Vacation deprivation Survey, 24
IRAs (Individual Retirement Accounts): description of, 111, 134; HSA account set up with trustee approved for, 59; three types of, 134–135
IRS (Internal Revenue Service): COBRA violations investigated by, 172; Educational Assistance Plan guidelines of, 108; fair market value of life insurance policy formula of, 139; 5500 Form required by, 16, 92, 163; 501(C)(3) tax exempt status, 160; 401(k) plan rules of the, 116, 123; nonqualified retirement plan not in compliance with, 135; special tax rules for various types of benefits, 109–110; tax penalty for HSA nonmedical withdrawals by, 63. See also Tax credits

J
January 1st start dates, 49–50
Jury duty policy, 32–34

L
Laid-off employees. See Former employees
Laser vision correction coverage, 80
Leave sharing bank, 25–26
Life event changes, 45–46
Life insurance. See Group term life insurance
Long-term care insurance, 151
Long-Term Disability (LTD), 143–144

M
"Make It Happen Day," 2
Matching gift programs, 159–160
Medicaid programs, 72
Medical plan components: copayments and deductibles, 184–185; coverage, 66; health advocates, 68–69; medical tourism, 66–67; prescription drug benefits, 67–68; self-funded versus fully insured, 69–70
Medical plan options: EPOs (Exclusive Provider Organizations), 56; HMO (Health Maintenance Organizations), 56–57; out-of-network coinsurance, 57; POS (Point of Service), 58; PPOs (Preferred Provider Organizations), 57; UCR (usual, customary, and reasonable) rates provision of, 58
Medical plans: BLS comparative information on, 48; choosing a, 71–72; communicating increased costs/changes to, 48–49; components of, 66–71; consumer-directed health care type of, 58–66; eligibility for state Medicaid, 72; employee nonparticipation in, 78; indemnity plans, 55–56; mini-medical, 70–71; options for, 56–58; prescription drug benefits, 67–68; self-

funded versus fully insured, 69–70. See also Health benefits
Medical plans. See Health benefits
Medical tourism coverage, 66–67
Medicare coverage, 46
Medicare payroll tax, 109–110
Mergers & Acquisitions, 93
Mini-medical plan, 70–71
Model COBRA Continuation Coverage Election Notice, 169
Mortgage assistance, 160–161

N
National Compensation Survey (BLS), 183
National Credit Union Administration (NCUA), 154
NetApp, 35
Notice of Early Termination of COBRA, 171

O
Online benefits enrollment, 43
Open enrollment: benefits education throughout year/not limited to, 50–51; checklist for a more effective, 47; common mistakes to avoid, 49; communicating increased costs or plan changes, 48–49; description of period for, 46; exceptions to, 46; 401(k) plans, 51–52; start dates for, 49–50
Orthodontia benefit, 76
Out-of-network coinsurance, 57
Overtime exempted employees, 23

P
Paid time off: bereavement leave, 34; birthdays and family events, 35; converting to Paid Time Off (PTO), 36–37; holidays, 27–29; importance of communication related to, 38; jury duty, 32–34; for part-time employees, 37–38; sick days, 29–32; time off to vote, 34–35; vacations, 17–27
Paid Time Off (PTO) policy, 36–37
Part-time employees: employee benefits of, 6–7; importance of defining, 7; paid time off for, 37–38
Partial days vacation, 23
Payroll deduction IRAs, 134
Payroll Savings Plan, 154
Payroll taxes: FUTA (Federal Unemployment), 109–110; income tax withholding, 109–110; IRS special rules for various types of benefits, 109–110; Social Security and Medicare, 109–110
Pension Benefits Guarantee Corporation (PBGC), 113–114
Pension plans: employer pros and cons related to, 112–113; PBGC regulations

for, 113–114; QDRO (qualified domestic relation order) to divide, 126
Pension Protection Act (PPA), 113, 115, 122
PEPM (per employee per month), 71
Per person charges [401(k) plans], 133
Personal property insurance, 150
Pet insurance, 151–152
Pharmacy Benefits Managers (PBMs), 67
PHI (protected health information), 71
Ping-pong tables, 162
POS (Point of Service) plans, 58
PPACA (Patient Protection and Affordable Care Act): cafeteria (Section 125) tax credits provision in, 95–96; coverage for dependents up to age 26 provision of, 192; coverage requirements of, 66; Form W-2 inclusion of health benefits value requirement of, 183; FSA changes under, 97, 98; full-time status eligibility by, 6; on health care reform impacting, 10–11; on health coverage waiting periods, 8; long-term care coverage changes under, 151; mini-med plan compliance with, 70–71; minimum coverage without cost sharing provision of, 184; wellness programs provision of, 186. *See also* Federal legislation; Health care reform
PPOs (Preferred Provider Organizations): dental plans, 74–75, 76; medical plans, 57
Preferred banking arrangements, 154
Premiums: comparing how cost sharing affects, 185; employee contributions toward, 182–183; employer percentage of, 184
Prepaid legal services, 152
Prescription drug benefits, 67–68
Preventative medical care: flu shots as, 61, 71; HDHPs structured to cover, 62
PTO (Paid Time OFF) policy, 17
Public transportation tax credit, 103–104

Q

QDRO (qualified domestic relation order), 126
Qualifying event (COBRA), 168, 169

R

Recruitment of employees, 2–3
Referral bonuses, 159
Retention of employees, 2–3
Retired employees: 401(k) plan rollovers/distributions to, 123–125; portability of HSAs for, 62–63. *See also* Former employees
Retirement plans: DB (defined benefit), 111, 112–116; DC (defined contribution), 111, 116–134; federal law governing employee-sponsored, 7; how to choose, 135; IRAs (Individual Retirement Arrangements), 59, 111, 134–135; nonqualified, 135; three basic formats of employer-sponsored, 111–112. *See also* Benefits
Roth 401(k) plans, 131–132

S

Safe Harbor 401(k) plans, 130–131
Same-sex domestic partners, 9
Section 125 tax credits (PPACA), 96
SEP plans, 134
Series EE and I savings bonds, 154
Severance package/COBRA eligibility, 170
Short-Term Disability (STD), 14, 142–143
Sick days policy: converting into Paid Time Off (PTO) policy, 36–37; determining number of sick days, 29–30; four specific issues to review for, 30–32; lack of federal requirements on sick day payments, 14; unused sick days when employee leaves, 32
SIMPLE IRA plan, 134–135
SIMPLE (Savings Investment Match Plan) 401(k) plan, 129, 130
Social Security payroll taxes, 109–110
SPDs (Summary Plan Descriptions): description of, 15–16; employee handbooks information on, 42; ERISA mandate on, 15–16, 43; "General Notice of COBRA Rights" included in, 167–168; limited ability to communicate information by, 53
Spouse's health benefits, 46
State requirements: allowing time off to vote, 34–35; COBRA coverage, 167; eligibility for state Medicaid programs, 72; on leave sharing bank program, 26; on Paid Time Off (PTO) policies, 37; Short-Term Disability (STD), 14; on unused vacations when employees leave, 26–27; on vacation accumulations, 24–25. *See also* Federal legislation
Supplemental life insurance, 139–140
Surveys: benefits requested on employee, 72; broker-provided benefits, 93

T

Tax credits: Dependent Care Tax Credit, 101; FSA Dependent Care category, 98–102; FSA health care expenditure category, 96–98; IRS special rules for various types of benefits, 109–110; PPACA cafeteria (Section 125) tax credits, 95–96; transportation benefits, 102–104; tuition assistance, 108. *See also* IRS (Internal Revenue Service)
Terminated employees. *See* Former employees
Third-party administrators (TPAs), 172–174

Time off to vote policy, 34–35

TPA (third-party administrator), 70

Transaction based costs [401(k) plans], 133

Transportation benefits: for commuting by bicycle, 102–103; for public transportation commuting, 103–104

Treasury Inflation-Protected Securities (TIPS), 154

TreasuryDirect, 154

Tuition assistance programs: eligibility for, 105; payment processes for, 106–107; purpose of, 104–105; tax credit through, 108; types of classes covered, 105–106

U

UCR (usual, customary, and reasonable): dental coverage, 75; medical coverage, 58

Unemployment insurance (UI): calculating your, 6; eligibility for, 13; federal legislation mandates on, 11; outsourcing claims management of, 13; understanding federal mandate on, 12–13

United States Bureau of Labor Statistics. *See* BLS (Bureau of Labor Statistics)

Universal enrollment form, 44

U.S. Department of Labor: COBRA violations investigated by, 172; Employee Benefits Security Administration (EBSA) of, 167–168

U.S. Savings Bonds, 154

V

Vacation policies: allowing partial days vacation, 23–24; BLS data on averages for, 18; converting into Paid Time Off (PTO) policy, 36–37; eligibility tailored to groups of staff, 18–19; example of vacation earnings and eligibility, 20–21; on how vacation days are earned, 19–20; issues to consider when creating, 17–18; leave sharing bank, 25–26; PTO (Paid Time OFF), 17; on timing of vacations, 21–22; on unused vacations when employees leave, 26–27; "use it or lose it," 25; on vacation accumulation, 24–25; on when employees can take vacations, 20; written acknowledgment as part of, 22

Vision plans: chain store discount program, 79; costs of, 80–81; description of coverage, 79–80; giveaways included with, 79; laser vision correction coverage, 80

Voluntary benefits: cancer or critical illness insurance, 149; description of, 148; elder care consultation and referral, 149; Identity Theft Protection, 150; insurance to cover personal property, 150; long-term care insurance, 151; making decision to offer, 152–153; pet insurance, 151–152; prepaid legal services, 152. *See also* Group term life insurance

Volunteer Time Off (VTO) program, 35

Voting policy, 34–35

W

Wellness programs: benefits of, 185; disease management and, 187–188; employee decisions about participating in, 186; legal issues related to, 187; on-site nurse and wellness coordinator, 188; PPACA impact on, 186; weight loss and exercise programs, 186–187

Workers' compensation: calculating your, 6; for company-sponsored soccer team injuries, 12; employer cost savings on, 11; federal legislation mandates on, 11–12; funding of, 11

Worth repeating tips: annual costs of 5500 reporting, 16; annual surveys evaluating benefit programs, 72; benefit costs renegotiated by brokers, 93; broker auditing of client bills, 91; caution against matching benefits with competitors, 4; clarifying medical plan coverage, 80; creating a consistent vacation policy, 26; creative benefits communications, 47; customized benefits Web site, 92; educational campaign on ER visits alternatives, 189; employee votes on benefit package, 148; employer contributions to 401(k) plan, 120; engineering master's degree tuition reimbursements, 105; flu shot coverage, 61; individual state PPOs plans, 69; investment education provided for 401(k) plans, 123; just-in-time college counseling, 157; lowering LTD premiums, 144; "Make It Happen Day" and ice cream treats, 2; managers who understand health benefits plan, 68; Memorial Day pay policy, 29; "Miles of Smiles" discount program, 162; on-site flu shots, 71; on-site nurse and wellness coordinator, 188; outsourcing unemployment insurance claims, 13; providing clear information on COBRA, 167; REI challenge Grant program, 156; scheduling meetings for overnight shift employees, 51; Seventh Generation's energy savings program, 160; taking enough time for explaining health plans, 65; value of vacation request rules, 23; verifying correct address of leaving employees, 166; video communication about 401(k) plans, 119; vision plans giveaways, 79; Volunteer Time Off (VTO) program, 35. *See also* Better forgotten tips

Pfeiffer Publications Guide

This guide is designed to familiarize you with the various types of Pfeiffer publications. The formats section describes the various types of products that we publish; the methodologies section describes the many different ways that content might be provided within a product. We also provide a list of the topic areas in which we publish.

FORMATS

In addition to its extensive book-publishing program, Pfeiffer offers content in an array of formats, from fieldbooks for the practitioner to complete, ready-to-use training packages that support group learning.

FIELDBOOK Designed to provide information and guidance to practitioners in the midst of action. Most fieldbooks are companions to another, sometimes earlier, work, from which its ideas are derived; the fieldbook makes practical what was theoretical in the original text. Fieldbooks can certainly be read from cover to cover. More likely, though, you'll find yourself bouncing around following a particular theme, or dipping in as the mood, and the situation, dictate.

HANDBOOK A contributed volume of work on a single topic, comprising an eclectic mix of ideas, case studies, and best practices sourced by practitioners and experts in the field.

An editor or team of editors usually is appointed to seek out contributors and to evaluate content for relevance to the topic. Think of a handbook not as a ready-to-eat meal, but as a cookbook of ingredients that enables you to create the most fitting experience for the occasion.

RESOURCE Materials designed to support group learning. They come in many forms: a complete, ready-to-use exercise (such as a game); a comprehensive resource on one topic (such as conflict management) containing a variety of methods and approaches; or a collection of like-minded activities (such as icebreakers) on multiple subjects and situations.

TRAINING PACKAGE An entire, ready-to-use learning program that focuses on a particular topic or skill. All packages comprise a guide for the facilitator/trainer and a workbook for the participants. Some packages are supported with additional media—such as video— or learning aids, instruments, or other devices to help participants understand concepts or practice and develop skills.

- *Facilitator/trainer's guide* Contains an introduction to the program, advice on how to organize and facilitate the learning event, and step-by-step instructor notes. The guide also contains copies of presentation materials—handouts, presentations, and overhead designs, for example—used in the program.

- *Participant's workbook* Contains exercises and reading materials that support the learning goal and serves as a valuable reference and support guide for participants in the weeks and months that follow the learning event. Typically, each participant will require his or her own workbook.

ELECTRONIC CD-ROMs and web-based products transform static Pfeiffer content into dynamic, interactive experiences. Designed to take advantage of the searchability, automation, and ease-of-use that technology provides, our e-products bring convenience and immediate accessibility to your workspace.

METHODOLOGIES

CASE STUDY A presentation, in narrative form, of an actual event that has occurred inside an organization. Case studies are not prescriptive, nor are they used to prove a point; they are designed to develop critical analysis and decision-making skills. A case study has a specific time frame, specifies a sequence of events, is narrative in structure, and contains a plot structure—an issue (what should be/have been done?). Use case studies when the goal is to enable participants to apply previously learned theories to the circumstances in the case, decide what is pertinent, identify the real issues, decide what should have been done, and develop a plan of action.

ENERGIZER A short activity that develops readiness for the next session or learning event. Energizers are most commonly used after a break or lunch to stimulate or refocus the group. Many involve some form of physical activity, so they are a useful way to counter post-lunch lethargy. Other uses include transitioning from one topic to another, where "mental" distancing is important.

EXPERIENTIAL LEARNING ACTIVITY (ELA) A facilitator-led intervention that moves participants through the learning cycle from experience to application (also known as a Structured Experience). ELAs are carefully thought-out designs in which there is a definite learning purpose and intended outcome. Each step—everything that participants do during the activity—facilitates the accomplishment of the stated goal. Each ELA includes complete instructions for facilitating the intervention and a clear statement of goals, suggested group size and timing, materials required, an explanation of the process, and, where appropriate, possible variations to the activity. (For more detail on Experiential Learning Activities, see the Introduction to the *Reference Guide to Handbooks and Annuals*, 1999 edition, Pfeiffer, San Francisco.)

GAME A group activity that has the purpose of fostering team spirit and togetherness in addition to the achievement of a pre-stated goal. Usually contrived—undertaking a desert expedition, for example—this type of learning method offers an engaging means for participants to demonstrate and practice business and interpersonal skills. Games are effective for team building and personal development mainly because the goal is subordinate to the process—the means through which participants reach decisions, collaborate, communicate, and generate trust and understanding. Games often engage teams in "friendly" competition.

ICEBREAKER A (usually) short activity designed to help participants overcome initial anxiety in a training session and/or to acquaint the participants with one another. An icebreaker can be a fun activity or can be tied to specific topics or training goals. While a useful tool in itself, the icebreaker comes into its own in situations where tension or resistance exists within a group.

INSTRUMENT A device used to assess, appraise, evaluate, describe, classify, and summarize various aspects of human behavior. The term used to describe an instrument depends primarily on its format and purpose. These terms include survey, questionnaire, inventory, diagnostic, survey, and poll. Some uses of instruments include providing instrumental feedback to group members, studying here-and-now processes or functioning within a group, manipulating group composition, and evaluating outcomes of training and other interventions.

Instruments are popular in the training and HR field because, in general, more growth can occur if an individual is provided with a method for focusing specifically on his or her own behavior. Instruments also are used to obtain information that will serve as a basis for change and to assist in workforce planning efforts.

Paper-and-pencil tests still dominate the instrument landscape with a typical package comprising a facilitator's guide, which offers advice on administering the instrument and interpreting the collected data, and an initial set of instruments. Additional instruments are available separately. Pfeiffer, though, is investing heavily in e-instruments. Electronic instrumentation provides effortless distribution and, for larger groups particularly, offers advantages over paper-and-pencil tests in the time it takes to analyze data and provide feedback.

LECTURETTE A short talk that provides an explanation of a principle, model, or process that is pertinent to the participants' current learning needs. A lecturette is intended to establish a common language bond between the trainer and the participants by providing a mutual frame of reference. Use a lecturette as an introduction to a group activity or event, as an interjection during an event, or as a handout.

MODEL A graphic depiction of a system or process and the relationship among its elements. Models provide a frame of reference and something more tangible, and more easily remembered, than a verbal explanation. They also give participants something to "go on," enabling them to track their own progress as they experience the dynamics, processes, and relationships being depicted in the model.

ROLE PLAY A technique in which people assume a role in a situation/scenario: a customer service rep in an angry-customer exchange, for example. The way in which the role is approached is then discussed and feedback is offered. The role play is often repeated using a different approach and/or incorporating changes made based on feedback received. In other words, role playing is a spontaneous interaction involving realistic behavior under artificial (and safe) conditions.

SIMULATION A methodology for understanding the interrelationships among components of a system or process. Simulations differ from games in that they test or use a model that depicts or mirrors some aspect of reality in form, if not necessarily in content. Learning occurs by studying the effects of change on one or more factors of the model. Simulations are commonly used to test hypotheses about what happens in a system—often referred to as "what if?" analysis—or to examine best-case/worst-case scenarios.

THEORY A presentation of an idea from a conjectural perspective. Theories are useful because they encourage us to examine behavior and phenomena through a different lens.

TOPICS

The twin goals of providing effective and practical solutions for workforce training and organization development and meeting the educational needs of training and human resource professionals shape Pfeiffer's publishing program. Core topics include the following:

Leadership & Management
Communication & Presentation
Coaching & Mentoring
Training & Development
E-Learning
Teams & Collaboration
OD & Strategic Planning
Human Resources
Consulting

What will you find on pfeiffer.com?

- The best in workplace performance solutions for training and HR professionals

- Downloadable training tools, exercises, and content

- Web-exclusive offers

- Training tips, articles, and news

- Seamless on-line ordering

- Author guidelines, information on becoming a Pfeiffer Partner, and much more

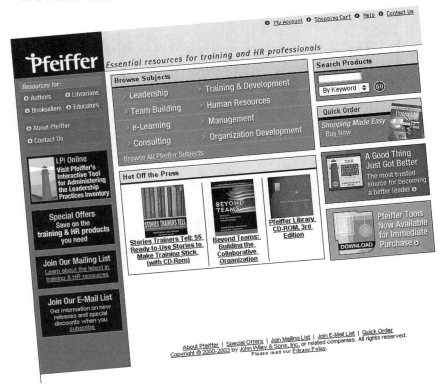

Discover more at www.pfeiffer.com